THE POWER OF THE FUTURE

Canadian Cataloguing in Publication Data

Cloutier, Guy, 1958-

The Power of the Future: The choice that transforms our lives

Translation of: Le Pouvoir du Futur.

ISBN 2-922541-01-0

1. Self-realization. 2. Autonomy (Psychology). 3. Life (Philosophy). 4. Creative ability in business. 5. Organizational change. 6. Quality of work. I. Zone Evolutionary Centre. II. Title.

BF637.S4C5713 1999 158.1 C99-941319-8

PUBLISHED BY ZONE EVOLUTIONARY CENTRE INC.
P.O. BOX 833 STATION A
Montréal (Québec) H3C 2V5
Tel: (514) 767-0601 • Fax: (514) 767-1107

Legal deposit: Bibliothèque nationale du Québec, 2000.
Legal deposit: National Library of Canada, 2000.

Cover: Richard Lord
Layout and Design: Olivier Lasser

ISBN 2-922541-01-0
Printed in Canada

GUY CLOUTIER

THE POWER OF THE FUTURE

THE CHOICE THAT TRANSFORMS OUR LIVES

ZONE EVOLUTIONARY CENTRE

Acknowledgements

To my parents Thérèse and Marcel who gave me life and through their integrity, showed me the path to follow,

To my brother Denis who taught me how to excel, my sister-in-law Joanne and their children Marc-Antoine, Katerine and Françoys,

To all my friends who made me what I am today,

To all my local, national and international business associates who allowed me to develop the concept of the family of enterprises,

To all my accounting clients who were business examples for me and who encouraged and supported me in my endeavour,

To all my students who were a source of inspiration and inestimable motivation,

To all the people, whose precious help gave me the moral support necessary to complete this book: Lise Paquette, Denis Boulanger, George Fajzel, Yolande Nesseth and Brigitte Morel.

To Josee Larivière for her supportive efforts, and her dedication in encouraging me to complete this book.

I would particularly like to thank Alec MacLeod for his supportive efforts in the translation of this book and for his belief in the Power of the Future.

Guy Cloutier

Table of contents

ACKNOWLEDGEMENTS 4
TABLE OF CONTENTS 5
AUTHOR'S NOTES 8
PROLOGUE 9
INTRODUCTION: TRANSFORMING OUR LIVES TO BECOME AUTONOMOUS 11

PART ONE: THE AWAKENING

Chapter 1 CHAOS 17
1) The Family: an evolutionary chain 19
2) Today's children 20
3) Human alienation 21
4) Organizational alienation 24

Chapter 2 TRANSFORMING TODAY'S ORGANIZATION INTO THE EVOLUTIONARY ORGANIZATION .. 33
1) The transformation of organizations 35
2) The challenges facing today's organizations 38
3) Today's organizational vision 47
4) My vision of the organization 48
5) The evolutionary organization 50

Chapter 3 HUMAN, WHERE DO YOU COME FROM? WHO ARE YOU? WHERE ARE YOU GOING? 61
1) Human, where do you come from? 63
2) Human, who are you? 69
3) Human, where are you going? 77

Chapter 4 ORGANIZATION, WHERE DO YOU COME FROM? WHO ARE YOU? WHERE ARE YOU GOING? 83
1) Organization, where do you come from? 84
2) Organization, who are you? 91
3) Organization, where are you going? 99

PART TWO: THE AWARENESS

Chapter 5 THE BALANCE OF LIFE'S NEEDS 111
1) Life's needs and universal values 112
2) Human needs versus life's needs........................... 114
3) Life's wheel of balance 116

Chapter 6 IN SEARCH OF ESSENCE 131
1) The definition of time 131
2) Money.. 134
3) The realization of the conscious dream................... 137

Chapter 7 THE QUEST FOR MEANING 167
1) The meaning of life...................................... 167
2) Our origins 169
3) Life's real needs.. 170
4) The process towards meaning.............................. 172

Chapter 8 EVOLUTIONARY THINKING................. 193
1) Evolutionary thinking.................................... 193
2) Intuitive intelligence 206
3) The cycle of an idea's realization....................... 210

Chapter 9 THE SYNERGY OF SEASONS 219
1) Seasonal cycles 220
2) The life force of nature 221
3) The synergy of the seasons 224
4) The influence of the seasons 231

PART THREE: REALIZATION

Chapter 10 FINANCIAL AUTONOMY 243
1) Financial autonomy for the Human 245
2) Financial autonomy for the Organization 260

Chapter 11 TOTAL AUTONOMY FOR THE HUMAN 275
1) The voyage or the road of life 277
2) The carriage or the body 278
3) The horse or the emotions 282
4) The driver or the spirit 285
5) The guide or the soul 287

Chapter 12 TOTAL AUTONOMY FOR THE ORGANIZATION 291
1) The voyage or the vision 293
2) The carriage or the organizational structure 295
3) The horse or the emotions and the resources of the organization 298
4) The driver or direction and daily management 302
5) The guide or the mission 306

Chapter 13 THE HUMAN AND THE ORGANIZATION OF THE FIFTH KINGDOM 311
1) The source of the Fifth Kingdom 312
2) The mission of the Human and the Organization of the Fifth Kingdom 314
3) The reason for being of the Human and the Organization of the Fifth Kingdom 316
4) The characteristics of the Human and the Organization of the Fifth Kingdom 317
5) The distinctive elements of the Human and the Organization of the Fifth Kingdom 319
6) The Human and the Organization of the Fifth Kingdom 321

CONCLUSION 327

Author's Notes

Everything begins with a wish; our life, life itself, a chance encounter, a desire to understand our life and our reason for being; all these simple things in every day life can ultimately allow us to reach true autonomy and freedom.

My wish is to share my life's experiences with others and encourage them to realize their dreams and give meaning to their lives. Writing this book allowed me to pursue the dream which gave meaning to my life: that of communicating my passions, what animates me and what makes me alive.

This work offers solutions inspired by my life, as well as personal reflections on the direction the Human and the Organization should take in the future to ensure their survival by being in harmony with life. In other words, it is a pathway that answers fundamental questions we often ask when we want to find meaning in our life and solve our inherent existential crises.

The life of every human
and organization is worth living
if we understand that our personal and collective
responsibility is to share and to express our
full creative power while respecting the life
that engendered us.

Prologue

Life has a meaning and we will only find our life's meaning when we discover the key to our full autonomy and freedom.

Over the last thirty years, advances in technology, science, genetics, society and economics have been phenomenal. Unfortunately, these rapid developments have proven to be powerless against the ills which plague our society: health problems, pollution, overpopulation, violence, unemployment, poverty and war. Indeed, our obsession with progress for its own sake may not have solved anything and the world of leisure that everyone was promised has turned out to be a mirage. What does the future really hold for us?

Up to now, the complexities of systems conceived by mankind have engendered in us, a certain kind of dependence, retarding our evolution to understand the meaning of our life. We have become totally dependent on others to find solutions for us instead of taking the initiative ourselves. If we want to master the future, we must first become autonomous. It is only by integrating the sources of their dependencies that the Human and the Organization can conquer their existential crises by no longer looking for solutions to problems outside themselves when the answers lie within them.

It was after becoming aware of my uniqueness that I decided to free myself from the values that society imposed on me. Doing so allowed me to view my life according to my personal values and find my own solutions to my existential problems. By realizing my dreams, I understood the importance of becoming autonomous and free. My profound desire to create a new conception of the world still leads me today to exploit my full potential and to continually excel in all my endeavours.

This work will deal with the Human and the Organization because both are integral parts of life's continuum as the Organization is an extension of the Human. Since the appearance of salaried work, humans in the organization have become disassociated from life. Their primary role should have been to bring their creativity to the organization, not only their energy. I would like this book to be the beacon that sheds light on what we are today and the transformation we must undergo to realize the Power of the Future. I see it as a pathway which demands that we integrate ourselves into the four existing kingdoms of mineral, plant, animal and Homo Sapiens to become what I call the *Autonomous Human and Organization of the Fifth Kingdom.*

I would like to guide you along this pathway and offer you the developmental tools necessary to help you attain total autonomy on both individual and organizational levels. Different keys will be offered to explore and exploit your full potential with the objective of transforming your life.

Our life can be a wonderful story once we realize it belongs to us and transforming our life through self-discovery will lead us to freedom and autonomy.

Autonomy is the fruit of a lifetime of effort
and the transformation of our lives
is the ladder to reach it.

Introduction

TRANSFORMING OUR LIVES TO BECOME AUTONOMOUS

To transform one's life is to create, to invent, to imagine.

Driven by a profound need to create, invent and imagine my life, while at the same time dreaming of seeing the world, I founded my own company. It exported products and inventions to world markets which may, in itself, seem rather tame. However, it ultimately became a stepping stone to my awakening and awareness of life and all its wonders. My discovery of Japan completely changed my life as I was assimilated into a culture which is based on the notion of the collective over the individual.

In Japan, individuals are an integral part of the decision-making process and the sense of belonging reigns at the heart of their organization. Japanese society is built on pride and loyalty above all else. Can we learn from this?

Why should we be interested in other countries when we are so well off at home in our oasis of peace? By considering the whole planet as our home and by opening up our spirit to the world, we will acquire a much broader vision of how to live our daily lives. We need this open-spiritedness if we want to transform our lives. It does not mean we have to travel the world. We can simply do something that frees, motivates and brings us happiness and an understanding of the meaning of our life. Establishing my business in Japan was an awakening for me because in the face of the unknown, the complexities, the seemingly impossible and all that was different, I discovered the meaning of my life.

Transforming our lives comes down to quite simply, realizing our conscious dreams. My conscious dreams stem from the essence of my life (what animates me) and each time I realize them, my life's journey is enriched. Everybody's dream can be an evolutionary process that brings them autonomy on every level: physical, intellectual and spiritual. However, the dream must be a conscious choice that we embrace to beautify our garden of life. It transports us, step by step, toward our autonomy, whether to find work, take a trip, buy a home, develop a business or invent a new product.

***Like a blossoming flower,
a conscious dream goes through the same
metamorphosis:***

***— the sowing or the formulation of a dream,
— the growth or the implementation of stages
for its realization,
— the blossoming or fulfilment of the dream,
— the wilting or the birth of a new conscious dream.***

In dreams as in life, everything has a cycle, a beginning and an end, a birth and a death. And every stage of the cycle brings us one step further in our quest for fulfilment. This is why it is of prime importance to live life to the fullest so that every conscious dream brings us well-being.

Life is a gift that should be considered the greatest blessing of all. It can be an extraordinary journey depending on what we make of it. This is why it is so important that we have meaning in our life.

This book's mission is to bring together the Human, the Organization and the elements of life towards a common goal: the creation of a better world.

Every life is worth living; but not everyone transforms or invents their life in the same way, since everyone is different. There are approximately six billion inhabitants on the planet and we all have the same objective: to ensure our survival. Beyond that, our interpretation of life differs vastly.

What motivates us to always want to go further in our life? Is it our aspirations, dreams or our lust for life? My greatest source of inspiration comes from my desire and determination to realize my conscious dreams. Once realized, I am filled with satisfaction and a joy for life. The dream accomplished is sweet music to my ear because it touches my soul and I then become the music. In this blissful state, I experience a profound inner peace. This is what the realization of the conscious dream can do for you.

There are many distractions in today's world which distance us from our true purpose in life, which is to realize our conscious dreams. We are too caught up in the daily grind to even take the time to dream. During our most active years, between 25 and 65, our complacency leads us to a self-sanctioned procrastination. Does society worship or put any value on the accomplishment of our individual dreams or is it more inclined to force us into its mould and follow its dreams? What is most regrettable is that by allowing ourselves to be lulled by society and its illusions, we eventually become creatures of habit... paralysed by lassitude.

The transformation of our lives begins with the awakening to and awareness of our potential to realize our dreams and become autonomous. By awakening to the experiences of our lives and life around us, an awareness emerges. This allows us to realize ourselves by creating, inventing and imagining a world that is propitious to our evolution to achieve total autonomy.

***To be alive is to dream.
To transform our life is
to realize this dream.***

This book is aimed at encouraging the Human and the Organization to bridge the gap that separates them from total autonomy. The process requires that they pass through three stages (Awakening, Awareness and Realization) which will serve to integrate them with all that surrounds them (the Mineral, Plant, Animal and their own Homo Sapiens kingdom) to emerge as a fifth distinct entity... that being the *Autonomous Human and Organization of the Fifth Kingdom.*

The first stage, Awakening, aims at sensitizing the Human and the Organization to the chaos they are experiencing by uncovering its source, to reach a new level of consciousness.

The second stage, Awareness, consists of leading the Human and the Organization to rediscover their uniqueness and integrate all life around them in order to bring about individual and collective well-being.

The third stage, Realization, focuses on the rise of the Human and the Organization toward their total autonomy to become the *Fifth Kingdom.*

***The transformation
of our conscious dreams into reality
attracts like-minded individuals and organizations
to share the same adventure.***

PART ONE
THE AWAKENING

Chapter 1

CHAOS

Chaos is the source of a new consciousness.

Transformation begins with an awakening to the past and present and their subsequent integration. In the context of this book, integration means recognizing, understanding and acting on everything that happens to us in our lives. It requires that we focus on where we came from and who we are to determine where we are going.

This chapter presents concrete examples of different problems which exist in our society. Its goal is to awaken us to the challenges which the Human and the Organization will have to face to ensure their survival.

For millennia, humans have developed different ways to create, invent and imagine the world, making Homo Sapiens the only species capable of going one step further, be it on the physical, intellectual or spiritual level. Unfortunately, this aspect sets them apart from all creation as it has a darker side: the conflict between the spiritual and the rational.

Have human beings really evolved since the beginning of their existence? Certainly we have created marvellous mechanical and societal extensions of ourselves, but at what cost? In the process, have we taken the time to stop and reflect on the meaning of our personal life or are we still more concerned with the material and emotional needs basic to our day-to-day survival? While nobody can deny the benefits of this somewhat limited evolution, there remains a number of glaring problems for which we have not yet found appropriate solutions. War, racism, violence, poverty, the degradation and depletion of natural resources are all negative by-products of our evolution. They are consequences which have certainly diverted us from our true mission, which is to understand the meaning of our lives. The more we look for solutions outside of ourselves, the greater the risk of these problems increasing. Should we not first look for the meaning of our own life before taking on the conquest of external worlds — those of information technology, cloning, and the exploration of the universe? To coin a phrase, clarity begins at home.

The meaning of our life will always be an enigma that needs to be demystified.

The answer lies in analyzing our problems and those of our society. The following are some personal reflections on society and the systems it imposes on us:

- Does society exist to control individuals to the extreme, through its coding system: employee number, social number, driver's license? If so, it creates an *impersonal society* where each individual becomes a number.

- Does society define us by what we know or what we have learned? If so, we are then a *society of specialists* who focus on specific disciplines, when, in fact everything in life is part and parcel of a whole and should not in any way be considered as a thing unto itself.

- Does society over-emphasize the material world? If so, it contributes to the creation of a *society of overconsumption,* where waste and pollution are rampant.

- Does society rob us of life in the process of our trying to make a living? We spend the greatest part of our lives working to pay off bills and debts imposed on us by a *society of over-taxation* while watching our purchasing power decline year after year.

- Does society smother us with rules and regulations which only legislators understand? Must life be defined by a pile of legal procedures and documentation rendering humans prisoners to a *bureaucratic society* of their own making?

While the drawbacks are obvious, there are two particular consequences generated by this type of society that are devastating: the breakdown of family values and the alienation of the Human and the Organization.

1) THE FAMILY: AN EVOLUTIONARY CHAIN

Nations could not exist without the notion of "family". Every nation is an extension of the family and every family is a building block in its formation. What makes the family important to life is the fact that it is an *evolutionary chain* that passes on the experience of life to succeeding generations. The breakdown of families severs this link and adds to the general chaos through separation, divorce, and subsequent restructuring. And even if a marriage does survive, parents today have little or no time to devote to their children, being overwhelmed by the increasing demands of day-to-day problems. As a result, the *evolutionary chain* is broken and the transmission of information vital to *intergenerational evolution* (the links binding grand-parents, parents and children) is severed. Consequently, we live in a state of imbalance which often requires the professional help of psychologists, therapists and so on.

In Asia, particularly Japan, the *evolutionary chain* is central to their culture. When a parent dies, respect and tradition dictate that the eldest of the family takes in the surviving parent and sees to their needs for the rest of their days. Do we, in North America, offer our elders anything like this? We tend to exclude them from the population-at-large by confining them to institutions far removed from the reality of life. We unwittingly break the *evolutionary chain* by cutting off information which is crucial to understanding ourselves and ultimately to our evolution.

The notion of family is the pillar of every nation.

2) TODAY'S CHILDREN

Rooted in a world of pure imagination, children have all the potential to be what they are in essence: natural individuals with their own identities, not beings forged by society. What is our understanding of what our children contribute as individuals to society? Are they sufficiently prepared to ensure their own survival? What values do we, as parents or society, pass on to them?

The situation of parents in today's world goes far beyond human understanding given their daily preoccupations, their lack of time, their numerous obligations and increasing responsibilities in the workplace. What would our children really like to tell us today? Do they feel isolated and insecure?

What ideas are we conveying to our children as they become adolescents and young adults? Are they relevant in a society with high unemployment, stress and violence? Consider that a child who has reached adolescence has already witnessed over 500,000 murders of every sort as seen on television, in films and video. Beyond this, they are likely targets of drug abuse, delinquency and depression. Living in isolation and deprived of "quality time", is it any wonder that the next generation seems to be demoralized and at times, suicidal? Does our world have solutions for any of this?

To understand the reality that youth is experiencing, I offer below, a comparative chart of attitudes to reacquaint us with our inner child and from there, re-establish the links which tie us to them.

COMPARATIVE CHART OF ATTITUDES

CHILD	ADULT
– ACCEPTS PEOPLE AS THEY ARE – UNCONDITIONAL LOVE – NAIVE – SPONTANEOUS – CANDID – OPEN-SPIRITED – IMAGINATIVE	– ENTERTAINS STEREOTYPES AND PREJUDICES – CONDITIONAL LOVE – CRITICAL – REFLECTIVE – OPPORTUNISTIC – CLOSED-MINDED – RATIONAL

Our inner child should reconnect us to the conductive wire of the evolutionary chain.

3) HUMAN ALIENATION

The Media

What influence do the media have on the family? With our eyes constantly riveted to television and with newspapers dwelling largely on negative rather than positive stories, are we not in fact vicariously living these chaotic events? Are we not the image of media projections? We owe it to ourselves to address this phenomena and understand how it undermines our existence. We must recognize that extreme violence on television, in newspapers and now the internet, is not only harmful in itself but also diverts us from our real evolution. It is time we made a choice in favour of "evolutionary" broadcasting which favours more positive human content and programming that contributes to our personal growth.

Evolutionary media awaken human consciousness to real values.

Technology

How does technology contribute to the family? By being increasingly attracted to this new way of living, are we not distancing ourselves from the *evolutionary chain*? As technology rapidly permeates every aspect of our lives, should we not be asking ourselves what its significance is to our evolution? Is it really adapted to serve our needs? Do we really need cellular phones, microwave ovens and virtual worlds? Does it in any way improve our quality of life? What would our ancestors have done with a cellular phone or an electronic game? Do we even know if they understood how important a simple game of cards around a table was to family unity? Unfortunately, with the arrival of modern technology, we tend to distance ourselves from these family values. The arrival of new technology has somehow given rise to a distorted perception of what life really means. It has contributed to today's familial chaos by rupturing the family bonds to which our ancestors accorded the greatest importance.

Are we about to witness a generation of technophiles so bent on overconsumption that "instant obsolescence" is no longer a concern? Will this lead them to a new order favouring human growth or a further loss of autonomy? In other words, will we master it or be enslaved by its ever-increasing costs and complexities?

A ball-point pen costs 30 cents whereas a computer with all its programs can run upwards of around $3000. This does not include the costs inherent in start-up, maintenance, lessons in its use, upgrading, user fees, etc. All this to arrive at the same result, that being the recording and transmission of information.

How many billions of dollars were spent to prepare for the arrival of the new millennium simply to replace the number one with the number two on all computer systems? The pencil does not render us dependent on these imponderables. In a few years time, we may well conclude that having taken the path of the technological revolution and having distanced ourselves from what is real in life, we would have been better served by exploiting the simplicity of the pencil, the symbol of a new universal consciousness.

If technology is to have meaning, it must respect the source of life which is the environment as well as the *evolutionary chain*. Technology must be as natural as walking and as simple to use as a pencil. However, humans tend to complicate their existence for the sake of simplicity. In so doing they increase their dependence on complex and expensive systems instead of gaining more autonomy by opting for a simple system which would be more suited to them. Will we ever witness a new era where the original computer (the human brain) will truly exercise its creativity by avenging itself on ultramodern technology?

The emergence of creative minds awakens human consciousness to the real needs of life.

The Organized Human

Faced with the reality of chaos, many people find themselves without hopes or dreams. The dreams they once had at the beginning of their careers lie buried in the scrapbooks of their minds, only to be remembered twenty or thirty years later. What causes such despair? Today's society overvalues work at the expense of family, leisure time and dreams. Demands on employers are constantly increased, leading to massive lay-offs of experienced people for the sake of economic and technological imperatives.

Greater financial obligations and responsibilities encroach on today's workers requiring them to earn as much as possible to support their daily needs, leaving them without the time or money to realize their dreams. This is why at retirement, they find themselves with less than they had at the beginning of their careers, taking into account inflation and taxation. Yet all they want is to reach retirement as soon as possible because they see it as a major accomplishment in their lives and a time to finally be happy.

I have a problem in seeing how anyone can spend their life dreaming of retirement. While there is certainly nothing wrong with giving it occasional consideration, a truly well-spent life is one in which work is enjoyable and dreams are achieved. In being self-employed, I have the advantage of realizing my dreams because I am doing what I like and my job security depends completely on my own personal efforts.

Work will always bring us satisfaction if it allows us to realize our dreams.

4) ORGANIZATIONAL ALIENATION

Technological Changes

What does business, with all its ultramodern technology, hold for us? Does it have room for human creativity? What is the real impact of the Machine on individual motivation in the organization? Insecurity, a sense of powerlessness and more stress? Has technology resulted in greater control over the human being? We are continually being overtaken by technology because it never stops developing, changing, "improving". Caught in a rat race, we find ourselves in constant, never-ending training programs for updating and integrating new applications.

Certainly, technology can be useful to our growth, but it must be evaluated beforehand, so we may determine whether it will bring us any real benefit. In the face of rapid technological advances, businesses have little time to analyze the relevance of technology's applications to human growth. The organization assumes that the human will adapt to technology and fails to even consider the reverse.

Many organizations have focused their future development on computer systems, resulting in the compartmentalization of the human being. Electronic communication has replaced human communication and this state of affairs has created an uncomfortable duality between the Human and the Machine within the organization. Has the arrival of technology contributed to the actual evolution of the Human and the Organization?

The mission of the organization should be to improve the quality of life of its members and clients. As an example, curative medicine is still favoured over preventive medicine as an approach to health problems. This tendency champions temporary relief and "miraculous" cures thanks to chemicals and technology, rather than encouraging people to find the real source of their problems and prevent illness in the first place. With the latter in mind, we should develop preventive schools grouping health professionals together in hospital centres where the public can be acquainted with preventive methods and take their health into their own hands. This would be beneficial to all and at the same time reduce the cost of global health care.

Technology should serve human consciousness for the development of humans.

Economic Changes

Caught napping in the face of the imbalance caused by the globalization of the marketplace, ever fiercer competition and the blind acquisition of technologies, our organizations have reacted with a short-term strategy in the hope of preserving their assets. They have thus resorted to massive lay-offs, foreign sub-contracting and over-indebtedness. Are the imperatives of today's private enterprises focused solely on financial gain to the exclusion of a long-term goal?

Through a lack of vision, business makes short-term gains but inevitably faces economic loss in the long run. To regain its original vision, the organization must recognize the human potential it already has by establishing a department whose first responsibilities are to evaluate, encourage and manage the creativity of its members through the development of new products, services and concepts.

***Creativity stimulates human potential
for the growth of both
the Human and the Organization.***

Environmental Changes

The economic profitability of a product today is often more important than its impact on the environment. But each product, as well as serving a need, should contribute to the collective betterment. As it comes from nature, so it must return to nature. In other words, like biodegradable products, it must not pollute.

What should we think of companies who excessively pollute the environment with their chemical and toxic wastes?

Should they not be re-thinking their reason for being or their mission? What is their justification? Many companies have polluted our environment without having a single restorative remedy at hand or any respect for the life which surrounds them. Instead, each company should exercise a social responsibility based on the added value that comes with preserving natural resources, eliminating pollution and protecting the environment. It should orient its activities toward a universal consciousness for the preservation of the planet.

The environment is a reflection of society.

Changes in the Organization of Labour

The end of the industrial era has given rise to profound changes in the organization of labour. Varied restructuring has created a scarcity of work and has thus given employers much greater power over the employees who survived the last round of downsizing. As such, the workers have seen their hours and responsibilities increase, their wages and social benefits diminish, and promotions all but disappear. We should ask ourselves if the organization is using chaos to regulate the human's life cycle to serve its needs. And have humans, in turn, sold their souls to the organization?

Endless restructurings have made organizations the authors of their own undoing by severing the conductive wire... the *intergenerational transmitter* of experience between its members. Thus the uncertainty which reigns inside businesses is a result of lack of communication between generations due to compartmentalization, short-term vision, time constraints and overwork which engenders a disappearance of loyalty and confidence within the company. We are witnessing the *categorization of experience* that separates the young from those who are in mid-career as well as those approaching retirement, leaving them all with only one concern; their own survival.

What the organization should really be is a structure that rallies members to a common goal and encourages them to integrate their experiences for the good of all. The organization should replace moroseness, despondency and stress with a new breath of life that harmonizes its life cycle with that of its members. In addition, it should create an environment that favours the sharing of ideas that will result in a unified and long-term vision.

The integration of human values into the organization will give members more confidence in re-establishing the inter-generational conductive wire.

In the face of this chaos which surrounds the Human and the Organization, a kind of *couldn't care less* attitude has arisen which is only making the problem worse. One solution might be the creation of a new order in organizations, by creating forward-looking industries endowed with a humane and environmental consciousness.

Irreparable disasters await us if we continue to go against the values which govern life. As hard as it is to imagine, our continued indifference may well lead to repetitive earthquakes, frequent floods, incurable diseases. The ozone layer will no longer offer protection, and violence and impoverishment on the planet will increase. This is why humans should transform their lives and take up the greatest challenge of all time: their survival on this planet.

What can we do to safeguard our planet and our lives and continue to evolve without destroying ourselves? We must first develop an awareness. Humans who are aware will then take it upon themselves to influence others and in doing so, bring about a universal collective consciousness which I call a *global awakening.* This awakening will activate in us a need to be in harmony with life, so that we may become at *one with all.*

At the moment, we are living the opposite. We content ourselves with *couldn't care less-ism,* saying "It's not my problem, it's someone else's fault and they can handle it." Society creates humans and organizations who simply want to take the most out of life without giving anything back. However, we all have the responsibility of integrating an awareness which respects the principles of life, in everything we do.

We should be asking ourselves what can be done to improve our present situation. When we experience personal and global chaos, it's always the same thing: we are discouraged and feel powerless about what we are experiencing. For example, when we lose a job, we go through many negative emotions: pain, hatred, fear, anger, discouragement and uncertainty. But in the end, we realize that we have survived our personal chaos. The lesson to be learned is that ultimately, the experience is just one more to add to life and that bad experiences can be rewarding for us and for others as well. From every chaotic situation there emerges a new consciousness and a new order. Therefore, to really understand the meaning of our life, we must integrate everything we experience into it.

***To avoid chaos in their lives,
the Human and the Organization must remove
themselves from all that links them to chaos
to become the life which lies within them.***

I often say that the best thing about life is TO BE ALIVE, to appreciate life for what it brings us, whether it be moments of happiness or sadness. Life courses through us; we are LIFE and we can all contribute to universal harmony.

Every flower that we cultivate in our garden of life
will brighten the garden of universal life.
We have the responsibility to cultivate the flowers
within us so that they become most resplendent.

I no longer live in chaos because I transcend it
to become a rose in my garden of life
as I am the master of my destiny.

WHAT CAN CHAOS BRING TO OUR LIFE?

- EMERGENCE OF A NEW CONSCIOUSNESS.
- REFLECTION ON OUR LIFE AND OUR MISSION.
- TIME TO STOP AND RETURN TO OUR SOURCES.
- DISCOVERY OF LIFE'S TRUE VALUES.
- GLOBAL AWAKENING TO A NEW SENSE OF GROWTH IN OUR LIFE.

What questions must be asked to develop an individual and collective consciousness?

1) What links can we make between our personal chaos and global chaos?

2) What information must we seek out to conquer our personal chaos?

3) What is the source of our personal and organizational chaos; how can we manage this source to raise our awareness?

4) What are the motivational sources which will resolve personal and collective chaos?

5) What balance must we establish in our life to obtain a better understanding of chaos?

6) What flowers must we cultivate in today's organization to give it a greater consciousness towards life?

7) What business communications program provides intergenerational sharing between the organization and its members?

8) What is the cost benefit for the Human and the Organization in living through and surviving chaos?

9) How can the individual, the community and society use chaotic information to bring harmony to their personal and collective gardens of life?

10) What do we experience from chaos and what are the lessons to be learned from it?

11) How do we integrate all the information generated by chaos into our life?

Chapter 2

TRANSFORMING TODAY'S ORGANIZATION INTO THE EVOLUTIONARY ORGANIZATION

Cultivate the tree within us
and we develop
the full potential of our forest.

We have just described the uncertainty which the Human and the Organization experience when faced with the unknown. This insecurity brings out an existential crisis in both. Consequently, we must ask how our organizations can profit from chaos.

To answer this question we will first discuss the transformation of existing organizations into *evolutionary organizations*, their traditional vision, their outlook on the future and the approaches that they must take. Then we will examine the challenges that traditional organizations are facing. In conclusion, we will propose a new approach to business, that being *the family of enterprises*, a concept aimed at gathering together independent organizations possessing specific expertise that are bound by a code of values and ethics which allow them to realize a common goal.

The dawning of the new millennium will see the organization undergo enormous economic, technological, environmental, political and social upheavals. Adapting to new global problems such as natural disasters, epidemics, the movement of international capital and corporate downsizing will require vision and futuristic solutions which concentrate more on prevention than reaction.

In the information revolution era, we are increasingly dependent on modern technology and its complexities. Who is encouraging the proliferation of these systems? The international elite or the large influential organizations of the world? What are their objectives? To better serve their own interests by pigeonholing humans and hampering their evolution, resulting in the loss of autonomy for the latter? Organizations have brought us to a point where profit is all that matters. Holding all the power, they decide on everything and leave us in a state of dependency which distracts us from mastering our life and taking on a more active role in our own evolution. To be truly responsible, the organization's mission should recognize the humans' need for autonomy that would allow them to realize their individual dreams.

Today's world is in the throes of the greatest generalized depletion of resources ever. It is on the verge of witnessing tremendous transformations such as human cloning, overpopulation, severe cataclysms and the loss of natural resources. The Human and the Organization will have to take a stand in the face of this chaos. Awakening to a new universal order will lead them to discover creative solutions for anticipating and mastering change.

The evolution of humanity will no longer only serve the specific interests of organizations but will also make individuals responsible for their own evolution. The *evolutionary being* understands and respects the fundamental links between nature, animals, humans and organizations.

In short, organizations should spend more time developing an understanding of "being" as part and parcel of the totality we call life. The arrival of the *evolutionary organization* means no longer creating needs and aspirations for individuals, but guiding them by respecting their real needs and aspirations.

The future of organizations will depend on their orientation: to continue to reinforce the dependency of human beings by "denaturing" them, or conversely, to encourage their autonomy by contributing to their global awakening.

1) THE TRANSFORMATION OF ORGANIZATIONS

The Denaturing of the Human Being.

There are two possible approaches for entry into tomorrow's world. The first, which would protract the status quo, is a product of the industrial and informational eras, which gave birth to automation, robotics and the mechanization of human beings. All these systems were designed to improve our quality of life but they evolved into an informational technology giving us the computer, the swipe card, the Internet and so on. In short, most modern technologies have contributed in some way to the "denaturing" of human beings by reinforcing their dependencies to the detriment of their own evolution.

Constant technological innovation means the human is continually being overtaken. But the pencil will always be the primary tool of the writer. The computer is a complementary tool but its cost and its tendency toward obsolescence are inevitable. After all, what is essential in transmitting a message: technology or the human behind it? What is it that pushes the organization to always want to be on the cutting edge of technology? To organize or become organized by the frenzy that feeds the technological revolution?

Why are all the industrialized nations in debt? Is there a causal relationship between indebtedness and the acquisition of technology? Certainly, computer systems are there to make life easier; but in adaptation, installation, application and maintenance, the costs involved make the organizations lose all contact with their primary mission, which is to contribute to the well-being of the individual and the collective. That notion has been usurped by the machine they are chained to and its mission is their unflagging servitude.

Should we not redefine technology's reason for being so that it favours the growth of the organization and not its dependence? Does technology really improve the performance of members by forcing them into a weekly schedule of over 50 hours of work in addition to demanding they be apprised of and able to master all the latest technological innovations? Unfortunately this is what employers must insist on to keep the company alive: the integration of a technology to peak performance instead of concentrating on their primary tasks.

We are progressing economically, but not in terms of human evolution. Technology was supposed to improve the quality of life of individuals by allowing them to devote more time to leisure, the pleasures of life and interpersonal relationships. Instead we find ourselves devoted to the technology that was supposed to free us.

Sooner or later, humans will be face to face with a major shift of consciousness, that being the re-establishment of universal order. We should therefore be prepared to determine which technology really contributes to our well-being and our evolution.

The Global Awakening

The second approach to consider calls for the Human and the Organization to anticipate and be ready for the global awakening facing their evolution and their environment — one that will allow them to reach their autonomy by doing what they like doing best. By telling us what to do, today's organization stifles our desire to take our life into our own hands. An evolved organization, by its very nature, would give us freedom to create, innovate or invent our own conception of tomorrow's world.

Since we are only custodians of everything that we have on this earth, it follows that we must protect nature and the life which surrounds us. Why, then, does our consumer society push us to buy, consume, waste and dispose without ever giving a single thought to respecting life? At the outset, was the organization concerned with the real usefulness of the consumer products it rushed to market? What social accountability can we ascribe to goods and services that are useless to the evolution of humans? Our major weakness is in determining our real needs over the superfluous. This is why goods and services should not only serve their initial purpose but also awaken an awareness of our evolution and environment.

For decades, the Human and the Organization have run counter to the natural order that is crucial to their evolution. The creation of societies, systems and organizations has resulted in an ever-increasing consolidation of power to the detriment of human development and life itself. In leaving to others the means to manage their lives, humans have lost their autonomy and the conductive wire that ties them to life.

Tomorrow's businesses will experience a major shift in the awareness of their responsibility towards life. Respecting life means being conscious that our daily behaviour does not go against nature. Respect for life is a criteria which cannot be disassociated from all of tomorrow's creative activities.

Mother Nature will return to Earth what belongs to Earth; what is and always has been.

In the future, harmony will consist of a balance between technology and the global awakening. By inducing this awakening, we will become more responsible, we will change and in doing so, subsequently transform our environment, community, country and our world. Our internal wisdom will radiate a wealth of optimism around us and create a synergy allowing humanity to take itself in hand and become true to itself and all that surrounds it. The Human and the Organization will then have a common mission: to become aware of the links that tie them to life and to finally become autonomous.

Life cannot be disassociated from our evolution.

We now come to the challenges that today's organizations must deal with and the unknown management problems which are likely to stem from them.

2) THE CHALLENGES FACING TODAY'S ORGANIZATIONS

Dependency on Work

The major challenge facing today's organizations, subjected as they are to constant transformations, lies in their inability to foresee the unforeseeable. The climate of uncertainty that reigns within the organizations results in major restructuring: downsizing, wage freezes and the loss of social benefits. An increased work load without financial compensation has become almost obligatory. Individuals are forced into multi-tasking resulting in overwork. As well, they feel devalued, lose their motivation, creativity and consequently, their sense of belonging to the enterprise. All that remains important is their personal and financial security. They view retirement as the only time they will be happy and lose all enthusiasm for completing the work at hand.

How can we explain this sad state of affairs? Can we blame it on new economic or technological realities? Certainly these changes have to some degree contributed to this uneasiness.

Economic Changes

Scarcity of work has perhaps created a sense of servitude on the part of employees toward their organization. Today's organization exerts greater control over humans because it has access to an abundance of qualified, low-cost workers. As employers demands increase, they must find top-notch, high-performance employees. Who are these rare pearls who are best suited to their needs? Has the organization created a system for finding and moulding ideal workers by measuring their performance levels through assessment programs, evaluations and psychological tests? Young graduates just out of school and eager to work must first respond to their pre-established criteria and act according to the norms of the business. In this way organizations exert greater control over manpower and control their behaviour. As well, they favour a certain dependency on technology because they need their members to be more and more efficient and quicker in the execution of their work, leaving aside their personal interests and creativity. In other words, the employee is incessantly driven to follow the agenda established by the business. The organization exercises ever-increasing control over employees much like control over a machine on which we impose job-time imperatives, schedules and efficiency criteria. Employees feel pushed to produce more for the sake of higher return and better quality which results in dissatisfaction, general discouragement and work-related problems. They no longer feel valued and as a result are no longer motivated to excel in their work. By adhering to these criteria, the members become alienated from their sense of creativity, gradually and unwittingly becoming bits in the corporate byte.

To increase performance, the solution for the organization is certainly not to increase the number of working hours but to listen to suggestions from its members in order to become more responsible and efficient in making decisions relative to the future of the enterprise. The organization and its directors, in tandem with the members, should work together to find evolutionary solutions to heighten performance instead of always depending on unilaterally imposed decisions. As well, upper management should entrust its members with the responsibility for finding proactive solutions through:

— a consensus on the common mission,
— a participatory management system,
— support for communicating their creative expression,
— a reward system for their creative efforts.

The organization should value humans for their personal creativity and how it distinguishes them from others.

Technological Changes

The other phenomenon which characterizes today's organizations is the conversion of the human into a *technophile, digital-human* or *homo-mechanus*. Society has come to a point where it requires individual performance to equal that of machines. The employees must be familiar with every new technological gadget. Is there any time left for them to do their job and fulfil their primary purpose within the organization, which is the accomplishment of their life's plan in relation to what they love or are passionate about? Or will they simply become puppets reduced to virtual servitude to the new technology? How will this affect the inner workings of our organizations? Will a dependency on work and a feeling of being overtaken by expensive new technology set in? The fear of being challenged and replaced by the Machine and the insecurity that stems from it can only smother initiative. Why do organizations force us to depend on these technologies? So that we can perform better only to suffer more stress, burnout and occupational illnesses? To what end? To quench the organization's thirst for excessive return on investments?

Can technology really replace the human? Certainly it can improve their performance, but at what price? A drop in motivation and limited creativity leading to organizational stagnation and engendering higher purchasing, maintenance and replacement costs?

With few exceptions, today's organizations often impose their decisions on their members. As a consequence, their work becomes dependent on mastering new technology, placing them on a treadmill leading nowhere, when in fact they should be creating a harmonious working environment. In their decision-making process, the organization should consider ways of introducing new technology with the real needs of their members in mind.

There should be at least one cognizant leader in the organization who can influence all those employees working in uncertainty. The job would mean sensitizing members into developing their creative potential by integrating their personal interests with the goal of the organization. Likewise, technology would no longer be a sinecure but more a process of integration and participation within the organization, aimed at encouraging the creative potential of the members.

The role of the organization
is to create a technological environment
which allows humans to evolve at their own pace.

Human Dependency

Another challenge facing today's organizations lies in the lack of communication between individuals within the enterprise. Employees are increasingly closeted inside a rigid system that defines them by their job title, a situation which can bring about lack of communication, fear and insecurity in anticipation of upcoming changes. Most of them create rules or defense mechanisms in order to protect themselves from the organization. To maintain power, they go as far as appropriating information vital to the growth of the business such as corporate strategies or professional secrets. With the risk of eventual downsizing always in mind, they develop a parallel system by creating false budgetary expenses (nest eggs) not pertinent to the growth of the company.

Pushed to the extreme, traditional companies reinforce the "denaturing" of the human being through the absence of a code of ethics necessary for the establishment of trust between members and directors. These organizations are so preoccupied with their short-term survival that they distance themselves from the essential element of their goal: encouraging the creative potential of their members to ensure survival in the long run.

What follows is some essential advice for the success of all companies caught up in dependency problems. These recommendations will help them to develop expertise for acquiring an overall vision through a detailed examination of their situation. Their new organizational values should be as follows:

- Invest as little as possible in hardware so that technology remains a complementary asset and not an operating imperative.

- Value human potential for its creativity, innovation and inventiveness.

- Team up with people who have a global vision of their activities and those of other organizations. Seek out people who are multi-disciplinarians, generalists, evolutionary thinkers.

- Live according to your means and not those of others; respect life's real needs in accordance with the environment.

- Fully understand the needs of existing and future clients through an evolutionary follow-up on the contribution of their products and services to life's real needs, and continually innovate to bring about harmony between the Organization, clients and life itself.

- Be honest and forthright in the development of activities and in relations with others.

- Appreciate communication with fellow workers and maintain good relations with business partners.

- Have a clear mission and transmit this message to everyone involved, including internal and external clients (those who constitute added value).

- Determine a collective conscious dream with members and collaborators, i.e. target a common interest and develop it to ensure growth for all.

- Develop "know-how" by respecting the "KISS" (Keep It Simple and Straightforward) principle.

To sum up, the Human and the Organization should formulate a common goal to:
— improve communication between members and collaborators,
— mobilise the intermediaries involved by having them participate,
— stimulate the development of creativity within the organization.

Communicating life's real values
is essential to build mutual confidence
within the organization.

Organizational Dependence

A major concern of today's organizations is their structure. The static organization, which in fact has been with us since the advent of industrialization, operates according to a pyramid system wherein each position is bound by a decision-making body. The static organization has contributed to interdependence among individuals (the chain of command) by pigeon-holing them within an hierarchical framework, and therefore limiting their creativity. The static organization is based on rigidity and control. Indeed, for decades this structure has served the particular interests of decision-making and the optimization of order within businesses. Even today, this structure predominates in organizations because of the insecurity that we feel in the face of the unforeseeable. For the Human and the Organization, it is more comforting to embrace what they know than imagine possible, as yet unknown futures.

In the chart below, we show the advantages and disadvantages of the static structure in organizations.

STATIC STRUCTURE

ADVANTAGES	DISADVANTAGES
SIMPLICITY OF EXECUTION.	RIGID AND LIMITING FOR ADVANCEMENT OF HUMANS, BEING CONFINED TO THE EXECUTION OF THEIR TASKS.
EASY CONTROL AND EVALUATION THROUGH HIERARCHIC SYSTEM.	NON-CREATIVE, NON-EVOLUTIONARY.
EASE IN EXECUTING WORK THROUGH COMPARTMENTALIZATION OF INDIVIDUALS.	INTERDEPENDENCE OF INDIVIDUALS WHO MUST RELY ON IMMEDIATE SUPERIORS.

Over the last decade, humans have felt destabilized by all of the new management models proposed. They always seem to bring with them a certain sense of duality: profitability and power versus autonomy and freedom. Who will be the new managers of tomorrow? Those who demand excessive workloads on a continual basis or those who mobilize their members by allowing them to improve their work through creativity?

To improve the atmosphere in today's workplace and to bring about a stronger interrelationship between the Human and the Organization, I am proposing a structure more favourable to creativity, which I call the *evolutionary structure*. This model puts members of the organization in contact with one another so that they can develop their creative potential to continually excel.

EVOLUTIONARY STRUCTURE

ADVANTAGES	OBSTACLES
INTERACTIVE.	FEAR OF CHANGE, RESISTANCE.
HIGH MOTIVATION.	REQUIRES OPEN-MINDEDNESS BY DIRECTORS AND EMPLOYEES.
CREATIVE, EVOLUTIONARY.	DIFFICULT TO CONTROL AND EVALUATE.
MORE FREEDOM AND FLEXIBILITY.	LACK OF FORMAL HIERARCHICAL STRUCTURE.
AUTONOMY AND FREEDOM OF INDIVIDUALS.	MORE PERSONAL RESPONSIBILITY.

This new organizational structure can be compared to a tree. The tree, which represents the organization, is the catalyst between the energy of the universe (via ideas and projects) and the earth (via their materialization). The members are the fruit of the tree. They are all alike whether they be employees or directors because by following their personal interests, they work toward a common goal (reason for being/mission) regardless of their different responsibilities. Thus the interrelation between the fruit and its source, the tree.

On the tree, the fruit passes through different stages: flowering, greening and ripening. Much like the fruit of a tree, members of an organization find themselves at different career stages: novice, intermediary, or senior employees. The fruit gives birth to the materialization of projects supported by the vision and the mission of the tree, the organization. The symbiotic bond of these elements brings about harmony among the members, better group participation and greater autonomy to each of them.

The *evolutionary structure* will allow humans to take their rightful place in the organization by exercising their personal convictions, through their abilities and the expression of their creativity. This is what differentiates it from traditional businesses who wish, above all, to serve their corporate interests. The *evolutionary organization* will be the tree which allows its members to foresee and deal with changes through their collective creativity instead of submitting to those changes. The objective will be to stimulate individuals into defining their role by exercising their expertise and their motivation to create their rightful place within the organization. Senior members will teach junior and intermediary members in order to strengthen the intergenerational link.

We recognize a tree by its fruit
as we recognize an organization by its members.

3) TODAY'S ORGANIZATIONAL VISION

What is the vision of today's organizations? What values do they espouse? Why do they create systems that only the world's elite understands, such as new computer languages, international investments, knowledge on a "need to know" basis? Throughout time, many problems have plagued humankind because we have placed monetary values above human ones. Society has glorified the financial objective: that money means power, and that power is almost exclusively associated with financial gain. They may well have been influenced by the food chain model where "big eats small". The proverb says it all: "money rules the world", meaning organizations can exercise control over humans. As long as we think that money drives us, we will in fact be driven by it. The Human and the Organization contribute to their own downfall by their inability to let go of what obsesses them: the lure of the short-term gain. They therefore become dependents and prisoners of the material aspects of their lives.

***If we cannot forego any single thing in life,
it is because that thing possesses us.***

Which organizations will survive in the future? The last few years have witnessed the mergers of companies in many sectors of world markets, such as professional services, the petroleum and automotive industries, and world banking, changing the face of the global business community. As future consumers, we will have no other choice but to deal with these mega-corporations which hold greater and greater power within their respective markets. These monopolies will manage to survive to tomorrow by increasing the dependency of consumers, but they will bring no real economic benefits in the long run. This trend toward corporate mergers creates many rumours in the marketplace and stirs up a great deal of insecurity amongst the members, who are afraid of losing their jobs.

Running counter to this, a new breed of entrepreneur has emerged; the freelance, contract or autonomous workers. They are the survivors of the last mergers, downsizings, mega-corporate creations, and so on. Left to their own devices, and necessity being the mother of invention, they have developed a network to market their skills and creativity. Their independence is the strength that will ensure their future survival. This new strength will force businesses to restructure into smaller and more efficient units with fewer human, financial and material resources to manage at source. This streamlining will lift a great weight from these businesses. In consequence, they will have more capital available to target their markets and concentrate on their basic skills.

4) MY VISION OF THE ORGANIZATION

As a professional accountant and consultant on international development, my vision of the organization of the future has been clarified by many meetings with directors of small and medium-sized businesses and multinationals. I was able to develop a new concept to allow the organizations I worked with to attain their autonomy. In this way I became an *evolutionary accountant,* that is to say a person who, for the sake of his clients, gives them personal and organizational information pertinent to their development. Beyond being an accountant, I taught them to become financially independent and helped them to create and market products designed for local, national and international markets.

Evolutionary accountants become the soul of the organization. They can orchestrate everything that emanates from the business, such as financing, marketing, human resources, research and development and exports. They have the capacity to see beyond numbers because their life experience has taught them how to interpret and integrate the knowledge acquired for the benefit of the organization's future, by establishing links between the Human, the Organization and life itself.

As an *evolutionary accountant,* I have always maintained that financial statements represent the history of any given business. Generally, my clients ask me to examine theirs and to bring them solutions based on the results obtained. Observations of clients and organizations revealed to me that the financial insecurity felt by the directors might have some bearing on their personalities.

Beginning with observations made of presidents and their associates, I was able to make links between their personality traits and their basic corporate values. I noticed that we attract what we are and that the values which drive the organization stem from the personalities of the directors. So people who love to control, attract or select people they can control. In contrast, directors who have confidence in themselves make sure they have a team made up of creative people who will help them to excel. In short, the analysis of directors and members of a business allowed me to bring creative solutions to the traditional problems they experienced and to improve their financial growth.

These observations led me to conclude that if tomorrow's organizations are to succeed, they will engage their members by giving them the information necessary to achieve their individual autonomy. This in turn will lead to a corporate approach which truly serves the consumer as a human, because, at the end of the day, every employee is a consumer. As an example, pharmaceutical companies should go beyond the fine print on the labelling of their products and openly sensitize the public to moderate its consumption of medications, to be aware of side-effects and to avoid dependency. The primary role of doctors will be to give sound medical advice on maintaining health; to prevent, instead of cure illnesses. They will then be more attentive to their patients and will get to know them and to investigate their family history instead of simply prescribing drugs.

The businesses that will survive in the future will be those that find solutions to clean up the environment and ensure the welfare of humans while offering information that will lead them to autonomy. They will therefore serve humans by improving their quality of life and by fostering their personal growth for the collective good.

Evolutionary organizations will favour the growth of humans by giving them the necessary tools to release the full potential within them.

5) THE EVOLUTIONARY ORGANIZATION

The management philosophy of my organization was inspired by Japanese values associated with a sense of the collective as well as North American values associated with creativity. Japanese society is based on collective values such as integrity and loyalty so they are therefore very respectful of people and their working environment. After the Second World War, they invested in the only resource available to them, their human capital. The industrialization of the country gave birth to "sogo shosha". These organizations started as trading companies negotiating the production, financing and distribution of Japanese products inside and outside the country. They established a family-like network with other Japanese companies (factories, banks, distribution centres, retail stores and international offices) to concentrate all these areas of expertise on developing their commercial activities. The establishment of "sogo shosha" was furthered by creating offices around the world which became the principal sources of information on goods and services. Thus, information coming from the exterior was filtered through the head office in Japan which determined what goods and services to produce and then dispatched this information throughout their business network. This network allows for a participatory relationship between manufacturers, distributors and exporters.

The "sogo shosha" today hold virtual control over the social and economic development of Japan. This "community" of Japanese businesses was formed primarily to serve the basic fundamental values of the country, that being the respect of the collectivity. The first lesson to be learned from Japanese philosophy is that the success of the organizations is largely due to integrating the notion of collective well-being.

Japan and North America allowed me to reconcile my notion of the collective with my desire to express my individual creativity. By integrating the two worlds, I introduced the concept of the family of enterprises in all of my business dealings. This network has allowed me to build my business around the essential component of each organization, that being the entrepreneur and at the same time, to work with people who share a common goal: collective well-being.

Is the family of enterprises tomorrow's new reality? This new type of organization is based on the traditional family structure except that the selection of each member stems from a conscious choice, such as choosing a friend, business associate, our partners and people who share our values. In creating a family of enterprises, we should know the strengths and weaknesses of each member and respect their basic skills as well as their aspirations. Each of them should assume a role within the family of enterprises and the collective should aim for a common goal. In the process, the family of enterprises is ethically bound to preserve the autonomy of each organization that comprises it.

Over the years, I have been applying the concept of the family of enterprises, acting as a master planner for different companies in areas as diverse as international commerce, inventions and business consultation. The consolidation of specific businesses allowed us to bring together a variety of expertise, human resources, raw materials and financing necessary to realize projects which, in the end, gave each member of the family of enterprises the strength of a multinational. This concept allowed the entrepreneurs, who shared a common business language, the opportunity to safeguard their autonomy while obtaining self-financing through the family of enterprises.

The concept of the family of enterprises is founded on five aspects:

- The definition of members
- The golden rules
- The selection of members
- Advantages of the family of enterprises
- Practical applications.

The financial principles of the family of enterprises will be dealt with in the chapter on financial autonomy.

The Definition of Members

A member of the family of enterprises is an autonomous organization possessing the capability of creating a product or service. This product or service allows the group to enrich itself by increasing its power on financial, human and material levels while pursuing the goal of the collective well-being.

The family of enterprises is an evolving chain in a free and autonomous continuum.

The Golden Rules

The family of enterprises is structured in a way that allows all members the freedom and autonomy to develop their full potential in harmony with the objectives and values of the group. They must follow seven golden rules to ensure group solidarity. The rules constitute an ethical code which goes beyond the general principles of business. They are designed to reinforce integrity, loyalty and a sense of belonging among the members.

Furthermore, they offer psychological support to the individuals by providing the synergy that is basic to any family structure.

The Golden Rules:

- **All members must be completely autonomous, free and independent of the group, meaning they must own their own business.**
- **All members must capitalize on their strengths, expertise and basic skills.**
- **All members must contribute to the collective mission of the project while pursuing their individual mission.**
- **Each member must respect fellow entrepreneurs and their interests. Members must help each other and build up relationships of confidence and trust.**
- **Each member must respect the commitments agreed upon by acting in good faith.**
- **Each member must respect the code of ethics and the values associated with it.**
- **All members must reinforce the weaker links in the chain to help them fulfil their commitments.**

The golden rules are based on the integrity of each member's reason for being.

The Selection of Members

The family of enterprises reflects the image of its founders. We attract what we are, therefore we surround ourselves with people who are like-minded: clients, suppliers, employees, business acquaintances. For maximum results, the selection of members must be based on their suitability to the family in terms of their affinity, their interests and their values, with the goal of achieving a group synergy to accomplish common projects.

The basic criteria in the selection of members are:

- Define the role of all members in terms of their respective fields of activity.
- Identify each member's real values in relation to the golden rules of the family of enterprises.
- Determine the interests of members in achieving the overall mission of the family of enterprises. Work together with businesses who have common interests.
- Specify the vision of the family of enterprises and its objectives.
- Recognize and target the strengths of every member in accomplishing a common goal. e.g. financial,intellectual and material input.
- Create mutual aid, a common understanding and group motivation. All members speak the same business language allowing them greater ease in solving problems.
- Develop a mutual aid network to strengthen the weaker members for a better collective project.
- Recruit members for their corporate mission and not only their financial interests. Take into account their track records: management philosophies towards their clients, suppliers and employees.
- Recruit members based on their basic skills. The family of enterprises will benefit from greater added value, better return on investment and an increased capacity for innovation.

The family of enterprises reflects its initiator through principles and values based on respect for individuals and organizations which comprise it.

Advantages of the Family of Enterprises

Hamstrung by the burden of regulations, standards, environmental concerns and the myriad of requirements from organizations, governments, municipalities, technology, education and so on, today's businesses feel increasingly removed from their primary goal which is to sell goods and services. With its vocation of gathering together like-minded organizations, the family of enterprises breaks this isolation by fusing together a variety of expertise, thereby allowing its members to resolve the problems of the moment and perform better in their primary field of activity. In short, the concept of the family confers the power of a multinational on small and medium-sized business.

The advantages that the family of enterprises offers for resolving problems of today's organizations are:

- More leverage in negotiations, greater buying power and individual and collective increases in revenues.
- Collective self-financing: increased financial leverage in relation to the family of enterprises.
- The grouping together of expertise for the purpose of the collective mission.
- The formulation of a collective mission to address problems in different sectors of economic activity.
- Group synergy through the creation of a common think-tank or research and development centre beneficial to the family of enterprises.

- The pooling of expertise, raw materials, financial and human resources to develop and invent new goods and services to gain a leading edge.

- The development of a common internal financial centre to realize common projects.

- The sense of belonging to a group; moral support and the collaboration of people we appreciate.

- The development of a central buying house.

- Self-financing of projects by all the members. Collective risk-sharing.

- Autonomy and freedom of members.

- Increased profit margins resulting from working in direct collaboration with other members united by a common goal.

The family of enterprises has the power of a multinational with the freedom and autonomy of a small company.

Practical Applications

Today's organizations are increasingly reluctant to trust each other. This lack of confidence results in a dependence on written contracts to overcome insecurity in the face of the lure of profit, instead of relying on a simple handshake based on mutual trust between two parties. The family of enterprises reinstates the notion of trust because its golden rules celebrate human values which go well beyond common business principles.

Practical applications of the family of enterprises concern:

- Relationships of trust and shared responsibilities.
- More flexible financial agreements, extended terms and conditions of payment in the event of unforeseen circumstances.
- Mutual understanding of each other's problems: being on the same wavelength.
- Transparency: be as good as your word in every stage of production and service (manufacturing, processing quality of the product and delivery deadlines).
- Willingness to discuss business problems or situations openly and honestly.
- Synchronization of production, distribution and assembly according to the "just in time" principle in order to minimize costs, losses and to respect delivery deadlines.
- Respect for the initial agreement but, in the event of unforseen set-backs, immediate communication with those concerned.
- Agreement in advance on an acceptable margin of error in production.
- Establishment of a preventive strategy to deal with all irregularities that may occur: quality of product, delivery deadlines and so on.
- Acquisition of financial, material and human resources on a permanent basis, supported by the integration of each corporation's expertise towards a common goal.

- Creation of a "think tank" grouping together different organizations from various sectors of the economy to gain a better vision of the future and to anticipate greater growth.

- Agreement on a percentage of group profits with all members and assurance that the consensus is respected.

- Encouragement of members through motivation, enthusiasm and ensuring that each is part of the evolutionary process of the family of enterprises.

Human values are the pillars of tomorrow and confidence will be the keystone to the success of the organization.

The proposed family of enterprises is an alternative organization able to respond to the need for solidarity felt by entrepreneurs. Uniting the strengths of each individual and organizational member allows them to realize their full potential to attain their autonomy.

As we have seen, the fundamental values of the family of enterprises are solidarity and respect for its human and organizational members. In light of this, I would like to share with you, by way of example, one of the products I marketed by following these principles. It was a simple marker designed to delineate property. It permitted me to put these values into practice by uniting different business organizations to bring the project to term. Together, we drew up the golden rules, and were able, without difficulty, to sell this product in over a hundred major stores across Canada for over a decade. In the beginning, when we presented it to retailers, they were sceptical with regard to the sales potential of this product, judging it too simplistic. However, I was convinced that the product would respond to a real consumer need and as master planner, I built up a family of enterprises in order to capitalize on the experience of each member, so that together, we realized unprecedented success. In real terms, the success of this approach resulted in the following:

- the development of the family to self-finance,
- the development of mutual trust between the members leading each to capitalize on their basic skills and efficiency for the benefit of the collective,
- the motivational development of each member in realizing a common objective in respect to their own autonomy.

This experience taught me that when we believe in the family of enterprises, its principles and values, we can summon up the potential of all members to reach a common goal while leaving them their freedom and autonomy.

***If you cannot recognize the tree that is within you,
how can you discover the forest
of your inner potential?***

WHAT CAN THE EVOLUTIONARY ORGANIZATION BRING ABOUT?

- THE VALUE OF CREATIVITY FOR THE IMPROVEMENT OF THE INDIVIDUAL AND THE COLLECTIVE.
- SELF-FINANCING AND POWER TO NEGOTIATE.
- GREATER AUTONOMY OF THE ORGANIZATION.
- EXPANSION OF THE ORGANIZATION BY EXTENDING ITS NETWORK OF CONTACTS.
- DECREASED UNCERTAINTY IN THE FACE OF CHANGE.

What questions must we ask relative to today's organization so that it will become an evolutionary organization?

1) What values drive my organization?

2) What will I gain by exploring a new evolutionary structure for my company?

3) Do I believe in the active participation of all members in my organization?

4) What practical applications are available to motivate the members to collaborate with each other?

5) Is my business distanced from its primary mission due to laws, standards and innumerable procedures?

6) What should I do to become evolutionary?

7) Is the family of enterprises a solution to my daily organizational problems: cash flow, purchasing, innovation and so on?

8) How can I create a family of enterprises to launch a common project?

9) Does the family model allow us to improve our organizational performance by adding our strengths to like-minded businesses?

10) Will the family enable us to realize substantial savings with greater buying power, better financing programs, new market sectors and so on?

11) What are the advantages our organization can gain by applying the fundamental principles of the family of enterprises?

Chapter 3

HUMAN, WHERE DO YOU COME FROM? WHO ARE YOU? WHERE ARE YOU GOING?

There are no coincidences in life, life is perfect.

This chapter will help us deal with our inherited behavioral dependencies so that we may take up our life's pathway towards freedom and autonomy. Throughout the course of our life, there will come a time to reflect on our situation so as not to repeat the mistakes of our ancestors. For as long as I can remember, I have been questioning the meaning of life: Where do we come from? Who are we? Where are we going? Life can be compared to a balance sheet which offers us a look at our past, to better understand how we will orient ourselves in the future. Having discovered where we come from, we will then be able to understand who we are by analyzing our three basic aspects which are the body, spirit and soul. In this way we will discover and develop our natural abilities. Finally, after having discovered who we really are, we must determine where we are going by manifesting today what we will become tomorrow. The road of our life is the one least travelled but nevertheless the most rewarding. It is the one which we have chosen to follow in terms of who we are. It represents a commitment towards a cause which is our mission in life.

One day, while I was walking alone on a mountain path, I felt compelled to stop and appreciate the beauty of nature around me and then of life itself. The idea came to me that in the end, everything has meaning. Life that surrounds us is part of a whole and everything that exists is there to help us understand the meaning of our life. Life is a learning experience and nature has kindly lent us the textbooks for our complete development. We have trees that give us the oxygen we breathe, clean water to nourish life on earth and sunshine to brighten and warm the planet.

I continued my ascent to the summit where I could admire the beauty of the city below me. I found myself asking if urban development was pertinent to our personal growth. Are cities in harmony with life? For a few moments I stood there, transfixed by the duality of a huge, over-developed urban centre against the backdrop of nature's simplicity. The interpretation of life can vary for each of the six billion people who live on this planet, but there is one aspect of life that is universal to all: our survival. Every one of us must survive and to succeed at it, a profound introspection is necessary. While staring at the city lights that flickered through the beauty of the mountain's foliage and danced across the surface of its lake, I came to the conclusion that absolutely everything has a purpose. This being so, what then is the greater meaning of life in terms of economic, social, cultural and universal development? The first question which came to mind was, "Human, where do you come from?" Before trying to understand ourselves, we must know where we come from, because our existence is the logical continuum of evolution.

The cycle of life began with the mineral kingdom which has existed for over ten billion years. The plant kingdom then evolved from it about one billion years ago, followed by the animal kingdom which is now about five hundred million years old. The Homo Sapiens kingdom is the fourth, aged barely forty thousand years. These kingdoms have always been present in our lives.

Homo Sapiens were therefore not the first on Earth. We have much to learn and understand about the workings of the kingdoms which preceded our own and how they survived and evolved to produce us. It was after this introspection that I began to ask myself what my role should be as an individual in the midst of this mineral, plant, animal and human collective. How can I contribute directly to this *evolutionary chain*?

There was no obvious answer forthcoming, but my intuition told me that the answer lay within me. In recalling the phrase: "To save ourselves is to save the world", I realized that I should begin by understanding the meaning of my own life. Every journey begins at home.

The beginning of every journey starts on our own door-step.

1) HUMAN, WHERE DO YOU COME FROM?

Where does the human being come from? This fundamental question has allowed me to learn and understand a number of things about my ancestors. Why, since the beginning, have humans not really understood the meaning of their lives? Where does this indifference to undertake such a personal search come from? Why must we deal with the same problems as our ancestors: war, violence, poverty, racism? Are we condemned to live with them forever? Even the presence of technology has not provided many solutions. We owe it to ourselves to stop and try to understand why we always repeat the same mistakes from generation to generation. Otherwise, our pride and inability to learn will bring us once more to the extinction that has cursed many great civilizations that preceded ours.

My interest in the mystery surrounding our existence has led me to the following conclusions about who we are: human beings can be considered the result of the fusion of mineral, plant and animal kingdoms because they retain chemical and genetic traces of each. As such, the human is the child of the preceding kingdoms and truly "nature's child". By the same token, I then made the link that ties us to our past: the family tree. When a man and woman come together to conceive a child, the latter inherits genetic baggage on three levels; the body, the spirit and the soul, which encompass all the strengths and weaknesses of the parents and ancestors.

TABLE OF INHERITED DEPENDENCIES

BODY:	CHARACTERISTICS, GENES AND HEREDITY.
SPIRIT:	PERSONALITY, BEHAVIOUR, EMOTIONS AND INTELLIGENCE.
SOUL:	VALUES, BELIEFS AND SPIRITUALITY.

By giving birth to us, our parents also engendered in us a number of dependencies. Children inherit both positive and negative elements from their parents and ancestors. From birth onward, their responsibility will be to learn and understand the inherited dependencies of not only their parents, but grand-parents and great-grand parents so their mistakes will not be constantly repeated.

The problem of dependence may explain why children seldom try to understand the strengths, weaknesses and all the other elements of their forebears. They would rather distance themselves from their parents by living their own experience and from there, perpetuate the same mistakes from generation to generation.

The analysis of our parents and grand-parents constitutes a primary source of information. My research brought me to develop a much closer rapport with my forebears by returning to this source of information which is, and always has been, the family I come from.

Our ancestors point out the challenges which we must rise to.

To truly understand ourselves, our primary source of information is as close as our parents and their families. What do I know of their personality, temperament, tastes, physical and mental state of health and their emotions — in short, all the elements that made them who they are? We should identify their strengths and weaknesses and use them as guides in our life. It is entirely up to us whether we integrate them or reject them. But once analyzed, they will reveal to us the dependence which we continually pass on from parent to child. We should understand them in order that they become strengths preventing us from repeating the same mistakes from generation to generation, such as alcoholism, conjugal violence, workaholism and parental irresponsibility.

To enhance our life on every level, we should recognize, understand and act on our ancestral dependencies which hinder us on our pathway of life. We can do this by recognizing the strengths and weaknesses of our kin, by understanding and accepting them, by integrating their strengths and by forgiving them their weaknesses while leaving them free to either solve or live with their own problems. By acting this way, we free ourselves from generational dependencies and are ready to begin our reflection on the meaning of our own life.

Nowadays, everything moves so fast that very few people have enough time to benefit from their primary source of information: their family. This rupture in the *evolutionary chain* stirs up internal conflicts responsible for many ills and suffering. It also makes for a long and arduous journey through darkness before seeing the light. In fact, many people today forsake the essential for egocentrism. They suffer from *acute navel-gazing*. They are so preoccupied with their work that they lose track of their ultimate goal, which is to find inner peace by living a life of contentment.

During many meetings with owners and presidents of corporations, I noticed similarities in their behaviour: the will, courage and determination to win and be financially successful. It is exciting to see them realize their goal, but will owning a company or exercising financial clout address the insecurities transmitted by their parents? The problem is that ambition and the need to succeed at all costs stops them from asking real questions about their dependencies. Whatever feeds our insecurities, we must recognize the deeper motives that keep us dependent on the false values we worship. Some thought on the matter would allow us to discover our real values and reach our rightful place. In other words, we can all be president of our company but before knowing whether this place suits us, we must first work on ourselves.

Our rightful place is determined by our reason for being and no one can take it away.

As president of a trading house, my personal vision was oriented, in the beginning, by what society glorified the most: financial success. Like everyone else, I pursued the dream of being at the head of an important corporation. However, I was plagued with questions which made me realize that success at any cost was in some ways related to a financial insecurity transmitted by my ancestors. I recognized this dependence, and understood, accepted and integrated it to free me from that situation. It led me to my rightful place. I now see life as much more than financial success. Life is what animates us and makes us what we should be. Happiness often comes from small pleasures: a stroll, the smile of a child, a conversation with friends or workmates, the exchange of ideas on the true values of life. When we think about it, only a few people make the connection between what animates them and what surrounds them and thus come to understand the meaning of their lives.

Problems at work can result from our past. Conflicting relationships with our parents can influence our behaviour with our workmates. Behaviour like egocentrism, aggressiveness and drug addiction reveal a difficulty in mastering our emotions. Professional burnout awaits the "workaholics" who want to prove to themselves and others, that they are able to succeed to the detriment of their self-esteem. All the problems of adaptation at work can be understood by asking the fundamental question: "Human, where do you come from?". It can be solved by comparing our behaviour at work to what we experienced in our family. This reality demands that we think, from time to time, about the positive and negative aspects that are the legacy of our ancestors. The integration of our behavioral traits will allow us to better understand our attitudes toward those around us.

Knowing where we come from is vital to understanding our nature and its origin.

WHAT CAN WE LEARN FROM THE ANSWERS TO THE QUESTION "HUMAN, WHERE DO YOU COME FROM?"

- EXPLAIN OUR PRESENT BEHAVIOUR.
- NO LONGER REPEAT THE ERRORS OF THE PAST.
- INTEGRATE THE LESSONS LEARNED FROM OUR ANCESTORS.
- GATHER UP THE STRENGTHS OF OUR PAST TO BUILD THE FUTURE.
- RECOGNIZE, UNDERSTAND AND INTEGRATE OUR DEPENDENCIES TO ATTAIN OUR FREEDOM AND AUTONOMY.

What questions should be asked in order to begin a thought process on our ancestors?

1) Why is it essential to understand where we come from to improve our life?

2) Where do my parents, grand-parents and ancestors come from? What are their strengths and weaknesses?

3) How do I behave in front of my parents? Is there a correlation between them and the nature of my relations with others?

4) What are the behavioral traits of my parents which have influenced me and how do I cope with this on a daily basis?

5) What steps should I follow to improve my attitude in my interpersonal relationships? Am I honest and upright towards myself?

6) What can I do to harmonize my life and brighten that of my parents and children.

7) Am I too dependent on values projected by society? How can that situation change my involvement towards my family and myself?

8) Do I impose my will on my family and my workmates instead of sharing or working with them to find harmonious solutions for all?

9) How do I better master my emotions and understand my behaviour in different situations?

10) Can I understand my parents, forgive them and be proud of what they are?

11) Do I have to prove anything to anyone? What should my contribution be to attain a greater harmony with all?

After having sought out our origins, this process of self-exploration brings us to the question: "Human, who are you?" It aims at gathering up our talents and our natural abilities from the body, the spirit and the soul in order to maximize the potential within us to realize our life's plan.

2) HUMAN, WHO ARE YOU?

Given the frantic pace that drives us in our life, have we enough time to analyze who we are? The question "Human, who are you?" is essential in helping us understand the meaning of our life. What does our body, spirit and soul reveal to us? What makes us unique? The answers to these questions will tell us who we really are. They reveal our strengths and weaknesses and consequently, we become much more tolerant towards others, because we come to understand and appreciate human complexity. This leads us to understanding and accepting others for what they are.

The question "Human, who are you?" touches three essential planes: the body, the spirit and the soul.

- The soul is our essence (the fuel for our vehicle).
- The spirit is our intelligence, our way of thinking, our internal strength (the motor of our vehicle).
- The body is the temple of the soul and the spirit (the chassis and the design of our vehicle).

These three planes will allow us to discover our reason for being. They must be balanced so that we can liberate our full potential. They are indivisible because they are part and parcel of the whole. For a car to be functional, it must possess three essential elements: Energy or the soul, represented by fuel; the brain or spirit, represented by the engine; the body or the physical, represented by the chassis.

The soul

The soul is the essence of the human and the reason for being of every form of existence on earth. It gives us the determination, motivation and the leadership necessary to go beyond our intellectual and physical capabilities. The soul is what animates our body in terms of our reason for being. It is the link between our imagination and reality. It is the energy which stimulates us to surpass ourselves by turning what I call the "imaginary world" into reality.

The soul is the bridge linking the unknown world with the known.

The soul guides us in the accomplishment of our life's plans. We are all here to accomplish a particular mission. Sooner or later, we must discover it in order to bring meaning to our life. Yet where do we begin? Getting in touch with our soul by becoming involved in something we love and cherish is a good place to start. The soul will then stimulate us in finding our rightful place in this world. The precious time that we devote to doing what we love brings us inner well-being. Being close to our soul means understanding our reason for being and our relationship with all things: the earth, the trees, the animals and all the people around us. In understanding our reason for being, we understand the message that each living being communicates to us, like a forester in touch with nature, a chef using only the best ingredients, a doctor with a good bed-side manner and the president of a business who values employees. This self-fulfilment then becomes a way for us to express ourselves without speaking. It leads us to compassion and empathy for those around us while remaining ourselves. We become at one with all we undertake. This means that we are in complete harmony with ourselves and others.

The Spirit

The spirit (our intelligence) is necessary for making decisions regarding our objectives in life. The spirit is the sum of all our previous experiences, beginning with infancy through adolescence and on to adulthood. It is the "pot-pourri" or the totality of everything we are. Each road of life is the sum of experiences and the lessons we learn from them.

Like any good manager, we should step back and take the time to foresee the future. We must think first before making important decisions, whether it be launching a business, changing jobs or starting a family. We must first ask ourselves fundamental questions in order to continue on our journey. Why do we want to change? To fill an emptiness? To respond to a need that is not our own? To impress a neighbour, our family, a friend? Or are we doing it for our own personal progress?

The spirit is often directed by emotions which are not understood or resolved and which make us prisoners of our own fears, rejections and in short, dependencies of every kind. The spirit should master, balance and focus what the soul inspires in us. To have success in our life instead of succeeding in life we should ask ourselves real questions. The choice of a career could be the result of our immediate environment or unresolved family problems when in fact it should be made for the sake of our personal well-being. Some people create a business to prove to others that they can succeed. Others get married in order to leave the family or to escape loneliness, which is often an expression of insecurity.

One day we will have to ask ourselves real questions to understand why we depend so much on others. Sooner or later, life will lead us to look for the link which should exist between the soul and the spirit. It is through the spirit that the soul will express itself within us to maximize our potential since the spirit is the conductive wire between the soul and the body. In today's society, people are reluctant to take time to think about their own identity. Our total preoccupation with the reality of our immediate environment leaves us little time to understand who we are.

The fishermen are confident they will catch fish today. They must tame their spirit so that their catch is plentiful and then thank life for the nourishment it brings them.

To realize our full potential in terms of our values and our well-being, we must familiarize ourselves with how our spirit works. Then, we must eliminate all behaviour and paradigms that hinder the emergence of our true self. In being aware of who we are, our vision will be focused by what we want to accomplish. Before becoming an entrepreneur, professor, professional or a business employee, we must first understand the reason behind our choice before considering what it will bring us in return. Our choice must be made without being influenced by society, material wealth or any other hold likely to hinder our progression in life. To avoid falling into this trap, the spirit distinguishes itself by its answers to these questions: what motivates me in life? What are my preferences, interests, passions, my skills? Are my fears, anxieties and dependencies jeopardizing my personal growth? Am I where I want to be? If we honestly question ourselves, the answers that emerge will be self-evident. All too often, we allow our dependencies to run our lives instead of following what inspires and motivates us.

The Body

The third plane is the body which is the physical manifestation of our essence: the soul and the spirit incarnate. Our physical features, our behaviour and our attitudes express what we are inside; in other words, our aspirations, our dreams and our vision. "You are what you eat." In fact, everything we eat, read and see shapes and builds our identity. Therefore, we have to wonder who we are when:

— Modern society gives us fast-food restaurants to save time but the "convenience" means the acceleration of life's pace as well as an increase in stress.

— Violence on television, video games and in the movies is so overwhelming that young people today express more verbal and physical violence than in the past.

— Most business people do not take or have the time to exercise. Their work load limits them to exercising their intellect at the expense of their physical health which would lead them to more efficiency and higher performance.

— Eating and breathing have become, to a certain extent, secondary, the priority being given to financial or personal success. We believe that our time is better spent working full-tilt to please our superiors, whatever the price, rather than going for a walk for a moment of rest and relaxation or enjoying a healthy meal.

Breathing allows for better oxygenation, something essential to clearer decision-making. Eating properly or giving oneself a moment's rest allows for recharging to occur. Caught up in the daily grind, many people do not take the time to please themselves. Nor do we take the time to appreciate life because today's employers incessantly increase our work load. They demand or subtly integrate the phenomena of the "workaholic" into their hiring criteria by proclaiming that performance-driven directors, managers and employees are corporate action heros when they are nothing more than potential victims of stress. Thus, we give heart and soul to our work to the detriment of our health. The frantic rhythm imposed on us does not respect our fundamental needs, such as sleeping, eating and breathing. It is only when we are totally exhausted that we think about balancing our life.

The body is the manifestation of our spirit and soul.

The study of human morphology seeks to distinguish the strengths and weaknesses of human beings through their physical features. In Asia they use morphology to recognize the characteristics of individuals and their personalities. It identifies physical strengths and weaknesses. Height, weight and facial features determine who we are and can be used to increase our potential to deal with problems which affect us on a daily basis.

The body is the barometer of our strengths and weaknesses.

In making the connection between our body and who we are, we can rely on our strengths and be ready to understand our weaknesses in order to learn from them and grow. The understanding and the harmonization of the three elements, the soul, the spirit and the body, allows us to determine what we must know, be and do to bring about total health. This is why we must pay particular attention to our morphology, our personality and our physical capacity.

The integration of the three planes allows humans to be where they want to be regardless of events in their lives.

WHAT CAN WE LEARN FROM THE ANSWER TO THE QUESTION "HUMAN, WHO ARE YOU?"

– IDENTIFY OUR REASON FOR BEING TO DISCOVER OUR FULL POTENTIAL.

– MASTER OUR DEPENDENCIES TO BECOME FREE AND AUTONOMOUS.

– UNDERSTAND OUR MORPHOLOGY TO KNOW OURSELVES BETTER.

– UNDERSTAND THE STRENGTHS AND WEAKNESSES ASSOCIATED WITH OUR THREE PLANES, THE BODY, SPIRIT AND SOUL, TO BE IN OUR RIGHTFUL PLACE.

– MAXIMISE OUR FULL POTENTIAL BY INTEGRATING THE THREE PLANES.

What questions must be asked to awaken us to a real understanding of our three planes?

1) What motivates me to find my reason for being?

2) What is the potential of my body, spirit and soul?

3) Do I use my talents or my personal interests to realize my full potential?

4) Do I master my spirit or my intelligence to make the right decisions in my life, or am I dependent on influences around me?

5) Do my decisions reflect my personal tastes and interests or are they those of others?

6) What are the strengths and weaknesses that distinguish me from others and allow me to find my rightful place?

7) What can I learn from my morphology? How can it raise basic questions on my progress through life?

8) Do I listen to my body by providing it with a well-balanced diet and regular physical exercise?

9) Do I take the time for breathing exercises and moments of reflection?

10) Do I take a break in the middle of my work in order to nourish my inner self?

11) Do I take time to analyze my body to understand my strengths and weaknesses in order to improve my physical performance?

After having integrated the three planes of the body, spirit and soul to determine who we are, we come to the question, "Human, where are you going?" which will project us into the future while manifesting in us today what we will become tomorrow.

3) HUMAN, WHERE ARE YOU GOING?

The third fundamental question: "Human, where are you going?" brings us naturally to reflect on the direction we will be taking along our road of life. Having understood where we come from and who we are, we can define and understand today what we will become tomorrow. In short, this means that a sensible diet, proper breathing and a healthy body will bring balance to our life and increase our chances of being in perfect health to face tomorrow's challenges.

By paying attention to our physical health and serving its needs, we will better understand the meaning of our life and be more inclined to act by prevention instead of being left to repair the damage resulting from our neglect. If truth be told, we tend to react to situations rather than prevent them. We take care of ourselves, or try to, by using temporary methods. For example, when we are injured we treat the wound without asking what the injury signifies in our life. Yet every ailment that appears in the course of our life has a meaning. Professional burnout can be interpreted as a need to stop, think, and understand that we may not have chosen the right path. Is every accident or illness which crosses our path not directly related to something we should have noticed before it happened? By a simple understanding of this type of event, we can act on its message and reroute our road of life.

When we know where to go, we become masters of our destiny. The road to take is an integration of our three planes: physical health, the mastering of the spirit and the harmonization of the soul with our deepest values. This balance gives birth to our life's plan. A unified life plan is a road which is clearly defined, organized, directed, mastered and integrated into reality. With it, we will manifest all that happens in our life and be responsible for whatever that may be, instead of depending on others to ensure our well being. Our dependencies will wither once we find ourselves in our rightful place.

Everyone must realize their own life plans since each mission is different. Once our mission is understood, we must communicate it to others to activate the process of awakening and awareness for the collective well-being. The more we manifest our life's plan, the more visible we become, attracting others who want to reach the same goal.

The future is created in the present.

In being conscious of this new dimension and in not putting off until tomorrow what we can do today, we will no longer have to endure the same plagues perpetuated from generation to generation. We will thus liberate ourselves from all our dependencies. This awareness will become the keystone of all intergenerational information flowing from the mineral, plant, animal and Homo Sapiens kingdoms. Humans will come to understand the evolutionary links coming from the world of perfection (nature in its purest state) in order to ensure their survival. The integration of this information will allow them to grasp the fundamental differences between black and white, war and peace, wealth and poverty, man and woman, in order to reconcile the past with the future and become the *evolutionary being of the Fifth Kingdom*: the one who forges the links between all that exists. Of all the kingdoms, the Homo Sapiens kingdom may be the only one with the choice to understand this dimension through the awakening of their consciousness. This information is the key to preserving the total order of life, the forerunner of our evolution.

The perfection of life
is the road to our evolution.

However, for preservation to begin, humans must first confront their transgressions against the kingdoms. They must own up to and correct pollution, environmental degradation, loss of bio-diversity, the extinction and near extinction of species, sickness, and natural disasters to ensure their survival. The paramount conditions for survival are awareness of and respect for the perfection of life. Once we understand this perfection, we will realize that our presence on earth is to improve life, not destroy it.

The integration of the four kingdoms in our daily life
will save the human from extinction.

Sooner or later, individuals will have to understand where they are going in order to become an inspirational source for all of humanity. This source of inspiration will guide us in crossing life's bridge by the awakening, awareness and the realization of our full potential in light of attaining autonomy and freedom. To cross it, we will have to adopt values in harmony with life: love, tolerance, understanding, a respect for oneself and others, the experiencing and understanding of our dependencies and a respect for the perfection of life.

The life within us
is the essential source of our survival.
Life preserves life.

Everything that exists is alive and everything that is in us is living; therefore we must make a link with all that surrounds us.

It will become very important to distinguish the true needs of life which surround us: the flowers, trees, animals, the forest, the earth, fellow-humans, in order to integrate their particularities and better respect them. We are all responsible for our garden of life and we are all an integral part of the global garden of life. In our own garden we can cultivate, then choose the components that we desire. However we have every responsibility towards humanity to spread the fruits of our labours to the collective universal garden of life.

"Where are you going?"
lies in the hope that one day humans
will understand what is essential to their survival.

WHAT CAN WE LEARN FROM THE ANSWERS TO THE QUESTION "HUMAN, WHERE ARE YOU GOING?"

- MANIFEST TODAY WHAT WE WILL BE TOMORROW.
- REALIZE OUR LIFE'S PLAN BY INTEGRATING OUR THREE PLANES: BODY, SPIRIT AND SOUL.
- RESPECT ALL LIFE AROUND US.
- BECOME ONE WITH THE KINGDOMS.
- RECOGNIZE THE PERFECTION OF LIFE TO ENSURE OUR SURVIVAL.

What questions must be asked relative to the road which must be taken to ensure our survival?

1) What is my contribution today to the collective betterment of tomorrow?

2) What motivates me to follow the road which I have chosen?

3) What is my vision of the future and does it reflect what I practice on a daily basis?

4) What should I do to realize my life's plan?

5) What are the intrinsic values which I cherish for my future development?

6) What essential information shows me the perfection of the kingdoms?

7) What is the essential source of our survival?

8) Do I believe in the coexistence of the kingdoms in my daily life, and in the well-being that this coexistence brings me?

9) Am I ready to respect the values that life dictates?

10) What is my contribution to the survival of humanity?

11) Is my garden of life well-maintained? How does it affect the global garden of life?

Chapter 4

ORGANIZATION, WHERE DO YOU COME FROM? WHO ARE YOU? WHERE ARE YOU GOING?

Our ultimate responsibility lies in creating goods and services that respect and serve the best interests of humans and the environment.

This chapter will analyze the origin of the organization. It will awaken us to the behavioral dependencies inherited from its organizational ancestors: the leaders, visionaries and directors who have made a mark on its evolution.

In their constant search for new areas of growth, today's organizations devote themselves almost exclusively to financial performance. This has forced them to restructure on an unprecedented level. How do they benefit by living in a perpetual cycle of transformation? Does it ensure their survival? In fact, mergers, downsizing, massive lay-offs and the omnipresence of technology which outmodes the human, create a sense of insecurity in the work place, reinforcing the dependencies which stem from financial insecurity.

Over the last few decades, the organization has undergone profound changes on economic, technological and organizational levels which have distanced it from the primary mission: to serve the human. To redefine its mission and clarify its vision of the future, today's organization must call itself to task by analyzing what it has inherited, "Organization, where do you come from?", its existing components, "Organization, who are you?" and its vision of the future to reach its rightful place, "Organization, where are you going?"

For some time now, organizations have leaned towards a system where human values and respect for life have been put on the back burner. They live in a world where profit is the bottom line. Faced with this grim reality which translates to over-consumption and the global pollution it represents, how can they address life's real problems when their own survival is caught up in this financial insecurity? This dependency has resulted in business mergers and budgetary constrictions under the pretext of the globalization of the marketplace. Uncertainties created by today's economy have propelled businesses into major down-sizing to please shareholders. The original mission of most organizations has been redirected to accommodate this reality. An international economic summit on the future of organizations is what is needed to arrive at new visions supported by new values.

What fundamental question must the organization ask itself at its inception or in the course of its existence to rediscover its primary mission? "Organization, where do you come from?", will allow it to discover its origins and to become its true self by being at the service of the Human.

1) ORGANIZATION, WHERE DO YOU COME FROM?

What is the origin of the organization? From were does it trace its beginnings? From the mineral, plant, animal or Homo Sapiens kingdoms? Do the kingdoms themselves constitute a type of organization? In imagining these as organized worlds, can we now give new meaning to the organization?

What do nature and life, these marvellous "organizations" which are perfect and harmonious, awaken in us? If life is perfect, why then are we the only species born of perfection yet imperfect?

The organization is defined as an organized grouping of humans with resources, expressing the desire to realize an idea, dream or concept. In practice, this means that our original sources of inspiration can be organizations found in the perfect world of nature, such as the forest, which gives us oxygen, the earth which nourishes us and the bees which give us honey. Which approach must the organization follow to understand the tools offered by the cycle of life and nature? The examples the kingdoms offer should influence our know-how and self-awareness in today's organizations. Bees give us an exemplary model of organized work where the hive is the organizational structure. The queen and her workers daily organize the "return on investment" from their labours. Each bee has a role to play and all the others respect it. Together, they succeed in attaining a common objective through their cycle of life while proliferating life around them as well as being in harmony with it.

The cycle of life is the organization's first lesson.

The meaning of life for the organization lies in the definition of its mission. It will find its reason for being by retracing its origins and by drawing on the information issuing from the perfection of this world. Somewhat like the human, the organization was engendered by the fusion of the mineral, plant, animal and Homo Sapiens kingdoms, retaining components from each. In other words, the evolution of the organization followed the chronological order of the kingdoms as:

- agriculture, can represent the exploitation of the mineral and plant kingdoms,
- industrialization, can represent the exploitation of the animal kingdom by calling upon the human's brute strength,
- creativity, can represent the exploitation of the Homo Sapiens kingdom by calling upon the intellectual strength of the human.

From this analogy, we see that from any organization's inception, the founders become the catalysts of "genetic" organizational baggage through their body, spirit and soul and this comprises the strengths and weaknesses of their organizational ancestors. This is why they must seek out the origin of all dependencies of the body, spirit and soul, and integrate them in order to avoid the errors of the past such as bankruptcies, loss of markets, mergers and so on.

TABLE OF INHERITED ORGANIZATIONAL DEPENDENCIES

BODY:	GOODS OR SERVICES, INDUSTRY OR SECTORS OF ACTIVITIES, HUMAN, MATERIAL AND FINANCIAL RESOURCES.
SPIRIT:	CULTURE, ETHICS, POLICIES.
SOUL:	MISSION, VALUES, MANAGEMENT PHILOSOPHY.

To ensure the success of the enterprise, the founder must recognize, understand and act on all the organizational dependencies obstructing the evolution of the organization: by identifying the strengths and weaknesses of organizational ancestors, by capitalizing on their strengths and by recognizing their weaknesses to know what they contributed in their time. In this way, the organization integrates its past, frees itself from inherited dependencies and is truly able to evolve.

In practical terms, the organization should examine the characteristics of similar businesses which existed before them. What goods or services did they offer? What did their human, financial and material resources consist of? What was the history of these businesses, their culture, ethics, policies, missions, their values and their management philosophy? What were the strengths, weaknesses and dependencies of their predecessors? How can their past contribute to the future growth of our organization?

In seeing what was done before, we can improve on today's organization. It is a matter of retracing the evolutionary origin of our organization in order to benefit from its strengths, such as a strong brand name and a notion of "family" in the business. As well, we can learn from past mistakes such as poor distribution networks, the exploitation of the workers, and so on. This exercise is vital for the organization if it is to integrate past experience for real evolution. Many of today's businesses have difficulty understanding the mistakes made by their predecessors because they have not as yet integrated their past. What is paralysing our businesses today? Labour problems, mergers, lay-offs, dissatisfied employees? Where do these conflicts come from? Today's organizations no longer ask questions but simply react to problems as they arise rather than prevent them. What links can be made between past and present problems? What solutions can emerge in light of lessons learned from the past? It has been said that the past is the guarantor of the future. Is this still true today?

Since the beginning, organizations have battled to conquer territory, create markets and protect themselves from competition and potential enemies. In short, they have strived to gain the high ground. Not surprisingly, the arms industry is the perfect manifestation of this type of thinking. Its original purpose and reason for being was to defend the collective. While in itself a very noble and necessary vocation, the notion was turned upside down to the point where the industry now encourages belligerence to sustain its growth. It justifies this paradox by operating under the pretext that war creates employment and contributes to the economic growth of nations. While there may be some truth in this perverse logic, the fact remains that it is not the arms industry or the destruction it promotes which is vital, but rather life and the preservation of the planet.

The organization which preoccupies itself by integrating the principles of life's cycles into its mission will give it a leading edge in the market. By integrating the dependencies of its predecessors, it will discover innovative solutions, bringing it back to its rightful place, which is where it really belongs in the market. Analysis of previous problems and their solutions will lead to anticipating the future with a preventive rather than reactive approach.

At the outset, the organization was concerned with the essential. It was oriented toward satisfying the immediate needs of individuals. The priorities were centred chiefly on what was vital: nourishment, housing and clothing. Today, the organization must deal with a profusion of new needs generating an endless supply of new and improved goods and services. The result is the proliferation of gadgets and consumer goods of every kind, created to the detriment of the environment. Because our society is developing exponentially and at the same time is caught up in the wave of overconsumption and the disposable, we have come to overly value the phenomena of "the super-hype", blindly believing in the *marketeers* or the *top guns* of consumerism. Consumers, inundated by goods, services and information of every kind, rely on the organization to determine what they need to live. This gives the organization free reign to foist new products on consumers which, in the past, would have been considered superfluous and unnecessary. Today, everything is based on the sales pitch without giving any thought towards the usefulness of a product. As an example of superficial needs, consider all the so-called options available in a new car. Not too long ago, these gadgets would have been considered useless. Nowadays, systems of every kind are automatically installed in our vehicles without the companies giving us a chance to evaluate their real usefulness in our life. Are we in danger of creating a world that exists in illusion rather than one which will bring a greater awakening to the essential elements of life? We should be asking ourselves why the electric or hydrogen-powered car has not yet replaced the gas-powered car. We should be questioning why cars that can run over two hundred kilometres (120 miles) an hour are on the market when the maximum speed limit in most countries is only one hundred kilometres (60 miles) an hour.

Tomorrow's organization will be able to anticipate the future by understanding its predecessors' mistakes. By integrating these inherited organizational dependencies, it will find itself and give new life to its mission.

Our organizational ancestors point out the lessons for our evolution.

HOW CAN THE ANSWERS TO THE QUESTION "ORGANIZATION, WHERE DO YOU COME FROM?" HELP THE ORGANIZATION?

- UNDERSTAND ITS ORIGINS.
- IDENTIFY, UNDERSTAND AND INTEGRATE ITS DEPENDENCIES ON ITS RESOURCES TO ATTAIN AUTONOMY.
- AVOID REPEATING MISTAKES OF THE PAST.
- INTEGRATE THE LESSONS LEARNED FROM ORGANIZATIONAL ANCESTORS.
- CAPITALIZE ON THE STRENGTHS OF PRECEDING BUSINESSES TO BUILD THE FUTURE.

What questions must be asked in order to identify the strengths and weaknesses of our organizational ancestors?

1) What sector-related businesses existed before us?

2) What were their strengths and weaknesses? Their vision in their time?

3) How do the missions of our organizational ancestors relate to today's organizations?

4) What can we learn from the similarities as well as the differences of our organizational ancestors?

5) Can our organization capitalize on past experience in order to manage its future growth?

6) Can business itself adapt to change over the course of time?

7) What major events have marked the industry since its beginning?

8) What is the direct contribution of our organization to the evolution of the industry?

9) How does our understanding of the past lead us to anticipate the future?

10) What is our mission? Are the goods and services offered adapted to today's real needs?

11) What is the link between our organization and the kingdoms? Are we in harmony with life?

Knowing where we come from is essential if we want to avoid repeating the mistakes of the past. We must integrate the past to be what we are in essence; in other words we must give new life to our reason for being by asking the second fundamental question: “Organization, who are you?”

2) ORGANIZATION, WHO ARE YOU?

Today’s organization, caught up in its fight for survival, must overcome a number of obstacles which distance it from its primary and original mission: to be at the service of the human. These obstacles demand that important questions be addressed if the organization is to redefine its true mission. What are the fundamental reasons for its existence? The question “Organization, who are you?” allows us to analyze the organization according to three essential planes in order to evaluate its potential to attain its objectives.

These planes are:

- The body, which represents the human, material and financial resources of the organization.
- The spirit, which encompasses the personality, culture, and the ethical code of the organization.
- The soul, which nourishes the mission, vision and the plan of the organization.

These three planes contain information which is useful to the organization in rediscovering its true nature and moving forward, in compliance with its basic mission. They must be in harmony and balanced if the organization is to free up its full potential. These planes are indivisible because they are part of the organization’s totality. Each organization is unique and must assume responsibility for its evolution.

The Body of the Organization

Human, Material and Financial Health

What is the human, material and financial state of health of the business? What is the physical condition of its employees and the directors? What state are its assets and ratio of indebtedness? What can it do to improve its present situation? An over-all balance sheet is imperative.

The deteriorating health of employees can be gauged by the rise in absenteeism, the increase in stress, the loss of motivation and so on. Businesses allow very little time for rest during the day and praise people who take their work home with them. So it should not come as a surprise that the majority of North American managers suffer from burnout.

Employers who survived the last round of downsizing and mergers demand much more from employees without giving them any job security whatsoever. Financial and material resources must also endure the repercussions of budgetary restrictions, leaving the members to do more with less. The result is work-overload, a great deal of stress and excessive fatigue.

One of the major factors in the deterioration of the human, material and financial health of the organization is its uncertainty towards the future and the financial insecurity which stems from it. What can the organization do to correct the situation?

- First, establish a communications system that will allow employees and directors to clarify the human, material and financial uncertainties which presently exist.
- Hold regular meetings with the members to determine their rightful place.
- Involve them in the decision-making process relative to organizational changes instead of having them always be the last to know.

These simple measures will invigorate employees and rejuvenate the health of the organization. They will instill confidence in the members and give them back the energy and motivation they need to realize their objectives.

Integrate uncertainty to develop certainty.

Strengths and Weaknesses

What are the strengths and weaknesses of the organization? Are they well-mastered? By identifying them, can we improve things such as after-sales service, the quality of goods or services, and personal interaction with clients? What distinguishes the organization from its competition? By knowing its strengths and weaknesses, the organization can consolidate its basic skills to find its rightful place in the market.

The organization must never assume it knows its strengths and weaknesses. It must rather continually seek them out because the knowledge obtained in the search for them awakens the organization to the need for improving the quality of its human, material and financial resources. Being aware of what makes it distinct will lead to better performance.

The integration of its strengths and weaknesses allows the organization to achieve its goals.

The Spirit of the Organization: Image and Culture

What is the image of the organization? Is it strong, weak, emotive, aggressive, competitive, dependent? What is its management approach: creative or rational, reactive or proactive, individual or collective? What of its culture, ethical code and policies? Its corporate image determines the way it operates. Does today's society prefer the creation of "personality-driven" businesses or is the collective approach more popular? Compare the image of Japanese businesses, valuing group unity, to that of North American organizations which favour individualism. Do these different approaches focus on the same long-term goal, being the collective well-being?

The Image and Culture of Japanese Organizations

Japanese organizations rely on integrated participation and the respect of tradition and group values. Individual expression gives way to the consensus of the collective. In Japan, labour disputes are manifested by wearing a black armband. Nobody suffers because work does not stop. In addition, socializing between members after normal working hours is important and valued by Japanese companies.

The Image and Culture of North American Organizations

Individualism, expressed through entrepreneurship and individual performance, is valued by North American organizations. Basic values are centred on individual creativity. Here, labour disputes can result in strikes affecting whole segments of the population without any concern for their interests. Socializing between members of the same organization after a day's work is not mandatory. Most are more inclined to return to personal interests such as family, friends or leisure.

To illustrate the advantages and disadvantages of each of these organizational cultures, here is a comparative chart of Japanese and North American organizations.

JAPANESE ORGANIZATION

ADVANTAGES	DISADVANTAGES
GROUP PARTICIPATION	LACK OF INDIVIDUAL CREATIVITY
SENSE OF BELONGING TO A GROUP	INDIVIDUAL NEVER MAKES DECISIONS ALONE
RESPECT FOR TRADITION	DEPENDENCE ON HIERARCHIES
HUMILITY	PREDOMINANCE OF GROUP OVER INDIVIDUAL
GROUP IS VALUED	FREEDOM OF EXPRESSION LIMITED

NORTH AMERICAN ORGANIZATION

ADVANTAGES	DISADVANTAGES
INDIVIDUALISM	EXHAUSTION OF LEADERS DUE TO CONSTANT EFFORT
CREATIVITY	EGOCENTRISM
PREDOMINANCE OF INDIVIDUAL VALUED	TEAM PERFORMANCE SECONDARY
CHIEF OR LEADER VALUED	COMPETITIVENESS AND OVERWORK
PERSONAL AUTONOMY	SOLITUDE

Despite the differences between these two approaches, there is a similarity in the common goals followed by these two cultures. Both aim to achieve greater economic performance.

As a solution for the future, the organization should opt for a corporate culture that unites and strengthens both approaches. It should stimulate individual creativity and integrate it into a collective goal. The balance between these two approaches can bring a new vision, inciting an awakening and awareness in tomorrow's organizations.

The family of enterprises thrives on this unity by putting the creativity of each member to the pursuit of the collective goal.

The spirit of the organization sculpts individual and collective creativity.

The Soul of the Organization

Mission

What is the organization's reason for being? Is it up-to-date and capable of effectively satisfying the real needs of today's market? Is it in harmony with life and its environment? These questions will allow it to objectively review its present situation in order to redefine its mission in accordance with its true nature.

Its reason for being is therefore to awaken the consciences of its members and consumers to a respect for life, by adopting the necessary measures for respecting the environment. In the future, integrity will be the most respected value and the only way for organizations to get away from the chaos which they themselves created by their obsession with profit. Their survival will depend on their ability to integrate their true mission.

Integrity defines the true nature of the mission.

Vision and Plan

After having defined its reason for being, the organization must solidify this vision by drawing up an action plan for realizing its mission. This plan must bring together its members so that they are united in a common objective.

Generally, management in modern organizations assigns responsibilities to people, regardless of whether they are comfortable with their assignment. However, in the case where members choose an assignment more suited to their own aspirations, their sense of belonging is enhanced, stimulating them to greater participation in the common mission. By reaping the creative potential of its members and by promoting collective progress, the organization will come to free up its full potential for achieving its objectives.

The plan is therefore a conceptual framework which allows the organization to capitalize on its true identity by releasing creativity. It is a matter of having members understand what their real vocations are in order to stimulate their interest, their motivation and their enthusiasm to create, innovate and invent while adhering to the mission of the organization.

The plan structures the creativity of the organization.

HOW CAN THE ANSWER TO THE QUESTION "ORGANIZATION, WHO ARE YOU?" HELP THE ORGANIZATION?

- IDENTIFY THE TRUE NATURE OF THE MISSION.
- LIBERATE POTENTIAL CREATIVITY.
- INTEGRATE STRENGTHS AND WEAKNESSES.
- REINFORCE A SENSE OF BELONGING.
- CREATE A CONDUCTIVE WIRE BETWEEN BODY, SPIRIT AND SOUL.

What questions must be asked to understand who our organization is?

1) What is the real mission? Is it well defined and understood by the members?
2) What is its image? What does it contribute to the collective well-being?
3) What are its human, material and financial strengths and weaknesses? What can be done to increase performance?
4) What are the problems in its sector(s) of activity? In understanding what the corporation is, can these problems be solved?
5) What can it do to settle its identity problems?
6) How healthy are its members? Has the rate of absenteeism risen?
7) Are mental and physical fitness programs offered to employees?
8) How does it awaken creativity in its members?
9) How can it treat the prevailing uncertainty without affecting the productivity of the members?
10) How does it get employees to participate in the formulation of common objectives?
11) What approaches are most favoured to bring the members into the initial vision?

In answering the question "Organization, who are you?", the organization will come to truly understand itself and can then proceed to realize its objectives and reach its rightful place. The third question, "Organization, where are you going?", will lead to manifesting today what it will be tomorrow.

3) ORGANIZATION, WHERE ARE YOU GOING?

Tormented by incessant questions about their future, organizations have to wonder whether they will live to see another day. Will they have the capital necessary to adapt to new technological demands? What will consumers' demands be tomorrow? What does industry expect of the future, knowing that the globalization of the marketplace will lead to competition coming not only from private corporations but companies that are subsidized by governments? Must the organization be reinvented and if so, how?

There is no question that the information revolution has brought about drastic changes and will certainly dictate the course of the organization's future. However, before blindly following its lead, we must seriously reflect on what it has brought us so far. Certainly innovative and inventive products that allow people to communicate faster, but what does this mean in the long run? Organizations with fewer employees, more specialists and a technology that rapidly answers consumers' needs may seem ideal, but what will the ultimate cost be? Living in a faster world means being more dependent on systems that are ever-increasingly complex, leaving us with little time and less freedom. Are there viable alternatives which will drive the organization successfully into the future?

Awakening to the Organization's New Mission

The most efficient way for the organization to manage the unforeseeable is to understand today what tomorrow will bring.

All unknowns can be very well-managed if it does not lose sight of its reason for being. A company which manufactures products to purify the planet manifests a clear mission of its true nature. Regardless of what changes the future brings, its objectives will never waver but rather be the mark of a solid commitment to its reason for being: the preservation of the planet.

***The organization serves the human.
The human serves life.***

The Real Needs of Consumers

Many of today's consumers have great difficulty in determining what is essential to their survival. They are often distracted by the media and by all that surrounds them. Is it important to eat properly? Consumers who eat poorly will eventually come to a turning point in their lives where they will see the need to change their lifestyles. The company that has properly understood its reason for being will gain by sensitizing consumers to a need for self-improvement rather than simply offering them goods and services. Tomorrow's organizations will develop products designed for the real needs of consumers. They will take responsibility by providing all information on the effects of their products. In this way, better-informed consumers will choose better products for their well-being and consequently improve their health.

***Goods and services to awaken
the consumer's well-being.***

Reinventing the Organization

With the emergence of more demanding and better-informed consumers, tomorrow's organization will have to undergo major transformations. It will have to provide more information regarding goods and services with a view to expanding awareness for individual and collective well-being.

The Consumer, the Organization and Life should be perceived as a single entity having a common goal which is to protect the planet. Thus the new role of the organization will be to awaken the awareness in human beings to their real needs so that they can take responsibility by becoming "ambassadors" for the preservation of life.

Each industry could develop a new approach to its goods and services. For example, the pharmaceutical sector can expand its information and educational services at point-of-purchase venues, or via the Internet and other media, in order to alert consumers about side effects of drugs and suggest alternatives. The food sector could also develop alternative and preventive services so that consumers know the potentially harmful and beneficial ingredients contained in the products and thus improve their quality of life.

Integrate the organization into life.

Today's Organization Towards Evolutionary Organization

In a world obsessed with competition and thereby focused on short-term gain, values such as respect for life and the environment are still far from being understood by today's organizations. Why are sales pitches always based on the supposed claims of the competition? While bench marks are fine and good, should we not transcend rather than improve? Why do organizations not invent distinctive goods and services that go beyond the competition and reinforce their uniqueness? The organization that distinguishes itself by its own identity will become one unto itself instead of being what society expects it to be.

Many organizations view the competition as a threat and have unwittingly placed all their hope on the cutting edge of technology to avoid being outpaced in their market. Unfortunately, the supposed solution means a massive acquisition of technology at enormous costs or off-shore subcontracting in the hopes of reducing production costs and keeping the industry alive. What are the real costs and impacts of these decisions? The organization must deal with an ever-increasing financial burden. The employees and managers are in a quandary; their job security is in question, they are reluctant to change and have lost motivation. Are there other solutions? One possibility would be for upper management to acknowledge its most creative individuals who have certainly been waiting for this moment to put their latent potential to use. They will now be in a perfect position to bring technical, scientific and human improvements to the company's development.

The following chart is a comparative table illustrating the advantages of creativity over high technology or off-shore subcontracting.

TECHNOLOGY AND SUBCONTRACTING	CREATIVITY
JOB LOSSES, INSECURITY.	INCREASED SELF-CONFIDENCE. JOB SATISFACTION.
LACK OF SUPPORT AND INTEREST FROM EMPLOYEES.	HEIGHTENED EMPLOYEE MOTIVATION. SENSE OF BELONGING TO THE ORGANIZATION.
FEARS/STRESS BURNOUT.	GOOD PHYSICAL AND MENTAL HEALTH. LOWER RATE OF ABSENTEEISM AND TURNOVER.
OFF-SHORE SUBCONTRACTING.	CAPITALIZE ON INTERNAL CREATIVITY AND INNOVATION.
SHORT-TERM GAIN. LACK OF COST CONTROL.	LONG-TERM GAIN. BETTER COST CONTROL.
BETTER RETURNS FOR OWNERS/SHAREHOLDERS.	DIRECT CONTRIBUTION FROM EMPLOYEES BY THEIR CREATIVE INPUT.
ACQUISITION OF NEW EQUIPMENT AND GREATER INDEBTEDNESS.	CAPITALIZE ON EXISTING RESOURCES. MAINTAIN EQUIPMENT AND SAVE.

A dynamic and humane business will attract members by valuing their creativity instead of ignoring it for the sake of short-term gain. This acknowledgement of human creativity can only strengthen long-term goals and develop the organization's autonomy and freedom.

Human creativity is the heart of the evolutionary organization.

Creativity in the Organization

Are we ready to become truly creative beings or is creativity merely an eccentricity best left to be expressed in our spare time? Where does it belong in our organizations? Why is there a reluctance to make use of creativity in the business world? Is it because the rigid and static hierarchical structures cannot accommodate it?

The evolutionary organization will harmonize its reason for being by establishing an action plan that draws on the creativity within its ranks. An open-minded organization would only be helping itself by informing its members and inviting them to participate in its new orientation.

By doing so, evolutionary organizations will be creating new managerial positions dealing with *organizational creativity: the integration of member-creativity to serve collective interests*. The task will be to liaise among employees, directors, technology, products and life itself to help each member find their rightful place. The idea will be to inspire cohesion between the personal interests of the employees and management toward a common goal. This position will require a creative person with experience in business, organizing, facilitating and motivating, in short, a generalist. In addition, the incumbents would be well-served if they also had some knowledge of human and organizational psychology.

These new managers will bring about more sharing, and an understanding of what is happening within the company. They will turn the individual dream into a collective reality for the prosperity of the organization, its members, their clients and life.

Creativity for the prosperity of the organization.

The Evolutionary Vision

The hierarchical structure of an organization may well hinder the development of both itself and its members. To get to the top, the game is musical chairs. This could be long and painful, not to mention the fact that we may never get the break we need. What is the organization's real objective? Is it smoke and mirrors or the stick and the carrot? Why don't businesses call into account their leaders, presidents, vice-presidents or any other members who are perhaps not in their rightful place? Is the role of every director carved in stone or can we modify it to better serve the organization? Are the presidents in their rightful places in terms of their true dreams, or would they be happier in public relations or production? Has anyone ever asked them? Have they ever asked themselves about their rightful place regarding the betterment of the organization? What drives them to hide behind walls of their own creation? What would happen if they were offered another role... one more in tune with their real aspirations and dreams? Perhaps the realization of their rightful place and a return to their reason for being.

When we have reached our peak as a president or vice president we should immediately begin to groom a successor who will continue the growth of the organization. This procedure will naturally require time in order to integrate each stage so that the transfer of power respects the intergenerational conductive wire that spans the organization.

Evolutionary vision for the growth of the organization.

The Globalization of Markets

Globalization leads organizations to think differently about their economic activities. In the years to come, it is obvious that we will all be part of a global village. To survive, businesses would be well served if they adopted a global management strategy based on the family of enterprises. Is this compatible with our present mentality, centred as it is on individualism or is it utopian? Presently, power is exercised through monolithic management, but in the future, survival will depend on each individual's quest for a common goal. What will the businesses of the 21st century look like? And what of their role?

I have always held that boldness and creativity coupled with the strength offered by the family of enterprises would bring about very promising results and I put this faith to the test while working on an invention. It was called "air solid" and consisted of a double-membraned, self-supported inflatable structure, serving to cover large surfaces such as tennis courts, amphitheatre, stadiums, airplanes, and so on. Exports of this product to Japan were very well-received. The creative and innovative spirit of the family of enterprises along with Japanese business savvy in terms of a collective approach guaranteed our commercial success.

The globalization of markets offers many possibilities for growth to the people in the global village. However, it cannot be achieved without a deep understanding of and respect for all cultures. The good news is that as the world gets smaller and smaller our inner world expands with the awakening to life's new vistas.

The abolishment of world trade barriers and the arrival of even newer technology will maximize returns by more efficient and less costly communication. The Internet, electronic highways, and multi-media will all allow the organization to be more efficient, profitable and achieve its objectives more quickly. Having said this, we must also be aware that these ever more powerful systems can be the source of enormous world problems.

Does constant technological improvement distance human beings from real communication? Does more advanced technology aimed at improving health in fact make us sicker? Does the overabundance and diversity of technology lead the human to a life of loneliness and isolation?

As more and more of us question the course the future seems to be taking, much of what we once took for granted will no longer be viable. The only reference points that will remain for the Human and the Organization after these questions are answered will be the lessons learned from the experience which contributed to their awakening and their evolution.

The future is rooted in the hope that one day the organization will integrate what is essential to its survival.

HOW CAN THE ANSWERS TO THE QUESTION, "ORGANIZATION, WHERE ARE YOU GOING?" HELP THE ORGANIZATION?

- DIFFERENTIATE IT FROM OTHER ORGANIZATIONS.
- MANIFEST TODAY WHAT IT WILL BE TOMORROW.
- BE IN ITS RIGHTFUL PLACE IN THE MARKET.
- RESPECT LIFE AND SERVE HUMANS BY AWAKENING THEIR CONSCIOUSNESS.
- ENSURE COLLECTIVE WELL-BEING.

What questions must be asked to determine how the organization sees its future?

1) What is its reason for being? Is it to serve the human and adapt to the real needs of life?

2) What link will it establish between the real needs of life and consumer demands?

3) How will it reach the consumer?

4) Will its goods and services awaken the consumer to a collective well-being?

5) What must it do to reinvent itself?

6) Is the new trend towards technologies in business pertinent to its evolution and that of its members?

7) What training programs will allow humans to raise their level of consciousness towards universal changes?

8) What fears do they face regarding the transformation to the "evolutionary organization"?

9) How will the organization convey the principles of "rightful place" to its members?

10) Why is it necessary to establish a management position dedicated to organizational creativity?

11) Considering world markets, what efforts must be made to remain competitive?

PART TWO

THE AWARENESS

Chapter 5

THE BALANCE OF LIFE'S NEEDS

We are all responsible for our lives and must assume responsibility for our survival.

The second part of this book deals with the awareness which will reunite the Human and the Organization with their sources through the integration of everything that connects them to life. This chapter is about the balance which the Human and the Organization must regain in order to be in harmony with the life around them. Analytical charts will show the parallel evolution of each, making us aware of their imbalances as well as offering solutions which will re-establish balance in their lives. What causes imbalance in the Human and the Organization? What values and needs must be established to attain ideal balance?

Balance is defined as having an inner peace and the feeling of being in one's rightful place. Why do we spend our whole life looking for our rightful place? To find a balance that will make accomplishing our life plan easier? What is a life plan? For humans it is the road of life they must follow to attain autonomy and freedom. For the organization, it is the road, fed by a vision, that must be travelled to attain autonomy and freedom.

To realize their life's plan and regain balance, humans must return to their source and the organization to its initial mission. To realize a life plan is to know in our heart of hearts that we are truly on the right road. Our own road is unique and every person or event that touches our life will bring us closer to our life's plan. We sometimes ask ourselves: "Am I in my rightful place? Am I on the road of my life's plan?" We must ask ourselves what we truly wish to accomplish so that every event becomes significant in attaining balance. Do the Human and the Organization feel distanced from their original sense of balance due to a lack of long-term vision? Our life's plan should be clearly defined so that maintaining this balance is easier.

Whatever happens to us in life has a purpose and one day we will understand this purpose.

1) LIFE'S NEEDS AND UNIVERSAL VALUES

Understanding the events in our life leads us to integrate life's needs and universal values which come from the world of perfection. What are these needs and values? They are principles well beyond human understanding which spring from everything that life has engendered and dictated.

The seven basic needs of life are fundamental to all the kingdoms that live with us on this planet. They constitute the foundation of all existence. They tell us what is essential to life. In themselves, they form the basic principles of balance in life.

THE SEVEN BASIC NEEDS OF LIFE

1- RESPECT FOR THE MINERAL, PLANT, ANIMAL AND HOMO SAPIENS KINGDOMS.

2- RESPECT FOR ALL HUMANS.

3- RESPECT FOR THE CYCLES OF LIFE AND NATURE.

4- MAINTAINING THE BALANCE OF LIFE AROUND US.

5- CONTRIBUTION TO COLLECTIVE AND GLOBAL WELL-BEING OF THE HUMAN, THE ORGANIZATION AND LIFE.

6- DISCERNMENT AND TOLERANCE FOR THE INTEGRATION AND EVOLUTION OF THE HUMAN AND THE ORGANIZATION.

7- SELF-SUFFICIENCY, AUTONOMY AND FREEDOM OF THE HUMAN AND THE ORGANIZATION.

The daily appreciation of life's needs allows us to raise our awareness so that we can attain individual and organizational balance. Appreciating these seven essential needs for our survival will lead us to respect all that surrounds us.

Life's needs preserve life.

The universal values are in fact laws which govern perfection. By calling for a common universal consciousness, their aim is respect for all life. They instill in us the knowledge that each life has within it an instinct for self-preservation which demands a respect for the world it inhabits. As such, they unify creation's original principle which is the interconnectedness of all existence. The Human and the Organization should never think they are outside this chain of life. What are these values that can connect us to the perfection of the universe?

THE SEVEN UNIVERSAL VALUES OF LIFE

1- RESPECT LIFE.

2- RESPECT YOURSELF AND OTHERS.

3- SERVE LIFE.

4- BE IN HARMONY WITH LIFE.

5- GIVE FREELY EXPECTING NOTHING IN RETURN.

6- UNDERSTAND THAT NOTHING IS TO BE TAKEN FOR GRANTED IN LIFE.

7- BECOME LIFE AND TRANSCEND IT.

These universal values are certainly uppermost in our minds in times of crises and international conflicts. However, we should always be thinking about them, as they themselves are the essence of our existence and stem from the balance of life and its perfection.

Universal values provide balance in the world of perfection.

2) HUMAN NEEDS VERSUS LIFE'S NEEDS

Are we able to determine our real needs? How do we distinguish life's real needs from immediate needs? Today, the Human and the Organization receive an enormous volume of information about all kinds of goods and services coming from different sources such as mass-media, information technology or marketing and publicity. Is this information overload useful?

Do we have filters to screen out information that is not essential to our evolution? This flood of information tends to distract humans from their real needs without bringing any real improvement to life. Does progress include inventing new products that have little or nothing to do with our development? Can we justify these products on a cost/benefit basis given the waste, excessive advertising, overconsumption and pollution that come with them?

Ultimately, we must take life's needs into consideration, and learn to choose products which are more suitable to our evolution and in harmony with life. The Human and the Organization of tomorrow will be able to imagine all sorts of creations and innovations based on life's real needs instead of superficial ones. Evolutionary marketing means creating and promoting goods and services that respect and answer the real needs of life, meaning products that are Earth-friendly and not ones that humans and organizations have been led to believe are essential to their own survival. Instead of wasting natural resources, we will have to ensure their abundance. In short, we need to nourish nature to preserve life instead of exploiting it to the extreme thereby precipitating its extinction.

Many inventions and innovations, developed with all the best intentions, have nevertheless had a disastrous impact on our growth by creating pollution, wars and the extinction of many life forms on the planet. New inventions should be evaluated and reviewed in terms of their impact on the environment and our survival. The Human and the Organization should have, as their life's goal, the preservation of life by determining their real needs as opposed to those that are not significant to their growth. The essence of life itself rests on the well-being of all that exists.

Life unites humans with the earth, sun, water, vegetation and animals so that together we can be in harmony, but only if our needs respect theirs.

If the Human and the Organization are to find their balance, they must first determine the essential needs of their lives and that of life around them.

3) LIFE'S WHEEL OF BALANCE

How can we attain a balance in our life while respecting life's needs and universal values? Life's wheel of balance is perfect but we have yet to truly understand the significance of this fact.

In the universe, everything is in balance. Otherwise the Earth would be engulfed by its oceans, scorched by the sun or destroyed by meteorites. Why do humans have so much trouble finding balance in their personal and organizational lives when it exists so perfectly in nature? Can we master this balance that we covet so much?

The balance of life therefore means harmonizing our needs with those of life itself so that we can better integrate and respect what is around us.

Life's wheel of balance includes different life cycles which must be experienced by the Human and the Organization as pictured in the following chart.

HUMAN AND ORGANIZATION LIFE CYCLES

Human Cycles		Organization Cycles	
0 TO 16 YEARS	INFANCY AND ADOLESCENCE	0 TO 2 YEARS	START-UP
17 TO 25 YEARS	YOUNG ADULT	3 TO 7 YEARS	EXPERI-MENTATION
26 TO 45 YEARS	ADULT	8 TO 14 YEARS	GROWTH
46 TO 65 YEARS	MATURE ADULT	15 TO 24 YEARS	MATURITY
66 YEARS AND OVER	ELDER	25 YEARS AND OVER	INTEGRATION AND REBIRTH

The schematic below demonstrates the importance of the five vital aspects (familial, social, financial, health and spiritual) necessary for the balance and interrelationship of the Human and the Organization. We will review the imbalances tied to these five aspects which the Human and the Organization may encounter at each stage of their life cycle.

LIFE'S WHEEL OF BALANCE

Life's wheel of balance implies that we understand the vital aspects of both our own evolution and the organization's to attain balance in our lives. Why are the Human and the Organization in the centre of the circle? The centre is the starting point, and pivotal to equilibrium that radiates to the external aspects. This point is like the ball of fire at the Earth's core which both gives birth and nourishes life. The more the Human and the Organization are focused and grounded, the more they radiate towards others. Everything stems from the "self" and the circle represents a continuity towards infinity. How can the Human and the Organization manage their changing priorities through the different cycles of their life? They must ensure that the priorities remain balanced so that the wheel keeps on turning.

We all have the responsibility of attaining balance in our lives to reach our autonomy.

The following chart describes the five aspects of life's wheel of balance which allow the Human and the Organization to define their real needs and attain balance in their lives.

**ASPECTS OF LIFE'S WHEEL OF BALANCE
FOR THE HUMAN AND THE ORGANIZATION**

ASPECTS	HUMAN	ORGANIZATION
FAMILIAL	FAMILY.	DIRECTORS AND MEMBERS.
SOCIAL	FRIENDS, RELATIVES, SOCIAL GROUPS.	CLIENTS, ASSOCIATIONS, COMPETITION, SUPPLIERS.
FINANCIAL	MONEY, MATERIAL GOODS ASSETS.	PROFITS, FINANCIAL AND MATERIAL RESOURCES.
HEALTH	SELF-IMPROVEMENT BODY, SPIRIT AND SOUL.	MOTIVATION OF MEMBERS, QUALITY OF LIFE.
SPIRITUAL	GROWTH THROUGH INSPIRATION, ACCOMPLISH LIFE'S PLAN.	MISSION, VISION, AND SURVIVAL.

Now, let us look at the links we can establish between birth and adolescence for the human and the start-up period for a new business. Is there a relationship between the wheel, the Human and the Organization and their respective growth processes towards attaining a balance in their lives? What are the predominant elements in life's wheel of balance for the human from birth to adolescence and the organization at the start-up stage?

HUMAN (0 TO 16 YEARS) From Birth to Adolescence	ORGANIZATION (0 TO 2 YEARS) Start-up
FAMILIAL: DEPENDENCE ON FAMILY, PARENTS.	**FAMILIAL:** NEED FOR MEMBERS (DIRECTORS AND EMPLOYEES) TO HELP ENTREPRENEUR REALIZE DREAM.
SOCIAL: ATTRACTION TO OTHERS.	**SOCIAL:** WEAK BRAND RECOGNITION AT THE OUTSET.
FINANCIAL: LITTLE OR NO FINANCIAL AUTONOMY.	**FINANCIAL:** FRAGILITY AND RISK.
HEALTH: VITAL NEEDS MUST BE MET.	**HEALTH:** OVERWORK DUE TO POSITION IN THE MARKET.
SPIRITUAL: FIRST DRAFT OF LIFE PLAN, LIFE'S FIRST LESSONS.	**SPIRITUAL:** DETERMINING INITIAL MISSION AND SURVIVAL DUE TO FEW SALES AND LIMITED FUNDS.

During the first phase, the Human and the Organization go through a learning period. Children can benefit from those around them and the organization can capitalize on the experience of the founder to conquer potential markets. This phase corresponds to a period of vulnerability for children, who depend entirely on their parents, and for the organization, which greatly needs the support of its employees and partners. Determination is of prime importance for the child and the organization. One must establish a life plan, the other a mission.

At this stage, an imbalance in the wheel of life may be caused by a lack of both spirituality and concern for health, since our concentration is on financial, familial and social aspects. To allow children to find their balance, parents should provide an environment filled with love and attention while stimulating creativity and innovation in their world. In the same way, the organization must clarify its mission to reinforce its vision. Then it must set up a tight financial budget, generating the least possible debt, or wait to be more financially secure before undertaking new ventures.

In the second phase, that of experimentation, the Human and the Organization continue their development by experiencing the meaning of their lives. What are the predominant elements in life's wheel of balance for the young adult and the young business?

HUMAN (17 TO 25 YEARS) Young Adult	ORGANIZATION (3 TO 7 YEARS) Experimentation
FAMILIAL: EARLY DETACHMENT FROM FAMILY.	**FAMILIAL:** VALUE DILIGENT WORK OF MEMBERS WITH AIM TO EXPANSION.
SOCIAL: IMPORTANCE OF SOCIALIZING. BE IN DIRECT CONTACT WITH ENVIRONMENT.	**SOCIAL:** CONSOLIDATE ASSETS AND POSITION IN MARKET, STRENGTHEN IMAGE. BECOME KNOWN.
FINANCIAL: CHOOSE CAREER TO GAIN INDEPENDENCE.	**FINANCIAL:** SHORT-TERM FINANCIAL NEEDS SHORT-TERM RETURN ON INVESTMENTS.
HEALTH: NOT A PRIORITY.	**HEALTH:** STRESS AND BURNOUT OF MEMBERS FROM OVERWORK.
SPIRITUAL: SEARCH TO DEFINE VALUES CAREER CHOICE: STUDIES OR JOB MARKET.	**SPIRITUAL:** SEEK BUSINESS CULTURE BY TRAINING EMPLOYEES AND DIRECTORS AS TO NEW VALUES.

During the second phase, that of experimentation, the Human and the Organization will concentrate on learning basic skills according to the values which motivate them. For the human, it means making a career choice and thinking about starting a family. Social aspects become their priority. As for the organization, it tries to distinguish itself from other companies by strengthening its image and position in the market with an exclusive product or service. It will encourage group cohesion by motivating employees to attain its present primary objective: increased financial return on investments.

At this stage, the wheel of life may still be out of balance. Humans are more concerned with the social and financial aspects of their lives and tend to ignore the other aspects which are family, spirituality and health.

The organization places enormous importance on its image and social attributes. On the financial side, it increases its capital investments to be more competitive. The imbalance comes from a spiritual weakness characterised by a lack of long-term vision and greater focus on values defined by the short term. Overwork creates health problems and work-family conflicts.

To regain their balance, young adults must ultimately return to their individual source by seeking advice from their parents and friends regarding their future. As well, the organization must look for practical means to encourage its members to create and innovate by supporting individual and collective creativity.

In the third stage, which is growth, the Human and the Organization continue their development towards attaining financial autonomy. Their efforts are more centred on acquiring capital for a better sense of security in the future. What are the predominant elements in life's wheel of balance for the adult human and the growing organization?

HUMAN (26 TO 45 YEARS) Adult	ORGANIZATION (8 TO 14 YEARS) Growth
FAMILIAL: FAMILY VERY IMPORTANT. MARRIAGE, STARTING A FAMILY.	**FAMILIAL:** MORE TIME DEVOTED TO WORK THAN FAMILY. MEETINGS BETWEEN MEMBERS ARE ENCOURAGED.
SOCIAL: SOCIAL LIFE IS ABANDONED FOR MONEY AND FAMILY.	**SOCIAL:** NETWORKING IMPORTANT: EMPHASIS ON BUSINESS RELATIONS.
FINANCIAL: FINANCIAL SECURITY AN ABSOLUTE PRIORITY, WORK IS THE MEANS TO BUILD CAPITAL.	**FINANCIAL:** PROFITS PARAMOUNT FOR FUTURE EXPANSION AND COMPANY SURVIVAL.
HEALTH: OVERWORK, EXHAUSTION, STRESS AND POSSIBLE BURNOUT.	**HEALTH:** URGE MEMBERS TO INCREASE PRODUCTIVITY TO THE POINT OF OVERWORK AND HEALTH PROBLEMS.
SPIRITUAL: DAILY PREOCCUPATIONS MAKE SPIRITUALITY SECONDARY.	**SPIRITUAL:** ALL EFFORTS CENTRED ON FINANCIAL ASPECT RATHER THAN SPIRITUAL, DEVIATING COMPANY FROM ORIGINAL MISSION.

At this stage, humans give priority to financial security and think about starting a family. These two choices can cause internal conflicts, the first leading to overwork and the other imposing personal sacrifice because of the time needed for the family. During this phase, many conflicts result from the opposing duality of finances and security versus the family and well-being. For its part, the organization consolidates its financial assets for expansion and mobilizes the employees to work harder for its growth.

During this phase, the wheel of life will still be out of balance. For the human, health is challenged by overwork and stress. Spirituality is set aside for the sake of capital gain. For the growing organization, constant demands for greater efficiency make the members more likely to develop health problems. The mission of the organization, in high-production periods, is abandoned for the sake of financial gain.

To regain their balance and realize their goals, humans must determine their personal objectives in terms of what they cherish without putting their mental and physical health in jeopardy. To do the same, the organization must reinforce its mission so that everyone can be in harmony and focus their efforts in the same direction, and by doing so, reduce stress and overwork.

In the fourth phase, that of maturity, the Human and the Organization continue on their roads, stabilizing and evaluating the meaning of their lives. All efforts are deployed to keep what has been gained and to look for the meaning of existence. What are the predominant elements in life's wheel of balance once the Human and the Organization have attained maturity?

HUMAN (46 TO 65 YEARS) Mature Adult	ORGANIZATION (15 TO 24 YEARS) Maturity
FAMILIAL SLOW DOWN OF PROFESSIONAL ACTIVITIES TO DEVOTE TIME FOR SELF, FAMILY AND LEISURE.	FAMILIAL: DOWNSIZING, REORGANIZATION, RESTRUCTURING.
SOCIAL: MORE FREE TIME. SOCIAL ACTIVITIES ARE FAVOURED.	SOCIAL: RETURN TO SOURCE, LISTEN TO NEW NEEDS, CONSOLIDATE BUSINESS NETWORK.
FINANCIAL: RE-EXAMINE VALUES, FINANCES BECOME SECONDARY.	FINANCIAL: REMAINS IMPORTANT BUT SECOND TO THE DEVELOPMENT OF THE COMPANY.
HEALTH: TAKES HEALTH SERIOUSLY, MORE CONCERNED WITH WELL-BEING.	HEALTH: IMPORTANCE OF DEVELOPING TRAINING PROGRAMS FOR MOTIVATION AND WELL-BEING.
SPIRITUAL: PREDOMINANT INTEREST IN SPIRITUALITY IN LIFE.	SPIRITUAL: RE-EXAMINES ORIGINAL MISSION. CONSIDERS NEW MISSION.

This phase of maturity in the human is marked by a greater concern with health and quality of life. At the same time, it represents the beginning of spiritual reflection on life. As for the organization, it is undergoing profound restructuring due to the important changes that its new orientation requires. This transformation demands adaptability on the part of employees and directors so that they can contribute to the new mission. During this phase of maturity, the Human and the Organization will concentrate on preserving assets and testing new values: those of life.

At this stage, the wheel of life may be off balance due to the duality which is inherent in both the Human and the Organization. The need to establish changes in their internal world or reason for being is pitted against expectations that society has imposed on them since birth. Internal turmoil is inevitable because they know their future will be determined by the decisions they make today.

The Human and the Organization can choose to evolve towards balance amidst the five aspects in the wheel by re-establishing order in the chaos that they themselves created. This imbalance is a result of a life centred on work, to the detriment of our health, and for the sole purpose of accumulating financial capital.

To regain their balance and at the same time retain their health, humans must give thought to their life's plan and capitalize on their personal interests. By the same token, the organization must integrate its members into their new mission so they can be in their rightful place and continue to create and grow within the ranks.

In the fifth phase, integration through rebirth, the Human and the Organization continue their evolution. They must recognize, understand and act on their past to live again through the increased awareness this brings them. In this way, balance will be restored to their wheel of life.

What are the predominant elements in life's wheel of balance for the Human and the Organization in the integration and rebirth phases?

HUMAN (66 YEARS PLUS) Elders	ORGANIZATION (25 YEARS PLUS) Integration and Rebirth
FAMILIAL: RETURN TO EVOLUTIONARY CHAIN AND INTRINSIC VALUES: FAMILY. LEGACY OF INTERGENERATIONAL VALUES.	FAMILIAL: RETURN TO MORE HUMAN VALUES AND INTERGENERATIONAL TRANSFER OF ACCUMULATED EXPERIENCE.
SOCIAL: INCLINATION TO LISTEN TO REAL NEEDS OF THOSE AROUND THEM.	SOCIAL: LISTEN MORE TO REAL NEEDS OF MEMBERS, CLIENTS, SUPPLIERS, ETC.
FINANCIAL: NO LONGER PRIMARY ASPECT, BECOMES AN ACCESSORY TO LIFE'S BASICS.	FINANCIAL: STILL IMPORTANT ASPECT IN SPITE OF SOLID FINANCIAL SECURITY BASED ON CORPORATE IMAGE.
HEALTH: VERY IMPORTANT IN MAINTAINING QUALITY OF LIFE.	HEALTH: MORE GENEROUS TO MEMBERS, PROTECT CORPORATE IMAGE (EMPLOYEE ASSISTANCE PROGRAMS, EMPLOYEE BENEFITS, SEVERANCE PAY).
SPIRITUAL: FOCUS ON REASON FOR BEING, GOOD DEEDS AND INTEGRATION OF THEIR LIVES BY REBIRTH.	SPIRITUAL: ELABORATION OF A NEW ORGANIZATIONAL MISSION, NEW VOCATION: REBIRTH.

For the Human and the Organization, this stage marks the awareness of the importance and fragility of life's wheel of balance. The experience acquired can lead them to collective and individual growth. Throughout this fifth phase, that of integration and rebirth, the Human and the Organization put emphasis on well-being and approach life in a more harmonious way. Suddenly, all planes have meaning: familial, social, financial, health and spiritual. Integration and rebirth bring to the individual and business greater balance and a healthier rhythm than that experienced in the earlier stages of their lives.

In this phase, we come to understand what is real for us. At the same time, it allows us to connect to all the events which surround us. We become calmer, more objective, thoughtful and in harmony with all that surrounds us. We see beauty in everything and marvel at the little things in life. We can hear our real needs and those of others. This stage is the one which allows us to respect universal values, to share with those around us expecting nothing in return, and to distinguish modern society's real needs from the superficial.

During this phase, those who have difficulty in recognizing the transformations which are occurring within them and feel that life has passed them by, be it on a human or organizational plane, may feel off balance. The phenomena of aging in the Human and the Organization allows us to learn from the wonders of our life and in doing so, attain balance.

Life is a cycle and the Human and the Organization are part of the cycle. The human cycle begins at birth and continues to old age. That of the organization begins with its inception and goes through the stage of integration and rebirth. What can we learn from this evolutionary process? Each stage of life is intimately connected to our respective lives. Every transformational phase requires personal reflection on the five aspects of life's wheel of balance and their respective contribution to our balance in life. Understanding the imbalances which occur allows us to attain well-being by better balancing the wheel. Attaining this ideal allows the Human and the Organization to integrate their evolution with all that ties them to life.

To be alive is to live;
to live is to respect the balance of life.

WHAT CAN LIFE'S WHEEL OF BALANCE BRING TO THE HUMAN?

- UNDERSTANDING THE IMPORTANCE OF EACH OF THE FIVE VITAL ASPECTS TO ATTAIN BALANCE.
- GREATER UNDERSTANDING OF LIFE'S CYCLE.
- RECOGNITION AND INTEGRATION OF THE IMBALANCES.
- GREATER MASTERING OF LIFE'S NEEDS AND UNIVERSAL VALUES TO ENSURE SURVIVAL.
- IDEAL BALANCE NECESSARY FOR AUTONOMY.

WHAT CAN LIFE'S WHEEL OF BALANCE BRING TO THE ORGANIZATION?

- RECOGNITION AND UNDERSTANDING OF THE IMPORTANCE OF EACH OF THE FIVE VITAL ASPECTS FOR MORE INTEGRATED MANAGEMENT.
- BETTER FORECAST OF THE FUTURE BY COUNTING ON THE BALANCE OF THE FIVE ASPECTS.
- THE IDENTIFICATION AND THE INTEGRATION OF EACH LIFE CYCLE TO IMPROVE PERFORMANCE.
- BALANCE BY RESPECTING LIFE'S NEEDS AND UNIVERSAL VALUES TO BECOME AUTONOMOUS.
- IDENTIFICATION AND CORRECTION OF IMBALANCE TO IMPROVE PERFORMANCE.

What questions must be asked to evaluate our life's wheel of balance?

1) Can you distinguish real from superficial needs in your life?

2) Do you respect life's needs?

3) What do you consider to be universal values and how important are they in your life?

4) What methods do you employ in your life to prevent imbalance in the wheel of life?

5) How much importance do you place on each phase in direct relation to the five aspects of the wheel of life?

6) Will you achieve balance in your organization if you recognize the five aspects of the wheel of life?

7) What place do life's needs occupy in the decision-making process of placing new products or services on the market?

8) Is your organization concerned with universal values?

9) How would you rate information you receive in your organization? Is it pertinent to your growth?

10) The cycles experienced by the Human and the Organization engender imbalances; what methods will prevent imbalance and fill in the gaps?

11) What methods are used to maintain balance in each of the cycles in your organization?

Chapter 6

IN SEARCH OF ESSENCE

Life is the greatest source of inspiration and being alive is the essence of life itself.

We have seen the importance of being in balance in order for the Human and the Organization to realize their lives' plans. Now we will explore the essence of life itself. Essence is in fact what we truly are because it stems from our original purpose. It differentiates us from everything else that exists. Every snowflake is different. Every leaf, flower, tree, animal expresses itself through its uniqueness.

This chapter deals with the discovery of an inner richness crucial to both our survival and evolution. It is the essence which distinguishes us from others. For the Human and the Organization, the search for essence means discovering what makes them different in their quest to become autonomous. Unfortunately, our daily preoccupations with time and money hinder us in this quest for the essence of our life. I would like to propose an approach which would allow the Human and the Organization to find their essence through the realization of their conscious dreams.

Are we the type of people who have enough money to realize our dreams but not enough time to live them? Or do we have a lot of time on our hands but not enough money? What is the relation between time and money?

1) THE DEFINITION OF TIME

What is this phenomena we call time? Why has it become so important in modern society? Why is it that every organizational system depends on it so desperately? Are we slaves to time? All these questions beg for personal reflection on the importance we attach to time in our lives. It has grown to mythical proportions and has become an obstacle in our search for meaning in our lives. Time must not be an end in itself, but rather an opportunity to understand who we are.

Look at life around us. Days go by, plants grow to the natural rhythm of life's cycle and animals feed as their instincts dictate. Time marks the continuum of the *evolutionary chain* which has existed since the beginning of creation. But in the universe, time as a commodity does not exist. Only humans categorize time: a time to eat, rest, work, and so on. We have thus succeeded in imposing our notion of time on the universe. In limiting ourselves to "real" time, we have surrendered all claims to intuition and creativity which stem from our imaginary world.

The only time that is important in our life is the present. The past is gone and the future will unfold as it may. This is why time may be a hindrance to the development of the Human and the Organization. Creativity, thought and the imaginary are not constrained or limited by time. They are free from it and follow a continuum to achieve perfect balance.

Human beings time everything they do, beginning with their rising which is dictated by the alarm clock. At any given moment, there are millions of individuals who are sleeping, eating, satisfying their needs, watching television and reading the newspaper habitually, like robots in a time and motion study created by society. Our lives are so constrained by time that any desire to stop and reflect on the essence of life is likely to be unfulfilled. For humans, time represents an organized system, a routine imposed by their external world.

The organization follows the same scenario. The employees come to work, take their coffee break, have lunch, and go through their working day always according to the same ritual.

They become prisoners of conditioned response, automatons shackled to the programming of time. This phenomena creates a permanent routine in the organization and consequently, a conspicuous loss of creativity and understanding of the members' real needs. Time can mean precision, discipline and efficiency but it can also limit creative input. We end up losing our identity for the sake of a value system imposed by society, creating a dichotomy between the real needs of our life and those of the organization.

Industrialization gave birth to systems which compartmentalized time to better pigeon-hole the Human and the Organization. Today's society teaches us that time is a method for measuring performance: efficiency, quality, profits, earnings, productivity and so on.

Humans function according to an internal time clock directly linked to the essence of their lives. For example, some people work better at night. Some eat at all hours while others prefer fixed times. It is therefore inconceivable to standardize time and confine all humans to a universal social framework, because we are all unique and must discover the way of life which best suits us.

To free ourselves from time and become autonomous, we must understand that it exists to structure and organize our life. It has no real meaning beyond this. Autonomy brings us a greater understanding of the place time should occupy in our life in terms of our personal needs and not those imposed on us by other people or their systems. In the event of power failures, floods and earthquakes, we do not find ourselves looking at the clock. There are more important concerns at hand.

Master time instead of being controlled by it.

As dawn breaks on the new millennium, we must consider a new approach to gradually free us from the grip that time has on us. We must get in touch with what is not constrained by time: our essence, our inherent creativity, our imaginary world, in order to properly reflect on the values society has imposed on us over generations. Only then will we find ourselves autonomous, free and masters of our own destiny. We will drink when we are thirsty, eat when hungry, and sleep when we are tired. We will be more in tune with our bodily needs and thus better able to integrate them into our daily lives.

The present is the real time in our life.

2) MONEY

What influence does money have on our lives? Can we live without it? Does it make us dependent on the great many systems that society has created? Dependence on money comes from a greater need to possess material wealth or to exercise power. How have we become so materialistic? Money can be a stepping stone to attaining freedom and at the same time a source of despair for those who let it guide them. Can money distract us from our personal and organizational progress?

Material wealth is increasingly valued by society,which is why the human places so much importance on money for survival. What role have we given to money? Does it exceed human values? Have we abandoned inner richness in favour of material wealth? In everyday life, money has a practical function: to pay bills, realize conscious dreams and help us attain a certain quality of life. Money should serve the growth of individual and collective human ideals. People who devote all their energy to accumulating financial wealth risk missing out on the greatest joys of life. Happiness can often be found in the simplest things of everyday life, like appreciating nature, playing with children, helping others. The small pleasures in life are often free and can be found in the appreciation of what we are and what we have accomplished over the course of our lives.

For the organization, money represents the motor of the enterprise, a vital resource in accomplishing its mission. Most organizations feel deprived when there is a shortage of capital. They therefore come up with all kinds of excuses to stay alive which ultimately result in indifference to the environment and downsizing or mergers with no regard for the interests of their members.

Without money, how can the organization manufacture or process its raw materials? Money is "the sword of Damocles" suspended above its head. It cannot grow without money, yet the pursuit of money often diverts the organization from its goal, thereby limiting real growth potential. Why does it endure the insecurity of this dichotomy? Why does it have difficulty in understanding the real meaning of money which is nothing more than the energy allowing it to realize individual and collective dreams? An organization that invests in human resources can generate a great many inspired ideas that will ultimately fill its coffers. The simple fact remains: inspiration breeds the investment necessary but investment does not necessarily breed inspiration.

Money is a means of exchange and not the essence of the realization of the mission.

For the Human or the Organization, money is the first thing that comes to mind when we want to carry out a project. Is it at all possible without money? Without cash, how can we make our conscious dreams come true. Lack of money is often associated with insecurity, obstacles, a delay that postpones the realization of dreams to an eternity of tomorrows.

I experienced the fears associated with the unknown and the financial risk that stems from it when I was involved in developing inventions. To conquer my financial insecurity when I take on an unknown world, I build up my faith by strengthening my personal convictions and I always work in terms of a realizable objective. Developing inventions allowed me to help my clients, friends and business acquaintances make real use of their abilities to create and innovate and to understand the meaning of their lives. My financial insecurity has therefore become secondary to my reason for being which is to realize my life's plan and to be happy.

The accumulation of small financial victories or realized dreams in life contributes to the success of our life's plan.

If we have difficulty in giving up material wealth, it is because we are possessed by it and that prevents us from realizing our conscious dreams. As a mental exercise and perhaps a solution, the Human and the Organization should imagine giving up everything they own to better integrate and conquer their financial insecurity with the goal of attaining their life's plan.

Visionaries have no fears of losing all they own because they understand that they are the fruit of their labours.

We become autonomous when money does not own us. We must therefore have trust in life. Money certainly represents a creative energy which helps us in accomplishing our life's plan but we must not be dependent on this energy. This dependence will always control our lives in relation to events outside of ourselves rather than allowing us to capitalize on a new source of income that comes from within us, such as inventions, books, a business or a work of art. Too often we entrust our financial success to others: the stock market, banks, lotteries and casinos, insurance, retirement savings plans... in short, all the systems that capitalize on human insecurity at the expense of potential human creativity. Conversely, by expressing our creativity, we master our own resources rather than depending on results from external sources.

The Human and the Organization must therefore rediscover the essence of their lives... what animates them beyond material concerns. In this way, they will achieve autonomy and freedom and gain the fullness and inner peace that come with the return to their original purpose. They must do what they love in order to succeed in their lives and not depend on others.

3) THE REALIZATION OF THE CONSCIOUS DREAM

Everything starts with desire. Our life, life itself, a smile, a business, an invention, a chance encounter... Desire is the source of what we are. The life within us is what animates us and allows us to manifest ourselves in the real world. It results from the desires which propel us to realize our life's plan. Only we can understand this plan because it is uniquely our own.

What animates us the most? What can we do to change, improve and transform our life so that our true essence emanates from us and is not society's persona? First, we must truly understand who we were, are and will be in the continuum of the *evolutionary chain* which has existed over billions of years. Even though we are born and die, we are not an end but rather a continuity of events swept along through time by an energetic and dynamic current.

Are we alive? Should we allow society, the media, governments and individuals to influence our lives? Are we able to understand what is best for us without being subjected to all sorts of interference that distances us from our essence, which is to be truly alive. To be alive is to take the time to watch birds in flight, to appreciate nature and the people around us. This awareness will lead humans to interact with their environment and start the process of realizing their conscious dreams.

Autonomy is the ability to get the process of the conscious dream into gear. To some degree, it means constructing a process or work plan which will allow the Human and the Organization to regain their essence through the realization of their conscious dreams. The proposed work plan is comprised of five elements: the dream, desire, willpower, patience and perseverance which will lead them to transform the imaginary into reality.

For the human, these five elements are the keys to understanding the imaginary world; to reflect on it, to materialize it by action and to integrate it by having faith in what must be attained, that being the realization of the individual dream.

For the organization, these five elements are the keys to formulating the mission that comes from a vision. We must choose a direction, adopt a plan, organize by consolidating resources, influence members to participate in the vision and master its role in terms of the goal ahead to realize the collective dream.

The following graphic represents the formation and the realization of the conscious dream.

THE PROCESS OF THE CONSCIOUS DREAM

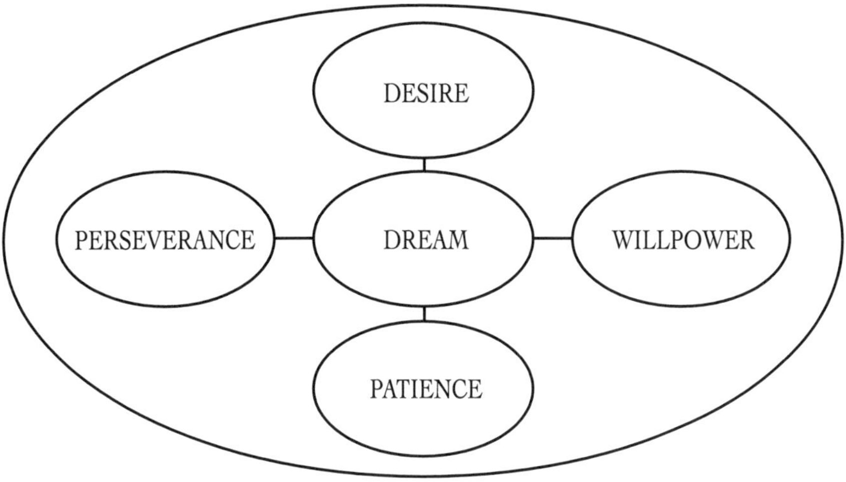

5 ELEMENTS	INDIVIDUAL DREAM	COLLECTIVE DREAM
DREAM	IMAGINARY	VISION/MISSION
DESIRE	REFLECTION	DIRECTION
WILLPOWER	ACTION	ORGANIZATION
PATIENCE	INTEGRATION	INFLUENCE
PERSEVERANCE	FAITH	MASTERING

The First Element: The Dream

What is the source of our dreams? What drives us to make our dreams come true? Does society value dreams? Today's society is not inclined to encourage and value those who wish to realize their dreams and as a result, most people prefer the security offered by a daily routine rather than the risks a dream implies. For many, the dream is associated with pie in the sky, idealism, the incredible, the unattainable... the dreamer is perceived as marginal, an eccentric. For most of us, the hard reality of life, the rational, is the only real world. Yet this sentiment stifles evolution.

What can be done to make people dream, but in a conscious way where they discover that their dreams can bring meaning to their lives and be a source of instant happiness? Can the conscious dream propel us to realize our life's plan?

The dream can come when we are alone with our thoughts. It can motivate us to follow our road of life which is, as we know, seldom easy. We are still a long way from the leisure society that shimmered before us not so long ago. Unfortunately, work still takes up most of our lives. Can work itself be converted to leisure? What sparks our dreams, our imaginary world? How many of us ever really call upon our imagination to understand and learn from our potential?

Very few people exploit their greatest resource which is the imagination. The imaginary world is a world without limits, one that is free and giving. It is a world that is entirely our own, without taxation levied on what we imagine. Yet why are so few people taking advantage of this inner resource? Our society prefers the material world where everything is evident and seemingly close at hand. However the imaginary world, by its very nature, gives us the energy to excel and realize the most cherished goals in our life.

The conscious dream is the essence of what we are. I have often found that music and dance help me to express what I feel when I realize a dream. At the sound of music that I like, I feel in tune with my soul and become the song. When I dance I become the dance and in that instant, I am the music. The soul within me emerges and radiates towards others and I realize my dream.

If you do what you love, you will realize your dreams. You will transcend work, music, the arts, dance and every other activity that comes from within you. At that moment you will radiate your enthusiasm to others and your environment will benefit from it. We do not have the power to change those around us but we can certainly change ourselves and, in doing so, spread a joy for life that will truly inspire them.

The dream is, in itself, the essence which allows humans to become one with themselves in terms of their deepest aspirations. In realizing their greatest dreams, they become the catalyst of their source of happiness.

The conscious dream is the source of all aspirations.

The individual dream sparks our energy, allowing us to realize all that we wish to accomplish. Our dreams can be the inspiration that keeps us alive. Following a dream is living life to the fullest. It is the stimulus to self-realization, the inner strength which allows us to surpass ourselves on physical and spiritual planes. The dream means being true to oneself. Having always been inspired by Japanese culture, my personal dream was to live in Japan. What is yours?

HERE IS SOME PRACTICAL ADVICE TO HELP YOU REALIZE YOUR DREAM.

- Identify what animates you: your interests, passions, ambitions (travel, business, fashion, helping others).

- Choose a role model whose achievements inspire you: a professional, inventor, politician, entrepreneur, artist or any other person who inspires you.

- Determine exactly what you wish to achieve.

- Focus on a very precise and realistic objective.

- Establish priorities in your life.

The following table lists examples of different aspirations that may stimulate certain people to choose a career that suits their personal dream.

PROFESSIONAL:	Guides people in their lives according to their specific discipline.
INVENTOR:	Creates products and concepts which can improve the quality of life of the consumer.
POLITICIAN:	Communicates ideas with the goal of helping society evolve towards a better world.
ENTREPRENEUR:	Contributes to the economic development of society.
ARTIST:	Expresses the life within us and sensitizes us to visible and invisible beauty.
YOU:	What are your aspirations? And to what end?

WHAT CAN THE CONSCIOUS DREAM BRING TO THE HUMAN?

– BEING ALIVE AND EXPRESSING JOY FOR LIFE.

– BEING POSITIVE, ENTHUSIASTIC AND HEALTHY.

– BEING CREATIVE, INNOVATIVE, INVENTIVE.

– BEING THE BEST IN A CHOSEN DISCIPLINE.

– STIMULATING EXCELLENCE.

Is it possible for the organization to dream? The *collective or organizational dream* results from the transformation of personal dreams to collective dreams which are integrated into a new vision. The collective dream unifies the members and inspires them to excel. Organizations which encourage their members to make their personal dreams collective ones are at one step ahead in the marketplace. The role of the dream in the organization is to keep the members abreast of new ways of doing things: to be more creative, imaginative and visionary. Therefore, teaching and encouraging members to dream allows them to contribute to the formulation of global and futuristic visions. My organizational dream was to sell inventions to the Japanese market.

HERE IS SOME PRACTICAL ADVICE TO HELP THE ORGANIZATION REALIZE ITS COLLECTIVE DREAM.

— Unite by brainstorming the personal dreams of each member to create a collective dream.

— Determine their basic skills to realize the collective dream.

— Identify corporate models with similar visions.

— Invent and create goods and services that will encourage the members to excel by developing their uniqueness in the market.

— Integrate the collective dream into a long-term vision. Concentrate efforts in the same direction.

The following table lists examples of different aspirations that the organization and its intermediaries may consider to realize their collective dream.

ORGANIZATION:	Spreads information relative to the collective betterment of clients by offering goods and services better suited to their real needs.
CLIENT OR SUPPLIER:	Supplies products favouring the evolution of humans and organizations around it according to an ethical code that respects life.
MEMBER OR EMPLOYEE:	Integrates the personal dream into the collective dream in order to evolve.
CONSUMER:	Acquires a greater understanding of reason for being in view of real needs: health and well-being.
STATE:	Informs the population and installs structures designed to improve the quality of life, e.g. promoting environmental policies.
YOU:	As an organization, what are your greatest aspirations?

WHAT CAN THE COLLECTIVE DREAM BRING TO THE ORGANIZATION?

- WORKING ENVIRONMENT FAVOURING CREATIVITY: ENTHUSIASM, OPEN-SPIRITEDNESS.
- PARTICIPATORY MANAGEMENT: RALLY PEOPLE TO A COMMON GOAL.
- ACCEPTANCE OF NEW IDEAS AND CHANGES.
- REDUCTION OF CONFLICT AND ABSENTEEISM.
- REDUCTION OF OVERWORK, STRESS AND BURNOUT.

The Second Element: Desire

After having defined the dream, we must now think about ways to bring it about. Desire is the motivation that drives us to realize our dream. Our desire is not simply a dream for its own sake, but is there to bring our imaginary world to life.

Desire is the driving force of the dream.

The role of desire is to generate thought and propel the dream to reality. The pursuit of my dream meant drawing on information pertinent to the viability of my project. I contacted the Japanese embassy and consulate, as well as other Japanese organizations. I tried to find out if what I intended to export respected the customs and culture of the Japanese people. I learned the language of the country and participated in oriental cultural events. I sought out and contacted local companies who already had business relations with the Orient. All of this was done because there was a desire that directed me to realize my dream. It is of paramount importance to understand that desire is a crucial element in deciding the direction to take in achieving a dream. In my case, it meant understanding the country by collecting useful information on its culture. By doing this, I was able to save time and money while preparing my personal plan and building up an interpersonal network with the Japanese.

HERE IS SOME PRACTICAL ADVICE TO HELP YOU EXPRESS YOUR DESIRE.

— Collect information pertinent to interests, passions and ambitions in light of building an action plan or changing direction.

— Look for information on people who inspire you.

— Verify the feasibility of dreams through what was learned from collected information. Determine the costs and sacrifices to be made.

— Think about the formulation of a plan that will make the dream come true.

— Decide on the steps to be taken to realize the plan.

The following table lists examples of different activities that may motivate certain people in their desire to choose a career.

PROFESSIONAL:	Researches and is aware of different professional educational programs.
INVENTOR:	Researches in the immediate environment for sources of inspiration that will lead to ideas for new goods and services.
POLITICIAN:	Meets with resource people from different political backgrounds.
ENTREPRENEUR:	Consults with business leaders to arrive at the best decisions relative to the launch of an enterprise.
ARTIST:	Identifies the inspirational sources which animate and motivate to practise a certain form of art in particular.
YOU:	What is your desire and motivation?

WHAT CAN DESIRE BRING TO THE HUMAN?

– CONCRETE STEPS AIMED AT THE REALIZATION OF A DESIRED DREAM.

– INFORMATION RESEARCH.

– DEVELOPMENT OF A NETWORK OF CONTACTS.

– EVALUATION OF THE VIABILITY OF THE DREAM.

– TIME AND MONEY SAVED.

The role of desire for the organization is to conceive the policies or strategies relative to the direction which must be taken to realize its collective dream. In my case, this meant looking for the necessary contacts to network the Japanese market and gather information on the country's businesses. It meant finding a local business leader who had succeeded in the target market as well as determining whether Japanese companies were interested in my products. The results of this endeavour were: developing an off-shore network of contacts, saving time and money with regard to the inception of the project, consolidating information obtained and preparing the action plan for exportation.

HERE IS SOME PRACTICAL ADVICE TO HELP THE ORGANIZATION EXPRESS ITS DESIRE.

– Research information relative to the feasibility of the collective dream.

– Research information on corporate role models that have succeeded in their fields.

– Proceed with quantitative and qualitative studies on the goods and services to launch the project. Determine the human, financial, material resources needed.

— Beginning with information gathered, formulate a plan to get the collective dream in motion and to determine a direction.

— Find a senior corporate leader or mentor that can advise on the steps that must be taken for its business.

The following table lists examples of different activities the organization and its intermediaries can pursue to motivate them to express their desire.

ORGANIZATION:	Establishes networks within its field of activity to gain information pertinent to the development of new products.
CLIENT OR SUPPLIER:	Compares its situation with that of contemporaries who have had prior experience in terms of what they wanted to accomplish, e.g. off-shore subcontracting.
MEMBER OR EMPLOYEE:	Compares their situation to other organizations with the goal of improving quality of life.
CONSUMER:	Examines existing information networks to ensure quality of goods and services. e.g. consumer protection studies etc.
STATE:	Develops local, national and international information networks to be aware of new trends and standards.
YOU:	As an organization, what is your motivation and desire?

**WHAT CAN DESIRE
BRING TO THE ORGANIZATION?**

- RESEARCH OF INFORMATION RELATIVE TO GOODS AND SERVICES.
- ENGAGEMENT OF ALL OTHER INTERMEDIARIES IN THE REALIZATION OF THE PROJECT.
- EVALUATION OF THE VIABILITY OF THE PROJECT.
- DETERMINATION OF DIRECTION AND REALIZATION THROUGH THE FORMULATION OF A PLAN.
- DEVELOPMENT OF A NETWORK OF CONTACTS.

The Third Element: Willpower

After having gathered together all the information pertinent to the realization of a conscious dream, willpower is the action for its materialization.

In life, there are four personality types with differing ideas about the notion of willpower:

- Those who organize parades;
- Those who participate in parades;
- Those who watch parades go by;
- Those who do not have the slightest idea parades exist.

In life we will always find leaders, those who can predict what is coming. Their clairvoyance sets them apart and they are the ones who organize parades.

There are always volunteers who are ready to take part in a parade. They are also people of action, determined to succeed in their lives.

Then there are those who love a parade and are content to watch it as it passes, without actively participating. They have the advantage of being up to date on all the latest.

Finally, there are the people who do not even know that parades exist and they constitute the majority of the population. They let things happen without the slightest idea of what is going on around them. They are robots who allow themselves to be seduced by contemporary fads without questioning their own existence. Which group do you belong to?

A lack of willpower is often tied to insecurities of every kind: lack of money, poor health, fear, time constraints, and so on. Willpower is marked by action, not reaction. Unfortunately, today's society often insists that we react to changes rather than anticipate them. What can we do to change this?

Willpower is characterized by action because it establishes an organized plan in view of attaining a common objective. The will is the bridge that allows the Human and the Organization to turn their imaginary world — their dreams or visions — into reality.

Willpower is the internal strength that allows the Human and the Organization to turn dream-inspired thought into reality.

For the human, willpower means accomplishing, through action, what has always been a dream. My willpower manifested itself in my leaving for Japan and once there, was tested by realizing the cultural gap, by trusting in the unknown and by integrating my conscious dream. This required investing considerable sums to consolidate my network of contacts, to learn Japanese, to live abroad and to make new friends and acquaintances.

HERE IS SOME PRACTICAL ADVICE TO HELP YOU EXPRESS YOUR WILL.

— Make your conscious dream a reality.

— Invest time and money.

— Overcome obstacles.

— Commit to the dream.

— Coordinate resources to realize the dream.

The following table lists examples of different ways for certain people to express their will in terms of their career choice.

PROFESSIONAL:	Takes on and succeeds in educational program for desired profession.
INVENTOR:	Creates final prototype.
POLITICIAN:	Develops a distinct approach and vision.
ENTREPRENEUR:	Incorporates and starts a business. Creates a project.
ARTIST:	Studies and practises art.
YOU:	What drives you to action?

WHAT CAN WILLPOWER BRING TO THE HUMAN?

- MAKING CONSCIOUS DREAMS A REALITY.
- FOCUS OF OUR ENERGY TO BRING EFFORTS TO FRUITION.
- INVESTMENT OF TIME AND MONEY.
- CREATION OF NEW PARADIGMS.
- SUCCESS THROUGH FOCUSED EFFORT.

For the organization, willpower means instilling in the spirit of its members, the realization and the organization of the initial plan. Willpower consolidates the members' sense of belonging to the organization through the confidence and interpersonal relationships that they share. In my case, I had to verify and organize information collected in Japan, understand what was financially at stake, market the products or services and build a company with a network of off-shore contacts. What resulted was considerable investment in on-site research into the possibility of exporting inventions and establishing confidence through my involvement in Japanese culture by actually being there. My absence required that I had to continually reinforce the sense of belonging in my family of enterprises back home.

HERE IS SOME PRACTICAL ADVICE TO HELP THE ORGANIZATION EXPRESS ITS WILL.

- Materialize the corporate plan to realize the collective dream.
- Consolidate the necessary material, financial and human resources to realize the dream.

— Invest time and money in equipment and technology necessary for expansion.

— Be open to the implementation of new concepts, policies and management philosophy.

— Take the necessary steps to market goods and services.

The following table lists examples of different ways the organization and its intermediaries can express their will.

ORGANIZATION:	Develops a research centre to create new products that can improve the quality of life in its community.
CLIENT OR SUPPLIER:	Establishes a "family of enterprises" network in order to integrate the client, organization and consumer.
MEMBER OR EMPLOYEE:	Puts into effect integrated programs of participation for employees in decision-making and profit sharing.
CONSUMER:	Establishes an information centre for all sectors of activity aimed at informing and protecting the consumer.
STATE:	Formulates a policy aimed at preserving life with better goods and services.
YOU:	As an organization, how willing are you to realize your collective dream?

WHAT CAN WILLPOWER BRING TO THE ORGANIZATION?

- MAKING THE PROJECT A REALITY.
- ESTABLISHMENT OF A BUDGET FOR INVESTMENT OF TIME AND MONEY.
- ESTABLISHMENT OF A BROAD-BASED NETWORK.
- MOBILIZATION OF MEMBERS TOWARDS A COLLECTIVE DREAM.
- REINFORCEMENT OF MEMBERS' SENSE OF BELONGING.

The Fourth Element: Patience

Patience is a virtue that we must practice throughout our life. It plays a pivotal role in the integration of our conscious dreams. It allows us to wait for the right moment to turn our efforts into reality. Patience is knowing how to wait for the opportune moment when life gives us a sign such as a chance encounter leading to a purchase order, or a business agreement. It is understanding that the results of our efforts do not entirely belong to us. Patience is the integration of our aspirations, our motivation and our actions and it is essential if we are to achieve what we set out to do.

Patience is a virtue which transforms us in the accomplishment of our dreams.

For my part, I had to exercise patience in learning Japanese, adapting to a different culture, respecting the values and traditions of that culture, and being at the service of my hosts. This patience taught me to adapt to their ways and customs, to develop a more global vision and to see my dream turn into reality. Yet patience differs from one culture to the next. While living in Japan, I noticed that business decisions took more time than in North America.

HERE IS SOME PRACTICAL ADVICE TO HELP INTEGRATE PATIENCE INTO YOUR LIFE.

– Know and understand your strengths and weaknesses to better adapt to change. Determine ways to overcome weaknesses to reach your objectives.

– Adapt to changing environments.

– Modify habits and behaviour. Transform "wanting" into "being".

– Take training courses, personal growth programs or ones in connection with your dreams to cultivate the desire to succeed.

– Wait for the right moment to appreciate success. "Don't count your chickens before they hatch."

The following table lists examples of different ways to integrate patience in certain people in the choice of their career.

PROFESSIONAL:	Develops a new vision in the exercise of one's profession. Confines oneself to the demands of the educational program.
INVENTOR:	Believes in the usefulness of a product or service for human growth. Develops that product or service.
POLITICIAN:	Develops an approach and an integrity conforming to what is being promoted. "Walk the talk".
ENTREPRENEUR:	Believes in a product or service which responds to the real needs of humans and life. Builds the business based on these principles.
ARTIST:	Brings understanding to the beauty of life by expressing it through the Arts.
YOU:	How patient are you?

WHAT CAN PATIENCE BRING TO THE HUMAN?

– UNDERSTANDING AND ADAPTING TO CHANGES.

– CHOOSING THE RIGHT MOMENT: BELIEF IN WHAT WE HAVE SOWN.

– DETACHMENT TO BECOME A SERVANT TO OUR CAUSE.

– ADOPTING A NEW ATTITUDE OR BEHAVIOUR.

– INTEGRATION OF THE RESULTS OF OUR EFFORTS.

For the organization, patience means establishing a value system which will influence its members and stimulate their efforts in order to realize a project. In my case, it meant establishing contacts with Japanese businesses by presenting our products, communicating with them and providing documentation in their own language and by respecting their traditions and professional ethics; all this while making the effort required to ensure the sale of our products. The results were the following: modification of products to suit local needs, mastering the business language of Japanese partners and consumers, adapting to national work norms, product regulations, international commercial law as well as Japanese customs and duties. The Japanese are much more patient than North Americans when it comes to business relations. In our modern organizations, characterized by constant change, decisions are made at the speed of light.

In most Japanese corporations, the approval of new products requires the consensus of all the participants. At the moment an order is placed, it has already been sold in advance. This decisional process can take from six months to two years, whereas in North America it only takes up to six months. Even the approval of orders requires dealing with the Japanese bureaucracy and the philosophy of a collective consensus. In North America, the reaction time to the launch of a new product is much shorter, so that unprofitable products soon find themselves replaced by better ones. The Japanese take much more time to measure the impact of new products on the market. This demands important initial costs in making a high-quality product that is profitable in the long run.

HERE IS SOME PRACTICAL ADVICE TO HELP THE ORGANIZATION INTEGRATE PATIENCE.

— Adaptation. Adapt goods or services to demands. Train the members to adapt to change.

— Develop a motivational program. Stimulate the members to pursue their efforts, to be enthusiastic about and open to other cultures.

— Adopt ways of doing things that will put you at the forefront of your market.

— Transform "know-how" into "know-how-to-be".

— Wait for the right moment to capitalize on success. Follow a tight budget to eliminate excessive costs that could jeopardize your success.

The following table lists examples of different ways to influence the organization and its intermediaries by integrating patience.

ORGANIZATION:	Establishes high standards of quality and dependability with the consensus of the members on the goods or services.
CLIENT OR SUPPLIER:	Brings improvements to the family of enterprises by coming up with new applications of goods and services to maintain harmonious relations.
MEMBER OR EMPLOYEE:	Maintains good working relations with employees and employers by having a common goal, i.e. individual and collective well-being.
CONSUMER;	Develops more evolutionary services to answer the real needs of the consumer, e.g. focus group on life's needs versus human needs, for improving the quality of life.
STATE:	Maintains policies that harmonize and promote the quality of life with a view to reaching a collective well-being.
YOU:	As an organization, how do you encourage patience?

WHAT CAN PATIENCE BRING TO THE ORGANIZATION?

- RESEARCH AND DEVELOPMENT ADAPTED TO NEW VALUES .
- APPRECIATION OF MEMBERS SO THAT THEY PERFORM WELL IN RELATION TO THE PROJECT.
- ORGANIZATIONAL EFFICIENCY, QUALITY.
- ABILITY TO ADAPT TO CHANGE.
- LONG-TERM PLANNING.

The Fifth Element: Perseverance

Perseverance is the faith that we have in our inner self that encourages us to follow through. The road least travelled by the Human and the Organization is their road of life. They are the only ones who know its glories and can deal with its obstacles. For humans, it represents their lives' plans or personal mission and for the organization, it is the mission or collective road.

Perseverance is the faith within us that propels us towards accomplishing our conscious dream.

For humans, the role of perseverance is the faith that allows them to realize their conscious dreams and continually surpass themselves in the pursuit of their lives' plans. My perseverance was believing in the possibility of marketing my inventions in Japan, trusting in the people who helped me through the process and having faith in my inner strength to accomplish my goal. The results were as follows: the sale of my products in Japan, assimilation into a new business culture and the satisfaction of having attained my objectives.

HERE IS SOME PRACTICAL ADVICE TO HELP YOU PERSEVERE.

— Believe in success of plan.

— Be certain that your efforts will bear fruit.

— Believe in your inner strength.

— Have faith: the power to move mountains.

— Excel, actualize self by realizing your full potential.

The following table lists examples of different manifestations of faith that can stimulate certain people to persevere in their career.

PROFESSIONAL:	Completes professional education until a diploma or degree is obtained.
INVENTOR:	Finishes final prototype so that it is functional.
POLITICIAN:	Acts on political aspirations to improve society.
ENTREPRENEUR:	Creates an organization focused on quality in the workplace.
ARTIST:	Creates art that will express what the artist wants to be to bring harmony to the life of humans and awaken their awareness.
YOU:	Are you perseverant? Do you have faith?

WHAT CAN PERSEVERANCE BRING TO THE HUMAN?

- INNER STRENGTH TO ACCOMPLISH OUR DREAMS.
- FINALIZATION OF OUR CONSCIOUS DREAMS.
- CERTAINTY THAT OUR EFFORTS WILL BE FRUITFUL.
- CULTIVATION OF INNER FAITH THROUGH DETERMINATION AND MOTIVATION.
- EXCELLING WITH THE GOAL OF GETTING CLOSE TO OUR ESSENCE.

For the organization, perseverance is the confidence in and the mastering of a project. If there is no faith in a given project, how will it be viewed by the employees? For a project to see the light of day, the employees and upper management should have a common interest. The collective dream is a generator which allows them to be responsible to each other. In contemporary society, there are certain principles and values to respect. We must follow these guidelines and build on solid values such as respect and integrity to complete a project, otherwise everything will collapse like a house of cards. Faith and mastering transform our individual and collective dreams into reality.

The role of perseverance for the organization is to cultivate a collective faith to realize a common mission. In my family of enterprises, faith was manifested by encouraging and motivating my intermediaries to make a success of our collective project, which was selling inventions in Japan. The result was the integrated participation of all the members of the family of enterprises to a global vision through the sale of inventions.

HERE IS SOME PRACTICAL ADVICE TO HELP THE ORGANIZATION TO PERSEVERE.

- Believe in the success of the project. Upper management must know how to present it to the members.
- Be certain that it will see profit and growth: the source of future revenue will ensure its survival.
- Encourage and motivate intermediaries to succeed and to accomplish the project. Aim for integrated participation.
- Cultivate and reinforce the guidelines and the basic values put forward at the outset: integrity, respect and honesty.
- Cultivate the faith of the members in terms of the goal at hand.

The following table lists examples of different ways of mastering that the organization and its intermediaries have, to be perseverant.

ORGANIZATION:	Establishes continuity with an internal policy for the manufacture of goods and services adapted to real needs, with the objective of better quality.
CLIENT OR SUPPLIER:	Establishes permanent and harmonious links between the family of enterprises while respecting the golden rules.
MEMBER OR EMPLOYEE:	Creates a symbiosis between the organization and its members in order to actualize the dream of each to constitute a collective dream. Establishes a creativity centre that encourages members to create, invent and innovate.
CONSUMER:	Maintains high standards of quality and ensures a follow-up on all that is contrary to the collective well-being.
STATE:	Maintains policies relative to the collective quality of life and well-being.
YOU:	As an organization, do you persevere? Are you the master of your project?

WHAT CAN PERSEVERANCE BRING TO THE ORGANIZATION?

- PROJECT COMPLETION.
- IMPLEMENTATION OF CONTROL SYSTEMS TO BETTER MASTER END RESULTS.
- ATTAINMENT OF INITIAL OBJECTIVES BY RESPECTING THE MEMBERS.
- STIMULATION OF MOTIVATION OF INTERMEDIARIES TO SUCCEED.
- CULTIVATION AND REINFORCEMENT OF BASIC VALUES: RESPECT, INTEGRITY AND HONESTY.

In this chapter, we have dealt with the relationship between time and money in contemporary society. We worked out a process for the Human and the Organization to materialize their conscious dreams by discussing the five crucial elements for the success of their life's plan: the dream, desire, willpower, patience and perseverance.

The role of essence for humans is to realize that time, money and the conscious dreams are building blocks in the accomplishment of their lives' plans. The closer they get to the essence of their lives' plans, the sooner they will reach autonomy. The essence of humans lies in the fact that they must continually learn and understand the phenomena of life around them. In this way, they will discover their inner potential for creating and realizing their conscious dreams.

The role of essence in the organization is to realize that managing time, money and the dream brings about a greater open-mindedness on the part of directors to stimulate every member to realize their personal dream and then create a collective dream. The essence of the organization is to stimulate creativity and accomplish the collective dream by establishing a common mission. This can encourage the members to contribute to the growth of the business while maintaining their personal identity.

Mastering dreams, desire, willpower, patience and perseverance allows the Human and the Organization to find their essence.

What are the questions we must ask to realize our personal and collective conscious dreams?

1) What are your dreams and what is stopping you from realizing them?

2) How much importance do you put on time and money in your life?

3) What motivates you to excel, based on the five essential elements to realize your conscious dream?

4) How can using the five basic elements change your life?

5) Will discovering your essence (reason for being) allow you to reach autonomy?

6) Do the directors of your organization put much importance on personal and collective dreams?

7) What methods does the organization use to encourage members to create, innovate and invent to realize their dreams?

8) Are managers open to creativity and how do they connect it to everyday life?

9) What are the incentives the organization uses to recognize people who distinguish themselves by using their willpower and perseverance to accomplish their dreams?

10) Does the organization value time and money to the detriment of creativity?

11) What methods are used to mobilize and unite the strengths of every member so that they can realize the organization's collective dream?

Chapter 7

THE QUEST FOR MEANING

We should stop looking beyond ourselves for the meaning of our life when all the answers can be found within us.

In this chapter, we will address the following concerns: the meaning of life, our origins, our life's real needs and the process towards meaning, in order that the Human and the Organization understand the true meaning of their lives.

What is the meaning of our life? What are our origins? What are life's vital needs? All these questions call for thorough introspection if the Human and the Organization are to find direction in realizing their personal life's plan or mission.

1) THE MEANING OF LIFE

Since the beginning, humans have always wondered about the meaning of their lives... their direction. Why do they question their existence? Is it to master their destiny? Yes, because we are the only species that can transform an idea into reality and have done so to both our benefit and detriment. Humans are the catalysts between the universe (ideas) and the earth (the materialization of ideas). In some sense, they are continuing the work of Creation. Yet an irony exists because if all creation is perfect, humans should be a perfect result of creation. However, the detrimental side-effects of many of our creations clearly indicate that we are far from perfect. Is it because we have not remained in contact with life and its natural cycles, the essence of all existence? If humans are to gain their direction and be in their rightful place, they must choose the road that respects life and the environment.

For the organization, the role of meaning consists of making choices which allow the members to move towards a common goal. By the strategic integration of its vision, the organization becomes the catalyst that drives the enthusiasm and motivation of all the members to find their rightful place and give the organization a competitive edge in the marketplace. In doing so, the Human and the Organization will find the meaning of their lives and make the right decisions regarding the actualization of their personal life's plan or mission.

Discovering meaning in our life will reunite us with the world of perfection.

If we are to become truly autonomous, we must first examine what distinguishes the mineral, plant and animal kingdoms from each other and what ties them together. In understanding their reason for being, we can apply their greater purpose to our way of living. By watching how animals behave, by appreciating the curative effects of plants and by realizing that the earth itself is the mother of all these marvels, we understand that nothing can exist on its own. These are well-established links in the continuum of life and to understand and appreciate them is to survive and evolve. When we accept this reality, we will finally understand our own life by understanding theirs. We will integrate them into our lives so that their existence and the way they benefit us will serve as an inspiration and a stepping stone to our evolution.

Earth nourishes, plants heal, animals teach and humans inspire.

2) OUR ORIGINS

Our being is the culmination flowing from a fundamental life cycle which is universal: we are the fourth kingdom... the issue of the three kingdoms which preceded us.

The First Kingdom, Mineral: Over ten billion years of existence. The creation of earth: a solid surface containing all the elements essential for the creation of life.

The Second Kingdom, Plant: Over one billion years of existence. Life form dependent on the Sun,endowed with sensitivity, extremely limited mobility, capable of self-nourishment and self-reproduction. Integrated with the mineral world.

The Third Kingdom, Animal: Over 500 million years of existence. Organized, instinctive, mobile and sentient beings that feed on organic matter. Integrated with mineral and plant worlds.

The Fourth Kingdom, Homo Sapiens: Over 40,000 years of existence. The descendant of primates now extinct. Endowed with intelligence and articulate language, has evolved to human in today's organization. Integrated with preceding kingdoms.

These kingdoms have all undergone major transformations since the beginning of their existence as part of the evolutionary process of life. The evolution of the mineral, plant and animal kingdoms made way for the arrival of the Homo Sapiens kingdom.

Our kingdom is distinguished by its intelligence and reason. Its ultimate role is to decode the meaning inherent in each of the other kingdoms and become imbued with them to discover their reason for being. In other words, it means recognizing the values and benefits that each kingdom has to offer. We can only become closer to the other kingdoms by learning from them. The realization of the human's full potential comes with the integration of the kingdoms and respect for universal values and life's needs. As long as the Human and the Organization concentrate primarily on the monetary aspects of their lives, they will continue to experience an existential void indicating that they have not yet discovered the meaning of their lives.

***The integration of the kingdoms
will fill the humans' existential void;
only then will they become one
with their life's plan.***

3) LIFE'S REAL NEEDS

What are our real or vital needs? What purpose do they serve? Are they in any way tied to the search for meaning? Vital needs are the following: breathing, nourishment, understanding, learning, loving, being loved and being alive to give our own life meaning. In our world, these needs are vital to our evolution, providing we are aware of their influence and give them the meaning that is their due; they can be listed as follows:

– To awaken to life's ultimate need: to be truly alive.

– To be aware of the creation of life: realize and appreciate what is around us.

— Materialize life's needs: respect and appreciate what is around us everyday.

— Integrate life's needs to universal needs: ensure our survival by a global respect for what is around us.

Have we ever wished to awaken to reality, to become aware of and realize life's real needs and take the time to pursue them? We can get closer to these real needs by properly using our five senses (sight, smell, taste, hearing and touch) in the way they were really meant to be used.

The following table concisely illustrates the real needs of the Human and the Organization in their quest for the meaning of their lives.

TABLE OF REAL NEEDS

	HUMAN	ORGANIZATION
To see what we no longer see:	The beauty of life around us versus the destruction of life.	The human behind the illness versus illness itself.
To smell what we no longer smell:	A field of flowers, the forest and clean air versus pollution.	Natural recycling versus toxic waste.
To taste what we no longer taste:	Natural and balanced food versus artificial and fast food products.	Natural food versus processed foods.
To hear what we no longer hear:	Bird songs versus noise pollution.	Harmony in the organization versus conflicts in the workplace.
To touch what we no longer touch:	Physical contact versus mechanical contact.	Inherent human creativity versus technology.

Do we take the time to stop and think about how these shifts in perception have affected life's natural cycle? What are the consequences of abandoning the true nature of life? Is all of this meaningful to the normal process of awareness such as seeing, smelling, tasting, touching and hearing life's real needs?

Autonomy comes with the integration of real needs and the Human and the Organization must recognize this reality to find their true direction.

Real needs are linked to everything that is true in life.

4) THE PROCESS TOWARDS MEANING

Being aware of our origins and having defined life's real needs, we must now question our direction. What is it that has not changed around us and will always remain? This question leads us to look, once again, at the meaning of our life in relation to the greater meaning of life around us.

We will now illustrate a thought process leading the Human and the Organization to find direction in the meaning of their lives. The approach hinges on the four principles of life: reflection, action, integration and retroaction. For humans, the end result of these four principles allows them to be themselves, to do what stimulates them and to understand what they have accomplished in order to find the meaning of their lives. For the organization, it means formulating a mission based on a clear vision, actualizing and aiming the mission in a precise direction and evaluating the vision to find an ideal orientation.

The following graphic illustrates the process towards meaning and demonstrates that the direction of one's life is intimately linked to the meaning of life.

PRINCIPLES OF LIFE : MEANING OF LIFE

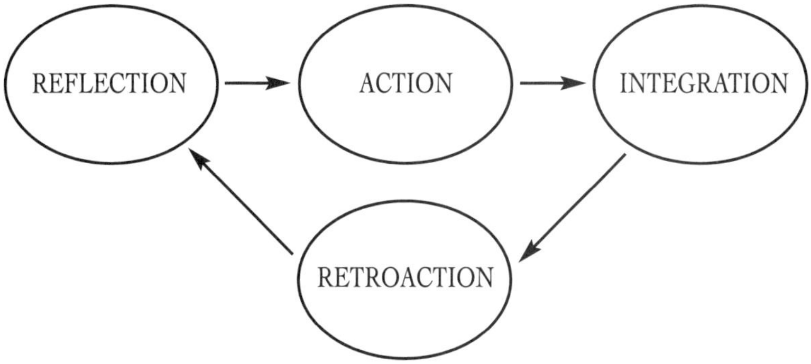

PRINCIPLES	HUMAN	ORGANIZATION
REFLECTION	BEING	MISSION
ACTION	DOING	ACTUALIZATION
INTEGRATION	UNDERSTANDING	EVALUATION
RETROACTION	MEANING	ORIENTATION

Reflection

How is reflection linked to the meaning or direction of our life? Does society give us time to think or does it do the thinking for us? Why is it that most people do not have time to think? Is it due to overwork, burnout, societal, familial, economic demands or are we simply not inclined towards this exercise? Yet if we had the time to think, would we conclude that our lives have no meaning?

The daily grind of *get up — go to work — go home — go to bed* has turned the human being into a robot. People's habits have become so anchored that they have created peak hours generating a lot of lost time on a daily basis. Even our week-end get-aways are preceded by traffic jams on Friday night and re-experienced on Sunday night to get back to Monday morning's routine. It is fascinating to realize how many of us are confined to repetitive routines. Tuned-out or alienated after a hard day at work, we still have enough strength left to "channel flip" or "surf the net" if not both at the same time so that even our free time contributes further to our "denaturing". What happened to the creativity we all had as children?

Have we become robots controlled by an internal punch clock? How often, through fear of losing a contract, missing an important call, being reprimanded by a boss or stopping the production line, have we denied mother nature's call? Are we overly manipulated by our so-called evolved society? We are trapped in a gridlock of our own creation and only we have the power to free ourselves from it by re-establishing our real needs.

People have been overburdened for too long. The days, weeks, months and years flow by without them ever questioning their dependence on the system. This dependence creates indifference and lack of interest, and inhibits any will to escape the vicious circle that we are unconsciously caught up in.

How to escape it? By returning to our principal source — our reason for being, through reflection on what has always existed around us since the beginning and will never change. Day and night, the cycle of days, sunrise and sunset... we should allow ourselves time for regular introspection to integrate the daily turmoil of our life. In doing so we will be able to break the cycle that programs us and find a new order more beneficial to our existence.

Insecurity and lack of self-confidence induce in us a certain reluctance to think, leaving others to control our daily decisions. We put much more confidence in others to handle our existential crises than we do in ourselves. We allow those who control us to think for us. Where has our lack of thinking and our mitigated decision-making led us? To a threshold of uncomfortable tolerance? To a more pronounced degradation of nature and life, marked by all sorts of crises: wars, unemployment, indebtedness, the failure of health and education systems, drugs and suicide? As a result, the Human and the Organization feel themselves less and less committed to taking an active role in their life's direction. They forget their obligation, which is to respect life. By letting others control their lives, humans become indifferent to all that surrounds them.

Reflection allows us to determine our aspirations, to understand the obligations which are connected to them and their implications for humanity. Everything we do stems from our thoughts and can have a positive or negative consequence on the survival of humanity. Consider the "domino effect" which implies that one person's actions can change the course of the world's history.

Are we ready to take up our collective and personal responsibilities by following our needs and aspirations? In the negative sense, following the illusory needs and aspirations dictated to us by others will only result in chaos. The solution consists of using our inner strength by thinking things through. We have to exercise our brain as much as we do our body. It is like a muscle and if we do not exercise it, it atrophies, becoming simply an organ for programming. The world of thought or the invisible is as important as the physical world because it often creates the world we live in. Thought creates because it has power. Every thought we have can influence or even change our life. What kind of thinker are you? Fast, meticulous, efficient, or dynamic?

To think properly, we must know how to direct our thoughts, to ask precise and pertinent questions if we want the right answers. How can we put this thought process into action? Get comfortable in a peaceful environment and breathe deeply for proper relaxation. Free yourself from what is around you through visualization, meditation, tai-chi, or any other form of relaxation that suits you. Conjure up a pleasant image such as a warm sandy beach, nature or any other sight that stimulates well-being. Then ask yourself a precise question and the answer will come to you. Repeat the exercise as often as you wish to fully integrate your preoccupations and find appropriate solutions.

We should set aside time for reflection every day. No matter what is bothering us, we owe ourselves a moment to stop and think about our problems and try to find solutions.

Think first, then act.

To achieve balance and inner peace, here are several approaches to help the Human and the Organization find their direction.

Focused Thoughts for the Human

What are my personal objectives in life? What goals do I want to achieve? For what end? Our thoughts should be focused on choices respecting our real needs: university, career, type of work (hired or self-employment, according to our aspirations or simply in terms of our quality of life). The object is to determine our goals and the means of attaining them by first thinking about them and then drawing up an action plan to achieve them.

THE MEANING OF REFLECTION FOR THE HUMAN:

- TAKE TIME TO DETERMINE DIRECTION.
- BE IN CONTACT WITH INNER-SELF.
- AWAKEN IN ONESELF THE ANSWER THROUGH QUESTIONING.
- DETERMINE WHAT IS REALLY WANTED.
- UNDERSTAND WHAT IS GOING ON AROUND YOU.

Focused Thoughts for the Organization

What kind of organization do we aspire to? What is our mission or vocation? Do we have a master plan? The organization can draw up a *universal integration strategy.* This strategy would link to all that exists, with the aim of serving the collective well-being of employees, directors, clients and ultimately the consumer, in the production of its goods or services. This would allow it to concentrate on its collective responsibilities which would include preventive measures in the production and expansion of its product line or services. Such reflection would bring greater focus to the organization and would unite the strengths of each member toward a common objective. For example, reflection can bring about the consensus of all the intermediaries associated with the formulation of a strategic plan and a forecast or pro-forma budget for the launch of a new product or service.

THE MEANING OF REFLECTION FOR THE ORGANIZATION:

- TAKE TIME TO THINK ABOUT ITS ORIENTATION.
- RE-EVALUATE ITS VISION.
- ADJUST VISION TO PRESENT REALITIES.
- ESTABLISH COMPATIBILITY BETWEEN INDIVIDUAL AND ORGANIZATIONAL OBJECTIVES.
- LIST OBJECTIVES AND DRAW UP A DEVELOPMENT PLAN: FOCUS GROUPS, CONSULTATIVE COMMITTEES.

What questions must be asked relative to the proposed methods of thinking?

1) Do we focus our thoughts to think better?
2) What are the objectives behind our thinking? Have they been satisfied?
3) Do we use our power of thought in everything we accomplish?
4) What tools do we use to think properly?
5) Do we allow others to make decisions for us?
6) What are the mechanisms the organization offers to help people think better?
7) Is thinking held in high regard by the organization?
8) Is there a value system that favours thinking in the organization?
9) Are ideas supported?
10) Is there follow-up on creative ideas?
11) Is the thought process well integrated and communicated to intermediaries?

Action

Action is turning thought into reality. It means implementing the established plan to allow the Human and the Organization to realize their respective aspirations and missions. The role of action is to secure the essential elements needed such as financial, material and intellectual resources, to make the idea a reality.

Does modern society encourage humans and organizations to be efficient and effective decision makers? Do we act for short or long-term goals? Action in life can be perceived as the implementation of a planned and well-organized approach. However, it must not be action for action's sake otherwise it will bear no fruit. Real action must be purposeful and well planned. Why do some people blindly throw themselves into a project without even thinking? Is society made up of people or organizations who only respond to problems? We are still looking for a way to cure the common cold instead of a way to prevent it. Today's health systems deal with emergencies instead of encouraging active prevention. In China, some doctors are only paid when their patients are in good health, their major role being the prevention of illness and not just its treatment.

Our economic system is tied to the "fast-lane" — the instant return on investments. The short-term takes precedence over the long. We build houses faster but they are less resistant to the ravages of time. We are witnessing record bankruptcies, unprecedented fraud and it is a well-established fact that 85% of new businesses will not make it beyond the five-year mark. Why? Because all too often entrepreneurs do not take the time necessary to properly plan the launch of their businesses. This problem results in part from a lack of cohesion between thought and action. Today's organization, at least in industrialized countries, tends to concentrate too much on short-term gain. With shareholders at the gate waiting for their returns, it is not surprising that when a problem arises, the corporate mind-set focuses on "band-aid" solutions and loses sight of the long term. We have every right to question what has become of the conscience and integrity of past organizations.

Very few people can get close to their aspirations because they feel enslaved by their debts and obligations. However, action, backed up by solid reflection will bring us closer to our real needs. Together, they will be the driving force that push us to excel.

Act to build.

The Implementation of Reflection for the Human

What are the financial, material and intellectual resources at my disposal? What choices do I have to turn my ideas into reality? Do I enrol in courses, launch a business or acquire property? In short, action consists of doing what we choose to do by thoughtfully applying the effort needed to attain our ideals.

THE MEANING OF ACTION FOR THE HUMAN:

- HAVE ALL THE TOOLS IN PLACE TO REALIZE OUR IDEAS.
- PUT OUR THOUGHTS INTO ACTION.
- CARRY OUT THE ACTION PLAN.
- FIND SOLUTIONS TO ATTAIN OBJECTIVES.
- ENSURE CONTINUITY IN REGARD TO THE INITIAL PLAN.

The Implementation of Reflection in the Organization

Is my sales force properly staffed? What is my production capacity? What is the efficiency of the existing network? Have we created enough momentum for the members to achieve forecast objectives? The pro-active organization will attain its rightful place in the local and international markets by fulfilling its ideas. Individual and collective efforts for the development of the mission, such as a new product launch, network development and marketing of the product are directly proportional to the benefits anticipated.

Proper reflection will result in specific action, bringing satisfaction and a greater return on investments because it is very difficult and expensive to revise the initial plan once we are in the midst of action. There is always a price to pay for having a bad idea. It can mean higher costs or irreparable damage for the organization if time has not been taken to understand and properly plan its basic mission.

THE MEANING OF ACTION FOR THE ORGANIZATION:

- BUILD AND ORGANIZE IN RELATION TO THE INITIAL PLAN.
- PUT IN PLACE INFRASTRUCTURES FOR REALIZING THE PLAN.
- CAPITALIZE ON THE COMPETENCE OF EACH MEMBER.
- CONCENTRATE EFFORTS IN DESIRED DIRECTION.
- EXERCISE CONTROLS TO REACH FORECAST RESULTS.

What questions must be asked relative to action?

1) Can we act instead of reacting?
2) What actions must be taken to turn our ideas into reality?
3) What objectives are we aiming for?
4) Are we active people, achievers, who go all out to realize the goal?
5) What are we doing to realize our aspirations according to our capabilities?
6) What are the steps taken by the organization to put its plan into action?
7) What structures allow the organization to develop a more efficient action plan?
8) Does the organization have a incentive program to stimulate the members to attain the initial plan?
9) What development plan has it installed to attain its objectives?
10) What are the financial, material and human resources needed to develop the action plan?
11) What incentive programs are there to generate enthusiasm in members to achieve the action plan?

Integration

Integration represents the downtime to take stock of our thoughts and actions to see if we are on the right path. Its role is to make us realize whether our thoughts and actions have brought us the expected results and if not, to make the necessary adjustments. Integration is understanding the lessons learned from the choices we have made, in order to move forward on our road of life. For students, integration will mean comparing their expectations with what they have actually achieved; for workers, it means evaluating their career choices against their initial aspirations. Do we take the time to objectively analyze where we are in our search for meaning in our life?

For the organization, integration can mean doing a follow-up study of the initial plan by realistically examining its budget in order to know where it stands and make the adjustments necessary to pursue its direction. The role of integration is to truly understand if the organization is still tied to its mission so that it will reap what it has sown. Integration will bring the organization considerable gains in time and money and keep it at the forefront of its market. The evaluation of results will allow it to act directly on its growth and maintain the enthusiasm of its members. At this stage, discouragement is to be expected since reality must be confronted: lack of financial, material and intellectual resources, and the unforeseen. The integration of all these variables is vital to ensure the future viability of the organization, and represents a springboard towards expansion.

Build to create.

The Evaluation of Actions Undertaken by the Human

What were the actual results? Have we satisfied our expectations regarding the time and money budgeted? Students should ask themselves if they are satisfied with their academic results. Employees should question their contribution to their employer. Integration means understanding that the choices made can contribute to our rise or fall. We must make sure that our choices are linked to our initial plan by making necessary adjustments to realize our full potential.

THE MEANING OF INTEGRATION FOR THE HUMAN:

- REAP THE HARVEST THAT FLOWS FROM REFLECTION.
- INTEGRATE THE LESSONS OF LIFE.
- FOCUS ON REALITY VERSUS EXPECTATIONS.
- DETERMINE IF DIRECTION IS STILL FOCUSED ON INITIAL CHOICES.
- MAKE THE NECESSARY ADJUSTMENTS TO RETAIN FOCUS.

Evaluation of Actions Undertaken by the Organization

What were the actual results? Were the demands regarding time and budget respected? Were the forecasts achieved? Was the decision to launch a new product wise? Was the new product well received by consumers? Was the product modified in accordance with the new demands of the market? Is it necessary to change our way of doing things? This stage is an evaluation of the business's activities... a follow-up on the initial plan. Integration will then come from the evaluation of actual results. This period is crucial for the organization because it may have to adjust itself to changes rather than maintain its present position.

Integration gives the Human and the Organization the understanding of life's lessons and reinforces the desire to continue their efforts towards the consolidation of their respective directions.

THE MEANING OF INTEGRATION FOR THE ORGANIZATION:

- ADJUST OR REINFORCE THE DIRECTION OF THE INITIAL PLAN.
- EVALUATE ACTUAL VERSUS FORECAST RESULTS.
- REVISE INITIAL STRATEGY: FEASIBILITY, PROFITABILITY AND EFFICIENCY.
- ENSURE THAT ALL MEMBERS UNDERSTAND AND COMPLY WITH ADJUSTMENTS TO THE PLAN.
- MOTIVATE MEMBERS' ENTHUSIASM TOWARDS DEVELOPMENT OF THE PLAN.

What questions should be asked relative to integration?

1) Have we properly integrated our initial plan, according to results achieved?

2) Should adjustments be made based on these results?

3) What lessons can be drawn from your personal experiences?

4) Have we adopted a "think first, then act" approach in accordance with our initial plan?

5) Have we reaped what we have sown? Why?

6) Has the organization properly integrated the participation of its members in carrying out its initial plan?

7) What is the reaction of the members vis-à-vis the actual results? Are they motivated to continue?

8) Has the organization chosen the right direction: mission, strategy, goods and services?

9) Do the members feel a part of the success of the initial plan?

10) What can we learn from the variation between actual results (material, financial and human) and what was forecast?

11) Should we change our initial plan or maintain our position? What adjustments should be made?

Retroaction

Retroaction is direction... the right meaning for the human and the right orientation for the organization. It means truly understanding what we want in terms of our being or our mission without following society's influences. Retroaction is the result of what we learn from the consequences of our actions. It brings us closer to our reason for being which is the quest for meaning.

For humans, the role of retroaction is to determine if they are on the right path. This stage will bring them back to what animates them to draw up a new life plan or reinforce what they have already accomplished. It means self-examination and questioning the road they have chosen to finally decide whether they are truly on the right path; all this to have greater confidence in what they hold dearly. It also allows them to reconsider their career choices, whether it be changing jobs or taking on new challenges within their professional lives.

The role of retroaction for the organization consists of verifying if its mission corresponds properly to its true orientation. Do the results of the plan fit with the mission? Returning to the basic mission and its values will let the organization discover the fundamentals of its activities; all this to focus their efforts on desired objectives, to redefine strategy for real needs and to reinforce the confidence of members in carrying out the plan.

Create to excel.

Evaluation of Integration for the Human

What is the next stage in finding the meaning of our life? Am I on the right road? Have I thought about what I have accomplished? Have I returned to my source without being diverted by anything? Am I myself or rather someone that others want me to be? These questions help in reviewing our reason for being and understanding where we are in our quest for meaning in our life. Thus, graduate students have the choice of starting a career or continuing their education by doing post-graduate work. Employees can keep their present job or ask for a different position within the company.

THE MEANING OF RETROACTION FOR THE HUMAN:

- CONTINUE ON PRESENT COURSE OR CHANGE DIRECTION.
- BE THEMSELVES AND NOT WHAT SOCIETY WANTS THEM TO BE.
- RETURN TO THEIR SOURCES AND REALIZE WHAT IS FUNDAMENTAL IN THEIR LIVES.
- TAKE THE TIME TO APPRECIATE WHAT ANIMATES THEM.
- REASSURE THEMSELVES THEY ARE STILL ON THE RIGHT PATH.

Evaluation of Integration for the Organization

Are we still on the right course or has it changed along the way? What direction should we choose? Should we change the vision of the project or support its continuation? When a project has been carried out, its results evaluated and the lessons learned, the organization should ask itself whether to continue in the same direction or redirect itself towards another market, product or service.

THE MEANING OF RETROACTION FOR THE ORGANIZATION:

- DETERMINE IF THE ORIENTATION IS IN ACCORDANCE WITH ITS INITIAL VISION.
- RE-EVALUATE INITIAL STRATEGY: CONTINUE OR CHANGE.
- REDEFINE OR REINFORCE BASIC MISSION, VALUES AND IMAGE.
- RALLY AND MOTIVATE MEMBERS TO CONTINUE INITIAL PLAN.
- STIMULATE MEMBERS' CONFIDENCE ACCORDING TO CHOSEN ORIENTATION.

To sum up, the process towards meaning requires that we practice the principles of life, which are reflection, action, integration and retroaction. They will help us to discover the true meaning of our life, that being the direction we must follow to attain our autonomy. The quest for meaning is the force which drives the Human and the Organization to realize their conscious dreams if that force is properly focused on their ultimate objective: the success of their lives.

What questions must be asked relative to retroaction?

1) What can retroaction bring us in the process of finding the meaning of our life?

2) Do we let ourselves be guided by external influences?

3) In what way do we apply the principles of life on a daily basis?

4) Does retroaction allow us to return to our source to better continue our journey?

5) Does retroaction allow us to excel in getting closer to the meaning of our life?

6) Are individuals in our organization encouraged to participate in the retroactive stage of the project's implementation?

7) Are managers capable of developing a new plan or supporting the existing project?

8) Do members participate in choosing the organization's direction?

9) Is upper management supportive of decisions made regarding the orientation of the organization or of changes to its initial plan?

10) Should original objectives be redefined or reinforced?

11) Can both meaning and direction be brought to the Human and the Organization so that they can live in harmony?

Chapter 8

EVOLUTIONARY THINKING

The imaginary world is the only real world that we own.

After becoming aware of the importance of developing a perspective on life's needs, of finding essence through the conscious dream and the meaning of life in terms of direction, I would now like to propose a new way of thinking which I call *evolutionary thinking*. When I saw to what lengths the Human and the Organization went beyond themselves to find solutions to problems which existed within them, I decided to develop an *evolutionary approach*. This process came from exploring my own imaginary world because I could not find answers to questions in the known world. I have always wanted to discover what I did not know about myself to better understand who I was.

This chapter will present different ways of applying *evolutionary thinking*, a concept that was born in my imaginary world. It will also deal with the notion of *intuitive intelligence* which is the materialization of our intuition. It is a gift we all possess but one which most of us are afraid to trust in. Finally, the cycle of an idea's realization will be offered as a conceptual framework bringing together different elements necessary for visualizing an idea and ultimately making it a reality.

1) EVOLUTIONARY THINKING

Over thousands of years, the evolution of thought has been influenced by School, State and Organization (genres of the "global elite") to bring about different ways of thinking. What were their objectives? Were they to lead the human to autonomy or merely serve their own personal interests by pigeon-holing humans and hindering their evolution? By nature, humans are always looking for the easy way out. This is one reason why they are content to let external systems guide their lives even if it means reinforcing the power of the elite. They develop, conceive and conceptualize in accordance with the world they know, their immediate environment. As such, humans have become dependent on the world they know instead of being creative by exploring the imaginary world; the world of "what could be". Human thought is a faculty that has seldom been fully exploited from within but more by external forces such as organizational systems created by the elite. It has been used over the centuries by these groups to create, support and justify systems of their own creation for their own self-interest. Our thoughts have never belonged to us because we have let others think for us. Humans innovate, create and invent products to improve their quality of life. They therefore concentrate on the material aspects of life: money and wealth. Power, in today's world is now more than ever measured by material wealth. The *evolutionary thinker* has been isolated and marginalized in favour of the excesses of materialism. Yet it is *evolutionary thinking* that can contribute to real growth for the Human and the Organization and ensure their survival in today's world.

We are living in a society that has become more dependent on complex systems that are born of modern technology and the information revolution. Is the international elite behind this as well? What are their objectives this time? To better serve the interests of this so-called revolution to the detriment of real evolution? Tomorrow's evolution will not come about exclusively through a myriad of technologies but more by understanding the notion of the being as both a total entity as well as part of the complete environment that stems from life itself. Faced with the harsh realities of life, the Human and the Organization, will be forced to make a choice: continue in their present state of chaos or awaken to a new way of thinking. By choosing the latter, they will find solutions which come from the unknown (imaginary) world leading them to real autonomy and freedom.

Evolutionary thinking, not revolutions, can contribute to real evolution for humanity.

What is *evolutionary thinking*? It is thought without limits or borders that finds its source in the world of the imaginary. By its very nature, it goes through many transformations to arrive at an idea that can be applied to the real world.

The evolution of human consciousness is directly proportional to the willingness to think.

This method of thinking is unique because it begins in a void. It exploits the unknown, or more specifically what we are unaware of. We are all conscious of the existence of this "unknown" but prefer to be guided by what we already know. The world of the "known" is the culmination of what we have perceived since birth. The approach based on this perception poses no risks, is effortless and encourages complacency. *Evolutionary thinking* extends our power of thinking beyond existing paradigms to encompass the unknown. The objective of this exercise is to allow the thinker to be aware of the unknown world's potential and its possibilities for innovation.

The unknown is the source of everything and it is incumbent on the human to discover it.

Evolutionary thinking stems from the faculty of active thinking that we all possess. It is born of the following inspirational sources of our being:

— The Imaginary: the dream,

— The Intuition: inner feeling,

— The Soul: essence,

— Other sources: the mineral, plant, animal and Homo Sapiens kingdoms.

SOURCES OF INSPIRATION

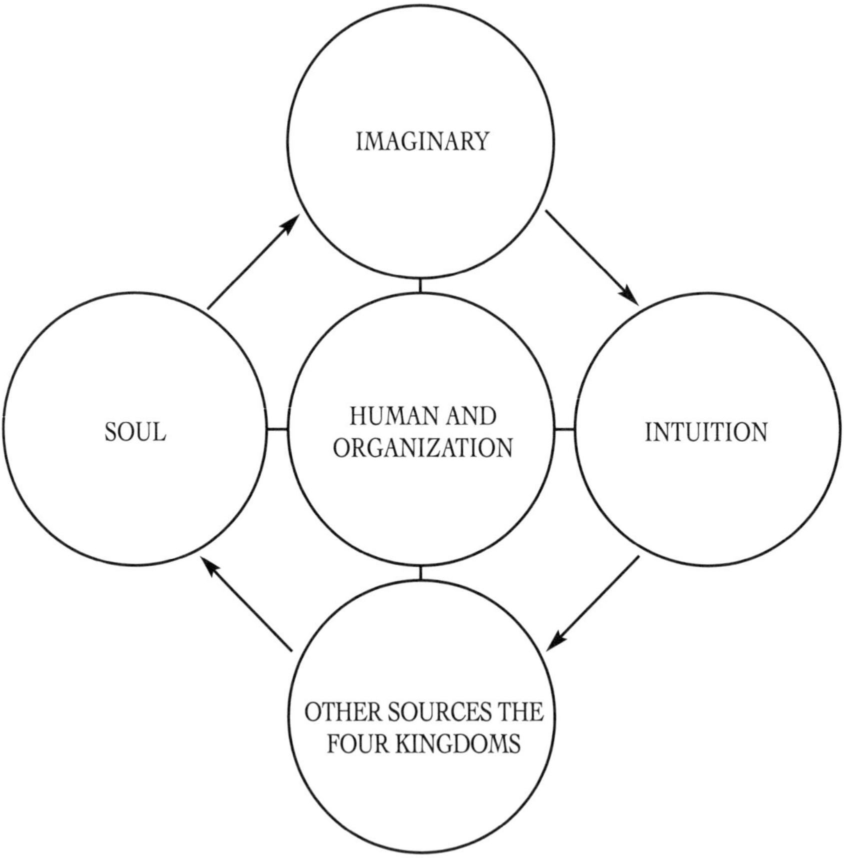

The Imaginary

The imaginary is our source of inspiration, the only real world that we own. It identifies us by its uniqueness and because it can belong to nobody else but us. It is a universe unto itself, made up of an internal richness, full of marvels and inspirational elements that spring from us and motivate us to realize our conscious dreams.

Through the imaginary, we are what we think. Finding its source allows us to understand who we really are and what we truly want. For instance, in our imaginary world, we can travel the globe and visit all the countries that interest us without ever leaving our living room. The next step is materializing the imaginary. As a source of creation, it is the concrete manifestation of a dream from the unknown world. It is the birthplace of reality. By experiencing my imaginary world, I discovered things about myself that I had not known before and acted on these discoveries to change my life.

The imaginary world is the source of everything.

The Intuition

Intuition is directly linked to our most inner feelings. It is that inner voice that speaks to us, giving us messages in relation to what we are living. It is a faculty that is inborn in the human being but often repressed by our reasoning. Unfortunately, very few people take advantage of their intuition to orient their lives or their businesses.

Intuition can be spontaneous, thought out, or even interpreted according to different choices we make. In business, for example, when encountering clients from different cultures, it is important to make a distinction between how we perceive them versus how we intuitively feel about them. Intuition is our only reference point to help us integrate cultures different from our own. In my negotiations with Japanese and Chinese corporations, the contracts were concluded in public places or even in their homes...places we would not normally consider in North America. In my case, I intuitively conformed to the culture of my hosts by understanding their cultural gestures and their ethics so that I was able to anticipate their reactions.

Intuition comes from feelings within us.

The Soul

The soul is the essence of our life. It nourishes our inner being and manifests itself in the external world. It is the most important element in *evolutionary thinking* because it sparks awareness of our reason for being which then motivates us to realize our life's plan. It is the energy allowing us to establish a direct link between our actions and our life's plan. Heeding our soul's message will guide us to the right decisions in order to fulfil the destiny entrusted to us at birth.

Unfortunately, many of us ignore this source of our existence which is vital in realizing our life's plan. The soul engenders within us the essence of our reason for being or mission and pushes us to excel throughout our life. As long as humans are united with their soul, they become true to themselves and the accomplishment of their original life's plan becomes feasible. In the same way, if the organization acts according to its reason for being, accomplishing its true mission becomes feasible. By taking full charge of their respective lives, the Human and the Organization can assume total responsibility by devoting themselves entirely to their undertakings. The soul allows the

Human and the Organization to manifest themselves by giving meaning to their lives while maintaining their authenticity.

The soul is the conductive wire of life.

Other Sources

The interrelation with other sources of inspiration is defined by what I call integration with the four kingdoms: the mineral, plant, animal and Homo Sapiens worlds. The Human and the Organization must enter into a symbiotic bond with all that exists around them. To achieve this, the imaginary, intuition and the soul, all born of the invisible world, must express themselves through the kingdoms of the visible world. These kingdoms are the essential components that make up the global life plan, the ecosystems we come from and therefore they are integral to our becoming *evolutionary thinkers*.

The mission of the kingdoms is to integrate the sources of inspiration into matter.

How do we integrate the kingdoms? We can start with an appreciation of their existence by understanding the role that they play in our development. The following chart illustrates how the Human and the Organization can integrate all the kingdoms to create a world that respects life's perfection.

THE WORLD OF THE INTEGRATED KINGDOMS

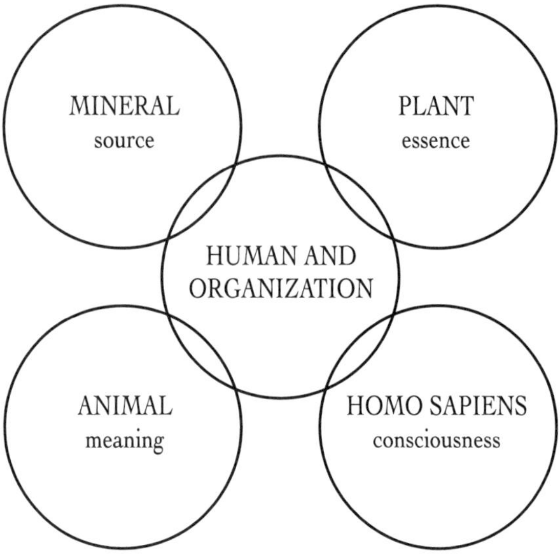

The premise of each of these kingdoms is:

— Mineral kingdom: the source of all life,

— Plant kingdom: the essence of life,

— Animal kingdom: meaning,

— Homo Sapiens: consciousness.

The integration of the four kingdoms will ultimately bring us to the *Fifth Kingdom* where we will become one with the rest of the universe and attain autonomy by reaching a universal consciousness through the respect of these kingdoms. For the *evolutionary thinkers* of tomorrow, the *Fifth Kingdom* signifies a return to our reason for being or our original purpose. To ensure their survival, the Human and the Organization must decode the origin of each of the kingdoms in order to understand and respect life's real needs. In this way, they become fully integrated with the kingdoms. In other words, *evolutionary thinking* is the spark that ignites universal growth... the evolution of all the kingdoms.

If life is to be, we must bring it light.
If life is to continue, we must give it breath.

Humans seem to believe that everything is eternal. They eat, pollute and consume excessively. Sooner or later, we have to understand that each of the kingdoms' components is very precious and that we must respect the balance of life around us. Once we are aware of this, we will be ready to interact with all that surrounds us. We will resonate with everything that exists and be integrated with the kingdoms which existed before, exist now and will exist after us. The interaction with the kingdoms will allow us to grow and evolve in harmony with all, thereby creating the essence of universal consciousness.

Resonating with or showing empathy towards a member of any kingdom will help us to understand its place in our universal family. We will therefore respect it instead of continually harming it. This awareness is based on new universal values and life's real needs. Instead of senselessly destroying what little remains in the world, we should protect what is dearest to us: life. Some organizations pride themselves by recycling when they should be preventing pollution in the first place. The destruction of the rain forests is not only abusive but accelerates the degeneration of life so that eventually humanity will find itself deprived of the medicinal plants necessary for its survival.

The preservation of life rather than its destruction is an example of the application of *evolutionary thinking*. The purification of water and air should come before the manufacturing of chemical products that destroy the environment. We must never forget that the kingdoms have always been present in our lives and are symbolic of the world of perfection.

The Role of "Evolutionary Thinking" for the Human and the Organization

The role of *evolutionary thinking* is to make humans consider aspects about life that have never been resolved, such as human frailties and the dependencies they create, with the objective of integrating the contributions of the four kingdoms into their development. This way of thinking requires a greater search for information as yet unknown in the real world. For humans, it represents the possibility of discovering the potential within themselves to gain their autonomy.

In our so-called modern organizations, little time is allotted to managers and employees to think. If they are to excel through *evolutionary thinking* they should take the time to:

— identify harmful and superfluous products on the market and those that were recalled or discontinued after their launch for any number of reasons,

— question the reasons for garbage and abusive waste of natural resources,

— understand the phenomena of overconsumption in some nations to the detriment of less favoured countries,

— give priority to respecting the environment.

Globalization of markets, the frenzy caused by new technology, the mergers of multinationals and the construction of mega corporations makes developing creativity in organizations very difficult. In general, members spend most of their time covering their backs while their businesses are rendered unsteady and fragile on both human and financial levels, by time and money constraints, staff lay-offs and salary reductions. They are forced by these circumstances to think reactively which is destructive and contributes to the withering of the Human and the Organization.

A corporation that is forced to produce for the sole purpose of maximizing profit will almost certainly have "respect for the environment" on the back burner. For example, the agricultural industry's excessive reliance on toxic products and chemical ingredients increases crop output but accelerates soil degradation. The end result is a classic example of "short-term gain — long-term pain".

For these organizations, trapped in old paradigms, one possible solution is to return to their initial mission and purpose by becoming *evolutionary thinkers*.

Thought emerges from life like a flower from a garden.

The role of *evolutionary thinking* consists of making the organization understand its contribution to a better collective well-being, in order to solve problems at the heart of its existence and integrate the contributions of the four kingdoms into its growth. This way of thinking allows the organization to create a new well of information essential to its development. It also stimulates the formulation of a *universal integration strategy* to find solutions from the imaginary world to attain its autonomy. In practical terms, the organization should not be exclusively concerned with return on investments; it should understand its basic mission to find its essence, which will engender a symbiosis with its reason for being and its profitability. By doing so, it will be able to deal with urgent problems in order to find its meaning, which is to be in harmony with life's values.

Practical Applications of "Evolutionary Thinking"

By applying the characteristics of *evolutionary thinking* to our daily lives, we become clairvoyant, self-healing, intuitive, imaginative and closer to the essence of the soul itself. By interacting with everything around it, the organization will become alive, dynamic and visionary, with a greater understanding of what is happening around it while manifesting today what it will be tomorrow. *Evolutionary thinking* is free-thinking which renders the Human and the Organization autonomous. It will stimulate them to be what they really are, transcending what existed to become what will exist. This approach demands personal discipline and focused thinking through our imaginary world and its materialization into reality. To achieve this, we have to interact with the kingdoms which exist around us, and be more respectful of the values and needs of life.

We must not forget that the other kingdoms sacrifice themselves so that we can integrate and receive their energy in order to become the *Fifth Kingdom*. What have we contributed to these kingdoms? Should we not be giving back to the earth what we received from the universe by learning to manage our resources with discernment, and understand that nothing on this planet should be taken for granted? Truly evolutionary beings think, create, conceive, invent and conceptualize in terms of their own evolution and the growth of all the kingdoms.

Should not our mission be
to teach others how to fish?

WHAT CAN EVOLUTIONARY THINKING BRING TO THE HUMAN?

– ABILITY TO CREATE, INNOVATE AND INVENT SOLUTIONS FROM THEIR UNKNOWN WORLD.

– CREATING A WORLD THAT RESPECTS PERFECTION.

– FINDING SOLUTIONS TO PROBLEMS BEFORE THEY OCCUR.

– INTEGRATING THE FOUR SOURCES OF INSPIRATION TO EXCEL.

– ENSURING OUR SURVIVAL AND FROM THERE, THAT OF HUMANITY.

WHAT CAN EVOLUTIONARY THINKING BRING TO THE ORGANIZATION?

– FINDING NEW SOLUTIONS FROM THE UNKNOWN WORLD.

– ENCOURAGING MEMBERS TO EXCEL THROUGH THEIR IMAGINARY WORLD.

– CONCENTRATING ON EVOLUTION NOT REVOLUTION.

– ESTABLISHING A FONT OF EVOLUTIONARY IDEAS.

– CONTRIBUTING TO A COLLECTIVE WELL-BEING.

What questions must be asked relative to evolutionary thinking?

1) What does "evolutionary thinking" evoke in you?
2) Does "evolutionary thinking" stimulate you to excel and understand the unknown world within you?
3) What stimulates you to excel when using your imagination?
4) Do you often follow your intuition?
5) What activity brings you closest to your soul?
6) Do you consider the kingdoms to be important in your life? What are you doing to preserve them? Do you consciously contribute to the clean-up and preservation of the environment?
7) How does "evolutionary thinking" bring about solutions to problems in the organization?
8) Do the kingdoms inspire the organization in the development of its products?
9) How does your organization stimulate the members to create through "evolutionary thinking"?
10) Does your organization prefer revolution over evolution?
11) Is your organization's ultimate objective to contribute to the collective well-being?

2) INTUITIVE INTELLIGENCE

What is intuitive intelligence? What is the link between intuitive intelligence and *evolutionary thinking*? What is its reason for being in our life and our organizations? How can it guide our actions in our chosen direction? What is its contribution on personal and organizational levels? How can we manage intuitive intelligence?

Intuitive intelligence means listening to that little voice inside us which points out the road that leads us to our life's plan. It offers us the means to act on what our inner world feels deeply, such as meeting our future partner in life. When that moment comes, something inside tells us that this person is important to us. In this instance, intuitive intelligence translates as making a choice based on feeling with the goal of developing a real and lasting relationship.

The role of intuitive intelligence is to give direction to what our intuition tells us. It is our ability to interpret our intuitions by turning them into reality. Intuitive intelligence is the conductive wire between intuition and realization.

The role of intuitive intelligence for the organization is to unite the intuitions of the directors with the other members. In reality, this means managing intuitions so that they become a realizable and a profitable asset for the organization.

What are the elements which will distinguish today's managers and entrepreneurs from tomorrow's with regard to their intuitive intelligence? The following chart shows a comparative analysis.

TODAY'S MANAGER AND ENTREPRENEUR	TOMORROW'S MANAGER AND ENTREPRENEUR
RATIONAL	INTUITIVE
STRUCTURAL	EVOLUTIONARY (SENSE, FEEL AND PRESCIENCE)
ORGANIZATIONAL	VIRTUAL
MANAGEMENT FUNCTIONS: PLANNING, ORGANIZING, DIRECTING, CONTROLLING.	MANAGEMENT FUNCTIONS: THINKING, FORESEEING, INFLUENCING, CREATING, INNOVATING, INVENTING.

Based on this chart, what transformations do we see taking place in the world of management? Many managers and entrepreneurs feel left behind by the speed of events and information. They have more work than ever and suffer additional stress brought on by budgetary restrictions. A 50 hour work week has become normal. Even worse, they shut themselves up in their ivory towers and bury themselves with ever-increasing responsibilities because they need to keep their title and the advantages that come with it. All of this is not lost on the employees, who become more demanding because they no longer have a sense of belonging to the business. To make up for their lack of recognition, they constantly demand more from their directors: more free time, better job security, daycare in the workplace and so on.

What can intuitive intelligence bring to the work place? It puts forward notions which are more likely to stem from within than without. Today we plan and manage, tomorrow we must foresee and create.

Confronted by constant changes, contemporary organizational structures must undergo drastic internal transformations. These require the establishment of a much more evolutionary program supported by a greater spirit of openness if the assimilation of new paradigms is to succeed. We must prevent instead of cure. Intuitive intelligence stems from the integration of these new archetypes by understanding and manifesting what we deeply feel and foresee in our life as well as that of the organization's. In other words, by expressing their creativity, members of every organization will become initiators of change. The organization should give all members the responsibility to exercise their creativity in accordance with its collective mission.

The intuition of a certain policeman can serve as an example here. He invented an emergency device ensuring that traffic lights would continue working during electrical blackouts. This invention prevented traffic accidents from happening and in the end, saved lives. In this case, intuition is represented by the need to prevent accidents for the collective well-being while intuitive intelligence is the means to get there by transforming the idea into a real and functional product.

Intuitive intelligence is therefore the evolutionary structure of human thinking to facilitate the manifestation of ideas in the real world. For the organization, it represents the *evolutionary organizational structure* allowing for *collective evolutionary thinking* to manifest itself into reality. In the same sense, this book comes from my imaginary world and intuitively, I pursue the goal of contributing to the well-being of humanity, while making sure that I find the means necessary to realize my ultimate goal.

Intuitive intelligence is the inner source that guides us towards individual and collective well-being.

WHAT CAN INTUITIVE INTELLIGENCE BRING TO THE HUMAN?

- ACTING ON DEEPLY FELT INTUITIONS.
- FINDING WAYS TO REALIZE THESE INTUITIONS.
- LEARNING TO FORESEE AND MANAGE OUR DIRECTION.
- BEING A CONDUCTIVE WIRE BETWEEN INTUITION AND ITS REALIZATION.
- BETTER DIRECTING OURSELVES IN REALIZING OUR LIFE'S PLAN.

WHAT CAN INTUITIVE INTELLIGENCE BRING TO THE ORGANIZATION?

- PREVENTION INSTEAD OF CURE.
- MANAGING IN AN EVOLUTIONARY WAY: FOLLOW A DIRECTION.
- STIMULATING MEMBERS TO FOLLOW THEIR INTUITION TO REDEFINE THEIR REASON FOR BEING.
- TEACHING MEMBERS TO BECOME INTUITIVE BEINGS TO REINFORCE A SENSE OF BELONGING.
- CAPITALIZING ON THE CREATIVITY OF MEMBERS TO FIND NEW AVENUES OF GROWTH.

3) THE CYCLE OF AN IDEA'S REALIZATION

What is the origin of ideas? How do we realize them? *Evolutionary thinking* stimulates the Human and the Organization to activate the cycle of an idea's realization. Can we make an idea profitable? What types of structures are needed to realize ideas? What is the process for developing an idea to its fruition?

Having described *evolutionary thinking* and intuitive intelligence, we now introduce the notion of the cycle of an idea's realization, starting from a conceptual framework, then working our way towards its materialization.

The idea is the fruit of evolutionary thinking.

The cycle of an idea's realization is the *evolutionary structure* allowing for the materialization of *evolutionary thinking* to occur just as we first imagined it. For the organization, this cycle manifests collective *evolutionary thinking* structured by a plan or conceptual framework. When we think about launching a product, a new company, or original art, we should truly understand what the mission entails. We should have a total overview of how we will realize the new idea. One way of doing this is to visualize the results of the finalized project in our imaginary world. By manifesting today our vision of tomorrow, we will create our future by simply thinking about it. What process should we follow to carry out our ideas? The visualization of an idea goes through four stages:

— Focused thinking, conceptualization of the idea.

— Creation of the idea.

— Transformation of an idea to a finished product.

— Commercialization of a product and achieving results.

VISUALIZATION OF AN IDEA

STAGES	HUMAN	ORGANIZATION
REFLECTION	IDEA	PLAN
CREATION	REALIZATION OF IDEA	PRODUCT OR SERVICE
TRANSFORMATION	MATERIALIZATION OF IDEA	PRODUCTION
COMMERCIALIZATION	COMMUNICATION OF IDEA	COMMERCIALIZATION OF PRODUCT OR SERVICE

For humans, visualization is for predicting definitive results before proceeding to the materialization of an idea. It consists of drawing an idea from their imaginary world, such as an invention, by realizing and creating a final prototype, then materializing the product or service and ultimately communicating its availability to potential clients, consumers and buyers.

For the organization, this process of visualization is to foresee definitive results before proceeding to action. It consists of building a plan to realize collective ideas resulting from brainstorming sessions, then choosing and creating a product or service according to the basic mission of the organization. Next comes production of the product or service and its commercialization in the market.

This step generates information with regard to the feasibility of an idea or project by a thorough analysis of the different norms (laws, costs, regulations and various constraints) which we encounter throughout the development of an idea or project. It brings a more precise vision to the realization of an idea or project and its economic, political, technological, sociological and environmental impact. For the Human and the Organization, this cycle represents the steps to take to realize their ideas for optimum results. This cycle is a conceptual framework which provides an overall view by the visualization of the full potential of the idea or project. Unfortunately, organizations today are made up of specialists who cannot see beyond their expertise. However, the formulation of a global vision is necessary to their survival. We can join our varied expertise to our conceptual framework for the materialization of the idea and thus generate the full potential of the organization and ensure its survival. Does the product we are manufacturing have an impact on the environment? What are its consequences on human growth? Is the product acceptable to local and international markets in terms of norms, laws, public health? These questions lead us to understand the interrelation between the Human and the Organization and more precisely, their role in the survival of humanity.

For humans, the role of the cycle of an idea's realization is to understand their global thinking to optimize their potential for the collective well-being. For the organization, the role consists of establishing a conceptual framework allowing the members to better understand their mission: formulate ideas and materialize them without losing sight of the ultimate objective – the collective well-being.

I applied this cycle to an event of international scope: The Japanese Art Festival held in Montreal, where I was one of the principal organizers. Within the framework of this event, 488 Japanese artists presented over 600 works. My greatest challenge was to develop a master plan for all the activities that would take place, according to the following steps:

- Describe the characteristics of the works according to the traditions of the country of origin.
- Obtain agreement from respective governments to show the works abroad.
- Arrange for the installation (location and display format) of the works according to security required.
- Arrange for the security and insurance of the works.
- Arrange the logistics, transport and the handling of fragile goods.
- Handle public relations and governmental protocol for the event.
- Plan the welcome and accommodation for the Japanese delegation.
- Organize sale of works and ensure the return of unsold works to country of origin.

The cycle of this idea's realization allowed me to visualize all the steps necessary to materialize a project. To understand and be ready to manage the unknown, we should expect the unexpected by contemplating the above.

In brief, the stages associated with this reflection were:

— Group reflection: formulate an overall vision relative to the feasibility of the project according to Japanese customs and traditions.

— Creation: organize the presentation of the artwork so that it respects Japanese culture and patrons can appreciate and understand these works according to Japanese traditions.

— Transformation: put together logistics allowing the works to arrive intact at destination; develop a comprehensive floor plan in accordance with the Japanese art director in respect of their traditions.

— Commercialization: publish a programme on the exhibition in conformity with ancient Japanese traditions.

Of all my accomplishments, the preparation of this major event was a most rewarding experience. The biggest lesson I learned from it was, without a doubt, that I was able to adapt to totally unknown situations arising from Japanese traditions. The associate artistic director kept insisting that the festival had to be an unprecedented success or he would lose all his credibility. In Japan, the image of the organization is vital in society and failure can lead to the instant dismissal of the director. As North Americans, we are not familiar with these notions of responsibility. In Japanese culture, the organization must be perfect in every way: mistakes are unacceptable. For the exhibition, that meant that every artist had to be presented according to an ancient chronological ascendancy.

In short, the progression of a project should begin with an overall vision and from there an idea, even in its embryonic stage (like the Japanese art festival), will see the light of day. Through the cycle of an idea's realization, reasoning gives way to an act of faith in bringing the idea to term by putting together all the intermediaries necessary to achieve a common goal. The success of every project is the manifestation of the idea, which takes its source from the unknown world and materializes into reality.

The visualization of an idea lets us anticipate results and avoid costly mistakes. Such is the power of thought.

WHAT CAN THE CYCLE OF AN IDEA'S REALIZATION BRING TO THE HUMAN?

- LINKING OF REFLECTION TO REALIZATION.
- REALIZING OPTIMUM POTENTIAL SUPPORTED BY OVERALL VISION.
- VISUALIZATION OF ACCOMPLISHMENT OF PROJECT AND ANTICIPATE THE PROBLEMS.
- MANIFESTATION OF A VISION TO LINK INTERMEDIARIES TO A COMMON PROJECT.
- BUILDING A CONCEPTUAL FRAMEWORK TO REALIZE IDEAS.

WHAT CAN THE CYCLE OF AN IDEA'S REALIZATION BRING TO THE ORGANIZATION?

- MATERIALIZING OF A COLLECTIVE VISION.
- ANTICIPATING THE UNKNOWN WORLD IN ORDER TO REALIZE THE IDEA.
- COMMUNICATING AN OVERALL VISION TO MEMBERS.
- BUILDING A CONCEPTUAL FRAMEWORK ALLOWING FOR ACTUALIZATION OF THE FULL POTENTIAL OF THE INITIAL IDEA.
- VISUALIZATION OF AN OVERALL PICTURE OF A PROJECT AND ALL ITS UNKNOWNS TO ANTICIPATE SOLUTIONS.

Evolutionary thinking is allied to the principle of life's wheel of balance. As such, the Human and the Organization should always seek their balance in all they accomplish and *evolutionary thinking* will bring them solutions which never before occurred to them. For the organization, this balance is necessary to its survival and *evolutionary thinking* instills in it solutions to the difficult problems it faces.

The concept of *evolutionary thinking* links all the essential components so that the Human and the Organization can realize their conscious dream. This way of thinking helps us to focus on the meaning of our daily actions both on an individual and organizational level.

What questions must be asked relative to intuitive intelligence and the cycle of an idea's realization?

1) Does intuitive intelligence allow us to structure our intuitions?

2) What advantages does applying intuitive intelligence bring us?

3) Does today's manager aspire to become an "evolutionary manager" by applying the principles of evolutionary management?

4) What is your management style? Preventive or reactive?

5) Does the intuitive intelligence of your organization's members allow them to build a collective vision?

6) Does understanding the cycle of an idea's realization allow us to manifest today what we will be tomorrow?

7) Does the cycle of an idea's realization help us to excel and optimize the potential of our ideas?

8) In accomplishing a project, what steps do you feel are most important to optimize your potential?

9) Can you visualize the accomplishment of your new project and respond to the unknown?

10) How does your organization communicate its overall vision to its members?

11) Do members apply the cycle of an idea's realization when launching new products? Do they analyze the costs and risks associated with it?

Chapter 9

THE SYNERGY OF THE SEASONS

Nature's perfection is the source of our inspiration.

This chapter deals with the impact natural phenomena and the seasons have on the Human and the Organization. It will illustrate how their cyclical nature can serve as a perfect example in our quest for meaning in our lives. We will examine natural cycles and how they affect our lives, what drives the life force of nature and how the synergy of the seasons influence us. The goal of this chapter is to encourage the Human and the Organization to consider the existing natural order as a model to achieve self-realization. If we apply our schedule to hers, we may find that we can benefit from the natural leverage she offers and increase individual and organizational performance, bringing a better "return on investment". The source of my inspiration comes from the links I establish between the perfection of nature and my own life's cycle. How do the seasons influence our lives? What transformations do we experience in their changing? Can organizations benefit from these changes? By considering these questions, I have come to understand how much natural phenomena directly influences the daily lives of humans and organizations. Nature's transformation over the four seasons, reveals vital information for our personal and organizational growth.

The seasons tell us that there is a time to work and a time to rest.

1) SEASONAL CYCLES

My observation of the cycle of seasons and its repetitiveness is another marvel that has made me aware of the perfection of this world. The spectacle of the seasons shows us how much this transformation is both simple and complex. This perfection unfolds right before our eyes throughout our life, regardless of our origins, yet have we ever considered the meaning that it can bring to our life?

Some cycles never change such as the sun rising in the east and setting in the west... the dawn, the day, sunset, night time and the four seasons. These universal phenomena are directly related to us but do we have any idea how they affect our life?

Can we gain from capitalizing on seasonal changes and the perfection of nature to build a personal development plan or business strategy? Can the information gleaned from understanding the benefits of changing seasons be applied to our management systems? How can we integrate these marvels of life or "ambassadors" of perfection? First of all, we must stop and look at what is happening around us. We must understand that the role of the seasons in our life is to show us how to properly use the resources of the kingdoms and integrate them into our life. The exploitive cycle of the earth has four stages: the sowing, nurturing, harvesting and rest. This cycle has served humanity since the beginning of time. Have we come so far that we can now afford to ignore it?

We should observe the characteristics of the seasons and their impact on our bodies, behaviour and attitudes as well as their contribution to our balance of life. Do shorter days, the light of day, the darkness of night and seasonal variations influence the Human and the Organization?

Watching life around us
will always bring us perfect answers.

2) THE LIFE FORCE OF NATURE

Consider the beauty that is a tree. What a wonderful source of inspiration. It changes itself altogether over the course of the year, freely following the normal cycle of its life. The tree is an integral part of life's continuum, just as we are, since we also undergo transformations. Through its roots, the apple tree draws its source from the mineral kingdom; through its sap, it ensures the perpetuation of the plant kingdom; through its leaves and flowers it nourishes the animal kingdom and through its fruit it nourishes the Homo Sapiens kingdom. This process allows the tree to follow its complete life's cycle while contributing to the other kingdoms. What is the tree's reason for being? To bring beauty to life, purify the air, feed the different kingdoms through its leaves, flowers and fruits, and transmit vital energy to ensure our survival.

Should the Human and the Organization not be valued by their fruits as well; meaning their essence, their vision, their love of life and their giving of self, in the same way that the other kingdoms give their lives for us. How far are we from this reality? Can we hope that our organizations, of which we are a part, will one day be in harmony with life and nature?

The tree is valued by its fruit,
humans by their values
and the organization by its mission.

Modern business was conceived by the human and for the human. At its conception, did anyone consider the environment, life, nature and their respective cycles? Does a relationship exist between nature's cycle of life and that of the Human and the Organization? Very few businesses think about the effect the seasons may have on their members when they establish their business plans.

Most modern organizations were conceived by profit-driven values transmitted by society. Consequently, the organizational structures put in place over the past are more and more called upon to undergo changes. However, these rigid systems make little room for new evolutionary concepts which take into consideration the integration of the four seasons in their business plan. Both the Human and the Organization can realize their plans in symbiosis with life, by letting nature inspire them to better realize their respective functions. A solid application of the seasonal cycle to both the Human and the Organization would see programs, products or services launched in the springtime when everything comes to life. Development could take place in the summer when life is in full bloom, and harvesting the fruits of their efforts would occur in the fall when nature is at its peak. Integrating the results of the cycle and formulating new resolutions for the future could be done in winter, a time of rest and reflection.

It is fundamental to consider the different seasonal cycles if we are to benefit from their added value in terms of working at times that best suit our personal preferences: night instead of day, spring instead of winter. The seasons can act as a perfect model for improving organizational performance and the development of all projects, goods and services. Does the educational system operate against normal seasonal cycles? Would not Fall and Winter sessions be preferable in Spring and Summer? Nature's four seasons tell us that there is a time to work and a time to rest. Should we completely dismiss this lesson? In general, organizations establish their budget in the Fall and often begin with restructuring and lay-offs in that period. Why can they not present their budgets and make the necessary adjustments in the Spring, a season more suited to change? The members would, at that time, be more receptive to dynamic and evolutionary solutions put forward to solve the business's problems.

The seasons allow humans to link up with the kingdoms that engendered them to find solutions viable to their evolution. The integration of what they have learned from the seasons (the time to reap and sow) will allow them to benefit from these real elements and lead them to their autonomy in a joyful and natural way. The four seasons become allies allowing humans to count on the benefits each season has to offer to attain their full potential.

The organization can integrate the seasons and nature to its initial business plan in order to attain optimal performance. Today's organization has denaturalized humans by standardizing their performance. As well, it continually runs afoul of nature and its cycle through pollution and the destruction it generates.

We are the fruit of an ancient sowing
and are the only ones who know when to harvest.

3) THE SYNERGY OF THE SEASONS

The plan below can help the Human and the Organization become aware of the essential elements needed to integrate the seasonal cycle into their daily lives. For the human, the synergy of the seasons is expressed as follows:

— Spring, by the sowing of ideas,

— Summer, by nurturing their growth,

— Autumn, by harvesting or transformation of ideas,

— Winter, by the integration of results and the formulation of new resolutions.

For the organization, this synergy is expressed as follows:

— Spring, by the elaboration of a plan and budget to launch new programs, goods and services,

— Summer, by developing the plan and putting it into action,

— Autumn, by the transformation of the project according to the results obtained,

— Winter, integrating forecast versus actual results and formulating new resolutions.

The following diagram shows the synergy and influence of the four seasons on our daily lives on both a personal and organizational level.

THE SYNERGY OF THE FOUR SEASONS

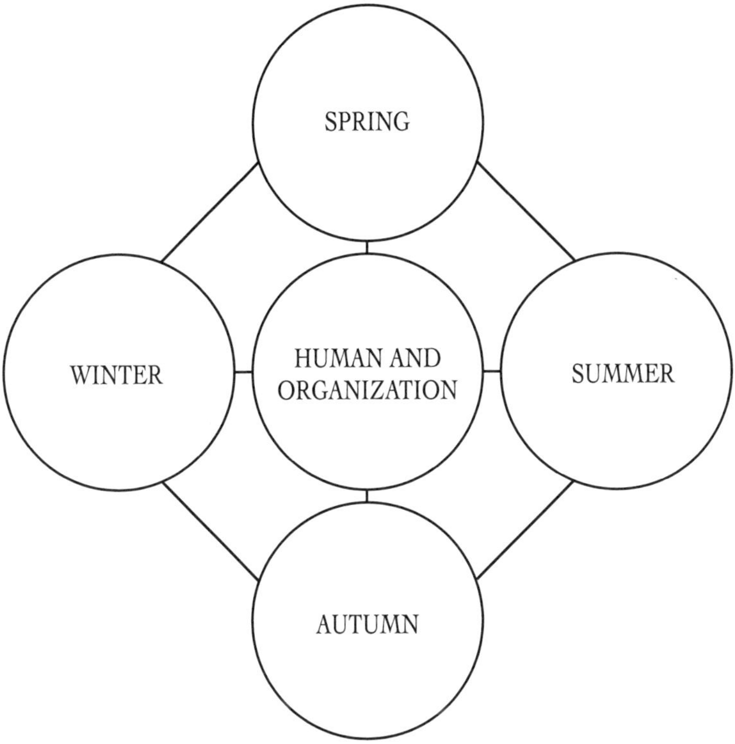

SEASONS	**HUMAN**	**ORGANIZATION**
SPRING	SOWING	LAUNCHING
SUMMER	NURTURING	DEVELOPMENT
AUTUMN	HARVESTING	TRANSFORMATION
WINTER	INTEGRATION	INTEGRATION

The Human and the Organization are at the centre of the diagram because they experience the influences of the four seasons. These phenomena are constant and applicable to our life's experiences. Based on what the seasons teach us, we should develop a plan for growth according to this source of life and benefit from the energy which emanates from it.

What effect do the seasons have on the Human and the Organization? What follows is a series of questions aimed at making us aware of the influence exerted by the seasons on the Human and the Organization.

Questions the human may ask:

SPRING: THE SOWING

— What excites you in Spring? Do you get back your lust for life? Do you feel an urge to do something different or to change your life?

— Are you enraptured by nature's rebirth? The birdsongs, budding trees and longer days?

— Does your body and your spirit undergo a change?

SUMMER: NURTURING

— Does the intensity of light have a positive effect on you? Does the sun energize you? Do you have the sensation that everything around you is alive and the kingdoms are displaying their most beautiful colours?

— Does the summer make you feel like developing new relationships, friends, and establishing a new network?

— What does the effervescence of summer evoke in you? Outdoor activities, travel, pleasure?

AUTUMN: THE HARVEST

— Does your harvest bring you gratification? If not, how can you make it so? Have you satisfied your initial objectives?

— Is autumn a driving force which pushes you to continue whether the harvest is good or bad?

— Do your habits and behaviour change in relation to the shorter days and cooler weather?

WINTER: INTEGRATION

— Does winter affect your metabolism? Does the change in temperature make you irritable, sensitive or depressed?

— Do you go into a period of introspection? Do you feel removed from life's flow? Is this season propitious for a return to your source?

— Are you inclined to question yourself more than usual? Do you integrate the lessons of the preceding year? Have you made any new resolutions?

Questions the organization may ask:

SPRING: LAUNCHING

— Are the members more receptive, motivated and dynamic in spring? Is the organizational climate more relaxed? Does nature encourage the members to a change of attitude or an openness towards creativity?

— Are the members more enthusiastic about starting anew in terms of launching a new plan aimed at the rebirth of their business?

— Is it a propitious season to launch new projects and products?

— Can we increase organizational performance by capitalizing on the rebirth of nature and the renewal of the members enthusiasm? Natural leverage consists of using nature to increase performance.

SUMMER: DEVELOPMENT

— Does summer offer a more propitious organizational climate for productivity and performance?

— Does increased daylight have a positive effect on communications between the members and upper management?

— Is summer a good time to implement a marketing network from the links created with new contacts?

— How can business capitalize on summertime to optimize the implementation of its plan? Should it organize outdoor activities such as golf tournaments and barbecues to create a sense of belonging?

AUTUMN: TRANSFORMATION

— Does the attitude and behaviour of the members change in autumn? Are they less or more productive? Does the rate of absenteeism rise or fall?

— How does autumn influence the results? What alternatives or corrections must be applied?

— Does autumn stimulate the members to excel to obtain forecasts? Did they reach the forecast?

WINTER: INTEGRATION

- Is this a good period to analyze the company's performance of the past year in order to make the necessary adjustments for the coming year?

- How would you rate the productivity and performance during this period? Do winter phenomena affect the organizational climate? Is there a drop in productivity, a lack of motivation or an increase in absenteeism and illness?

- Does the integration of the variation between forecasted and actual results call for adjustments to the initial plan in order to avoid repeating the same mistakes in the upcoming year?

The four seasons can constitute a conceptual model allowing the Human and the Organization to establish links with each of them to improve financial, physical and spiritual performance. This reflection leads us to understand that our life can follow a cycle similar to the seasons. Unfortunately, many of us ignore the beneficial effects that the seasons have on our lives and we tend to pay scant attention to the passage of time that they reveal to us. This process of transformation, emerging from nature's perfection, is governed solely by life's values.

Today's organizations strive for profitability on a perpetual basis. They want more and more profit to please the shareholders and directors without taking into account the values which come from the synergy of the seasons. Consequently, we are swept away by chaos: bankruptcies, professional burnout, lay-offs, downsizing or mergers of every kind. When we sow, we should wait until the time is right before drawing benefits or reaping the fruit. We can hope to make profits, but in a more harmonious way, in accordance with the global and natural order of life. Universal balance is necessary for the survival of the Human and the Organization.

In freeing ourselves from results,
we become the fruit we have sown.

To summarize the influence of the seasons on our lives, the following chart will serve as a model showing the impact they have on us.

	HUMAN	ORGANIZATION
SPRING:	PLAN A PROJECT, FORMULATION OF AN ACTION PLAN. E.G. LAUNCH A NEW PROJECT, DRAW UP A PLAN FOR A HOUSE.	MAKE MISSION PROFITABLE BY FORMULATION OF A BUDGET INTEGRATING NATURE TO THE INITIAL PLAN. E.G. LAUNCHING OF GOODS AND SERVICES.
SUMMER:	ACT, DEVELOP A NETWORK OF CONTACTS, FRIENDS. MATERIALIZATION OF PROJECT. E.G. BUILD HOUSE.	PUT INTO ACTION FINANCIAL, HUMAN AND MATERIAL RESOURCES FOR THE REALIZATION OF PLAN. E.G. ESTABLISH COMMERCIAL NETWORK.
AUTUMN:	HARVEST, RESULTS OF PROJECT. EVALUATE RESULTS OF IDEA. E.G. OCCUPY HOUSE	EVALUATION OF PLAN REGARDING ITS PROFITABILITY. E.G. ORDERS, SALES OR CONTRACTS.
WINTER:	INTEGRATION, ANALYZE RESULTS. IMPROVEMENT AND CHANGE ACCORDING TO ORIGINAL PLAN BY NEW RESOLUTIONS. E.G. INTERIOR ARRANGEMENT OF HOUSE.	INTEGRATION OF RESULTS ON THE BUDGET. CONTRIBUTION, IMPROVEMENT OR MODIFICATION OF INITIAL PLAN. E.G. PROFIT OR LOSS. ADJUSTMENTS FOLLOWING THE ANALYSIS OF BUDGETARY VARIATIONS.

The chain of seasons links
the Human and the Organization
to the cycle of life.

4) THE INFLUENCE OF THE SEASONS

Spring

For the human, springtime is magic. Everything is reborn. It is the first metamorphosis that we undergo marking a new start. The buds are bursting, flowers are blooming, the sun is fiery and hot and everything is brighter as the days get longer. It is the planting season that sees the growth of food reanimated. We want to fill our lungs with fresh spring air to reawaken all our senses to the reborn glory of this life which was temporarily sleeping.

Spring is an ideal time for new projects. We naturally tend to look forward to new friendships. We buy property, sow our garden, develop new ideas and even determine the subject of a new book. In short, it is a time to take on what stimulates us. Spring stirs us once again to address our life's plan which we were carefully pondering over the past winter.

WHAT CAN SPRINGTIME BRING TO THE HUMAN?

- INTERRELATION WITH WHAT STEMS FROM THE PERFECTION OF LIFE.
- RENEWAL AND REBIRTH.
- ENTHUSIASM AND MOTIVATION TO UNDERTAKE NEW PROJECTS.
- AWAKENING OF OUR DREAMS: REFLECTION, THE IMAGINARY AND BEING ALIVE.
- CONCEPTION OF OUR ACTION PLAN.

For the organization, spring can be a time to consider a new project or product. It is the time to plan for the acquisition of new equipment, to establish new associations or to hire new recruits and to formulate new strategic plans, budgets or any other project. Spring stimulates reflection on the formulation of a strategic plan in relation to the four seasons to attain pre-established objectives. By starting in spring, the organization can improve the performance of its members by integrating the cycle of the four seasons to its management plan. From that moment, being in harmony with life's cycle can energize the members to greater productivity.

WHAT CAN SPRINGTIME BRING TO THE ORGANIZATION?

- FORMULATION OF A COLLECTIVE DREAM THROUGH THE PLAN AND THE MISSION.
- CONCEPTION OF A STRATEGIC PLAN BY INTEGRATING ALL FOUR SEASONS.
- ENTHUSIASM AND OPENNESS OF MEMBERS TO A NEW PROJECT/NEW APPROACH.
- NEW MISSION AND PRODUCT LAUNCH.
- RENEWAL AND REBIRTH.

Summer

For humans, summer is the time to act, to implement their plans to realize their personal objectives. Thus, summer is an ideal time to develop new relationships through outdoor activities. It is a good time to build a house, tend a garden, materialize an idea, write a book or any other project that we wish to see completed. Summer is the time to build, to materialize our thoughts or any other personal project that we cherish. Why is this period more propitious for the realization of our project? Summer is the season of maximal luminescence. There is more sunshine, therefore we capture more energy. The days are longer; it is time to nurture what we have sown in the spring. Why do we have more energy? Sunlight stimulates all creation. Nature's growth is at its peak.

Summer is the ideal time to stimulate creativity and put our plan into action. We are more inclined to take the time to try new things. Summer is the season when all life is at its fullest. It is the most opportune time to take advantage of life's bounty and vitality for our personal growth.

The Sun is the source of all life.

WHAT CAN SUMMERTIME BRING TO THE HUMAN?

– OPPORTUNITY TO ACT ON THEIR DREAMS.

– IMPLEMENTATION OF PROJECTS VITAL TO THE REALIZATION OF THEIR PLANS.

– DEVELOPMENT OF AN INTERPERSONAL NETWORK.

– INTIMATE CONTACT WITH LIFE, NATURE AND THE AWARENESS OF THEIR PERFECTION.

– RENEWED ENERGY, MORE OPEN TO SHARE AND EXCHANGE.

For the organization, summer also signifies a time of action and development for the implementation of mechanisms to achieve forecast results. It is the season to apply strategic plans: acquisition of equipment, the development of a product, the approbation of new employees, the establishment of a new network. In summer, the organization should count on the productivity and creativity within its ranks. This period is ideal to re-energize the members so that they are more open to technological changes and new ideas. It is the period when we feel at our best on a physical, intellectual and spiritual level. The atmosphere is much more relaxed and we have the feeling of being closer to nature, which is at its fullest. The organization should encourage its members to participate in social activities. The summer is also an ideal time to develop new markets and to exchange and share ideas with the members at company outings and sports activities. It is much easier to establish an atmosphere of confidence on the golf course than in the office.

The cycle of the seasons has always been part of our lives and is therefore perfect.

WHAT CAN SUMMER BRING TO THE ORGANIZATION?

- MATERIALIZATION OF THE COLLECTIVE DREAM BY TRANSFORMATION OF MISSION INTO REALITY.
- IMPLEMENTATION INTO ACTION OF THE STRATEGIC PLAN.
- GROUP SYNERGY: EXCHANGING AND SHARING BETWEEN THE MEMBERS.
- DEVELOPMENT OF NEW LOCAL, NATIONAL AND INTERNATIONAL NETWORKS.
- MATERIALIZATION OF CREATIVE IDEAS.

Autumn

For humans, autumn signifies the harvest, the transformation of their initial project and the evaluation of their actions: keeping in touch with new acquaintances, the completion of a house, the harvesting of a garden, the result of an idea's materialization, the satisfaction that comes with a book's completion. It is the harvesting of all that is sown, the crowning moment of our efforts, because nature is undergoing another transformation which is the fulfilment of life. She transforms herself to give us her fruit. She metamorphoses in an explosion of colours, year after year. This period can bring about great personal satisfaction by harvesting the fruits of work accomplished or revising the initial plan. Regardless of results attained, they are integrated as a lesson in life. We can now enter the upcoming period of introspection by bringing with us, the improvements and changes necessary to our initial objective.

WHAT CAN AUTUMN BRING TO THE HUMAN?

- REALIZATION OF DREAMS BY UNDERSTANDING THEM.
- PERSONAL GROWTH THROUGH REALIZATION.
- EVALUATION OF ACTUAL RESULTS.
- ADJUSTMENTS TO THE INITIAL PLAN.
- REAPING THE FRUITS OF OUR EFFORTS.

For the organization, autumn is the reaping and evaluation of results that were forecast in Spring. Was there a return on investments? Was our new product a success? Were the members satisfied with their performance? Was the budget respected according to the initial plan? In this period, a new routine asserts itself. The passage of autumn marks the end of a cycle of great growth and gives nature a chance to slow down. The organization now has the time to evaluate the actual results and learn from them, in order to make improvements and continue following the goal of the initial plan.

Autumn is the pivotal point of transformation, propelling the organization's growth.

WHAT CAN AUTUMN BRING TO THE ORGANIZATION?

- REALIZATION OF THE COLLECTIVE DREAM BY MOTIVATION OF MEMBERS.
- EVALUATION OF THE PLAN AND MISSION.
- MEMBER CONFIDENCE OR INSECURITY ACCORDING TO RESULTS OBTAINED.
- ADJUSTMENTS TO THE INITIAL STRATEGIC PLAN.
- MOBILIZATION OF MEMBERS' EFFORTS TO ATTAIN THE INITIAL PLAN.

Winter

For humans, winter marks a period of integration: rekindling new relationships, adjusting to a new property, contemplating nature's beauty, analyzing the results of a book launch, integrating the progress of an idea. It constitutes a period of introspection and analysis of final results. It means integrating the lessons we have learned in order to better prepare our resolutions for the upcoming year. Winter should be a time of analysis and integration. During this period, the human may experience a drop in energy. It is a time for rest, to take a vacation and to think about new strategies for spring. Winter is a period of *cocooning* which is ideal for the integration of the past year's results, in order to be prepared for all the new projects that may occur in the continuum of our life.

WHAT CAN WINTER BRING TO THE HUMAN?

- INTEGRATION OF RESULTS.
- LESSONS LEARNED FROM THE PAST YEAR.
- FORMULATION OF NEW RESOLUTIONS.
- SELF INTROSPECTION.
- CONTEMPLATION OF A NEW START.

For the organization, winter is a period of integration that should be used to revise initial strategies by an in-depth analysis of final results: employees, equipment, new products, distributors, and so on. Winter is a difficult period to live through because of excessive cold, the lack of sunlight and the hibernative aspects of nature. Employees and directors feel less in shape, are more often absent from work and experience a decrease in vital energy. The information transmitted by nature demands a general introspection on the part of the organization, calling for members to regroup in order to analyze the major events of the last year's performance. What were its strengths and weaknesses in relation to the initial plan? The organization could then implement a bonus system on creativity to encourage new ideas. This period of integration is ideal to bring the members to task by contributing to a better collective well-being. Winter prepares us for a new start which will take place in spring.

The silence of winter allows us to integrate the existence of life and to awaken us to a greater state of consciousness.

WHAT CAN WINTER BRING TO THE ORGANIZATION?

- INTEGRATION OF THE COLLECTIVE DREAM AS MASTERED BY ITS MEMBERS.
- RE-QUESTIONING ITS MISSION.
- INTEGRATION OF FINAL RESULTS AND THE APPLICATION OF NEW RESOLUTIONS.
- NEW ORIENTATION OR THE CONTINUATION OF THE INITIAL PLAN BASED ON STRENGTHS AND WEAKNESSES.
- VALORIZATION OF MEMBERS TO MAINTAIN OR IMPROVE THEIR PERFORMANCE.

The synergy of the seasons is part of a global and natural cycle of life. The four seasons teach us the principle of nature's transformation and its influence on us. These perpetual changes are intimately connected to the evolution of the Human and the Organization. The cycle of each season can be beneficial to us if we learn to recognize understand and act on their individual virtues. Life holds for us the key to success and if we know how to master what is around us, we will ensure our survival and evolution.

There is meaning to everything and this meaning comes from the perfection of life. We can all count on real things, such as nature and the seasons to direct our life and the organization's mission. When we look for truth, we will find it in the perfection of nature. All truth lies in perfection. Why are we always trying to reinvent life when it is right in front of us, telling us what is essential, which is to BE ALIVE? Are you ready to make the necessary efforts to rediscover life?

The seasons mark the time for the awakening, awareness and realization of our life's plan.

What questions must be asked relative to the four seasons?

1) Why is Spring an ideal time to make plans?

2) In springtime, what methods does the organization use to encourage interaction between the members for the formulation of a plan?

3) In Summer, am I acting according to my initial plan?

4) In Summer, what are the practical applications to implement an organizational action plan for its realization?

5) In autumn, how do actual results compare to our initial plan?

6) In autumn, what is the analysis of actual results versus those forecast? What adjustments are necessary for the organization to respond to its initial objectives?

7) In winter, what lessons can be learned from the integration of the actual results?

8) In winter, how does the integration of final results contribute to improvements in the performance of the organization?

9) Can the synergy of the four seasons help the organization reach a greater performance?

10) What are the important elements for the Human and the Organization to remember, regarding the integration of the four seasons as natural leverage to their initial plan?

11) What can result from the application of the cycle of seasons to the Human and the Organization for the realization of their plan?

PART THREE
REALIZATION

Chapter 10

FINANCIAL AUTONOMY

If we cannot let go of something in life, it is because we are possessed by it and no longer masters of our destiny.

We are now ready to broach the third theme, which is the realization of our full autonomy and freedom towards reaching the *Fifth Kingdom*. This chapter will offer inroads that can be followed by the Human and the Organization to attain financial autonomy. It will examine financial insecurity that we all experience as well as offer different tools to help us become financially independent.

Why do we associate money with power? Are they inseparable? Why are we so dependent on money? What drives some organizations to develop strategies aimed at reinforcing people's dependencies? Can contemporary society function without the world of finance?

As a professional accountant, I am often asked about the role of money in our society. Money has given birth to a number of cliches such as: "money can't buy happiness" and "without money, you're nothing". Why does money hold such an important place in our life? Is it lack of self-confidence that pushes us to accumulate financial and material wealth to boost our self-esteem? Or is it to blindly follow the trends that society has imposed on us; that of "keeping up with the Joneses" without thinking about our real needs.

Nowadays, fear of being without money defines our existence. This fear provokes tremendous insecurities which repress our creativity and the desire to discover our full potential. We are often caught in a vicious circle that sees us living for the sole purpose of satisfying our creditors. In addition, constant changes and the time needed to make more money as quickly as possible have robbed us of the time needed for personal reflection and growth.

In fact, the Achilles' heel of the Human and the Organization is to constantly have to generate financial resources or short-term gain respectively. Experience teaches us that the apple seed, which metamorphoses into a tree, takes five to ten years before producing an apple. The Human and the Organization should follow the same example if nature's cycle is to be respected. The better the sowing, the more the likelihood of an exceptional harvest. We cannot pull on a carrot and hope it grows faster. Yet we accelerate the normal growth process in life by using chemicals to enrich the earth without respecting nature's timetable.

What is true financial health? Does it mean always wanting more, or can we manage by simply following the course of nature? The Human and the Organization live a dichotomy between short-term gain for their immediate survival and long-term gains necessary for the collective well-being of humanity.

Where does the financial insecurity that impedes human creativity come from? When our world was less obsessed with material values, everything had to be built, created, invented in its own time... our grandparents were very happy with what they had and put much more stock on human values than we do today. They placed great importance on the family and people were satisfied with the life they were leading. Today, we are never happy with what we have and always want more. Where does this obsession come from? Can it be justified by the power it brings us and is this power real or illusory?

We have created a world of illusions based on the notion of gain. The International Monetary Fund counts on the economic performances of the industrialized nations and, curiously, most of them are hugely in debt. Why have the richest countries in the world generated such a high ratio of indebtedness? In today's world, society glorifies individuals who have large financial holdings without taking into account how these fortunes were built. Some companies generate billions of dollars in profit by selling products that are harmful to the environment. Yet, these same companies invest several millions of dollars for research and development in areas of health and the war against pollution. What is the real meaning of their mission? On one hand, they pollute the environment and on the other they contribute to the research of well-being. As a society, do we want organizations that buy their way out of their global responsibilities because their mission is purely profit-driven. Would not the ideal organization be one which served humans without harming the planet?

The questions raised above and the situation we are living, inspired me to find concrete solutions to major problems that are preventing the Human and the Organization from attaining financial autonomy.

1) FINANCIAL AUTONOMY FOR THE HUMAN

Personal Finances

Given that we are never better served than by ourselves, financial balance understandably begins with the health of our personal finances. There are any number of people who are more than ready to offer financial advice to others. It is always easier to understand the problems of others instead of our own because it is their money, not ours. However, when we discuss our own finances, it is a different story. The lesson to be learned is that we should never depend on others to find solutions to our personal money problems. We can always ask for advice from financial experts, but at the end of the day, the final decision is up to us.

Credit Cards

Many financial institutions capitalize on the convenience credit offers by providing cards to people knowing full well that most of them are unable to fulfil their obligations before the end of the month. What is the mission of these institutions? Are they banking on the emotional and impulsive nature of people, knowing that they will spend more on credit than they normally would with cash? Are they counting on them to overextend themselves so that they can profit on interest charges? The good news is that if we manage to control our impulses and pay off our accounts at the end of each month, we can actually save money by benefiting from the interest free delay, rather than fill the coffers of the institutions. The system is certainly in place for their benefit but we must never forget it can serve us just as well if we know what it offers and avoid the pitfalls of rampant consumerism.

Financial Institutions

We use bank services to carry out personal transactions and pay our bills. There is a certain built-in convenience to all of this but everyone who uses these services must assume the charges. The real question is; do financial institutions base their reason for being on our real needs or our emotional impulses? Do they contribute to our dependencies in order to make more money by imposing discretionary user fees?

A more disciplined use of the different services offered by these institutions can result in substantial savings. Wiser use of the bank card, Internet services, personal cheques and savings in high interest accounts are easy methods to help you control your personal finances. The bright side of financial institutions is that they do offer service, but only if you are prepared to thoroughly research all their options and then decide on what is best for you.

Financial Systems Versus Our Reality

As consumers, we can save to our advantage, by putting greater importance on life's reality instead of believing in a system based on global human indebtedness. The first exercise consists of carefully analyzing our buying habits. To do this, we must understand that our economic system has created a world of illusion that is fed by overconsumption. In this way, the more we consume, the more we support the existing system and the greater in debt we become. In the same way, this contributes to the increased indebtedness of all the industrialized nations. If every nation suffers indebtedness, it is because we have individually and collectively brought it on by unwisely using the financial systems at our disposal. We have therefore become dependent through this indebtedness.

One of the factors responsible for our indebtedness is the compulsion to overconsume in moments when we are most vulnerable such as annual holidays, St. Valentine's Day, Easter and other events promoted by businesses to increase their profit margins at our expense. To avoid indebtedness in these critical moments we should exercise common sense by waiting until we have the necessary resources or the buying power to purchase the goods.

***Live according to our life's reality
and not that of others.***

Life's Essential Needs

What is vital to our survival? Can we objectively determine what is really necessary to our quality of life? Take for example, day-to-day life. Have you ever truly considered the importance of:

Breathing: It is free, non-taxable and not assessable. Contemplate nature; your surroundings. Go for a walk, meditate, take the time to be yourself. Good breathing prevents health problems, absence from work and the consequences that ensue.

Nourishment: Proper nourishment need not be expensive. Junk food is and lacks nutrition. We can save by buying fruits and vegetables as they are less expensive in season and at their best, being rich in vitamins. Proper eating brings us the energy necessary to do our work more efficiently and thus increase our earning power.

Clothing: Buy durable, quality clothing instead of what is merely passing fashion. Wait for the sales and buy off-season. Take care of your clothes so that they last longer. Choosing a style that is practical will help you save on your wardrobe.

Transport: Use economic methods of transport such as public transit systems. Buy a car with the smallest and most efficient engine (every vehicle can reach the maximum allowable speed) to save on cost, maintenance and insurance. Fix your buying criteria according to the cost of acquisition, the price of gas and long term durability and maintenance. Buying a car according to how it will actually be used (work or leisure) can result in substantial savings.

Lodging: Buying or renting a house or apartment within our means is much more profitable in the long run than "keeping up with the Joneses".Wait until you have as much cash as possible to have a lower mortgage and a faster depreciation schedule in order to pay less interest. Waiting for the right moment to buy your oasis of peace can lead to substantial savings in purchasing and renovation costs. Timing is everything.

Clearly, drawing up a list of essential needs is the right thing to do. Be as objective as possible, eliminating all that is superfluous in your life. Try not to be influenced by friends, media and everything else around you. You will quickly realize that there are many products you can forego completely and that your buying habits are often induced by "marketeers" of illusion. By limiting our spending to what is essential to our real needs, we can realize substantial savings and invest them into our conscious dream.

When we limit our spending to our life's essential needs, we can invest in the realization of our conscious dreams.

The Dream

What are your conscious dreams? What motivates you to realize your dreams? Are you ready to make sacrifices to achieve them? When we cherish a dream, we discipline ourselves to save money so we can make it happen. How often have we dreamt about a trip, a house, a university degree, and so on? The dream is the inspiration that drives us to harness the time, money and energy necessary for its realization. The sooner we know our dream, the faster we can achieve it and benefit from it.

Building up financial capital can be a great source of joy and personal satisfaction. Most people who have realized their dreams will tell you that their greatest satisfaction was not achieved solely in attaining their final objective. They consider the decision-making process and preliminary steps as being just as worthwhile. The conscious dream is therefore a great motivational source for attaining our financial autonomy.

The dream drives us to the realization of our financial autonomy.

The Emotions

Why is mastering our emotions essential to attaining a financial balance? They could well be the first step in the downfall of our society, as they lead to the global indebtedness we are now living. Businesses use a variety of techniques to gauge our buying tendencies. Surveys, focus groups and statistical data bases lead to the development of consumer profiles that help to serve these interests. These companies make fortunes through their skills in perceiving the behavioral habits of consumers and by capitalizing on our weak points. What comes of their research is slick advertising that prods and seduces us to overconsume.

How often have we found ourselves buying when the prices are at their peak instead of waiting for post-holiday sales? By waiting two or three weeks longer, we can benefit from substantial savings on what we really need. Why are we always so eager to jump on anything that catches our eye? If you are addicted to every kind of gadgetry on the market or are an incurable technophile; if you are a *shopaholic*, or are always looking for an excuse to go to restaurants, bars or clubs, have you ever asked yourself why? What makes you so dependent on these distractions? Is it your lack of self-confidence, your fear of being out of touch or alone?

Your answers will reveal the real reasons that drive you towards reckless spending. Whatever they are, you should recognize and master your impulses. The technophile and the gadget freak should evaluate the real and immediate usefulness of the products in question. Those who go out regularly should think about why they are unable to be alone. The *shopaholics* should recognize their dependence and ask themselves if they really need the items at hand. All these questions will allow us to become masters of our emotions as well as our destinies. We will then truly save by avoiding the pitfalls which have trapped this consumer society. We will become evolutionary consumers, conscious of our real needs.

Recognition and acceptance of our emotions allow us to regain mastery of our destiny.

Social Status

What does social status really mean? Who creates and imposes it on us? Who benefits? Why do people aspire to be part of an elite? Why do we have trouble accepting who we really are? Does social status really bring us any value? Since society confers a particular status on everyone, humans are faced with the duality of who they really are and who they want to be in the eyes of their peers.

The importance placed on social status leads companies to focus much of their marketing efforts on different social levels to the extent that lifestyles are advertised rather than the product itself. In the process, they create a rift between our true identity and the one they are imposing on us. People try to buy their way into society through the acquisition of vehicles, luxury items and property to become recognized as part of an exclusive elite. Yet, above all, they do it to counter the fear of being rejected or associated with a less prestigious social class. This dependence distances us from realizing our life's plan. We always think that the grass is greener on the other side. However, we should always think twice by returning to our source and asking ourselves:

— Does my acquisition of "things" have anything to do with my real needs or am I trying to keep up with the Joneses?

— Do my purchases give me permanent, temporary or no satisfaction?

— What is the real usefulness of these goods?

Once we answer these questions, we will realize that what drove us to overconsume in the first place was the need to reach an illusory status. Only then will we start to make substantial savings.

The closer we are to our essence,
the less important social status becomes
and the more our true nature emerges.
We become one with ourselves and regardless
of our social status, we will always remain the same.

Phobias

Many people suffer phobias: rejection, loneliness, lack of money and love, to name but a few. What price do we pay in having these fears and what are the advantages of understanding and conquering them? We have to understand that they are created by humans for humans. These different fears, human and social, inherited and amplified over the course of our lives, are a boon to many industries. To get to the root of our fears, we must first ask ourselves the following questions to understand what they are about: who or what are we afraid of? Losing our job? Not having money? Where does our existential anxiety come from; our parents' experiences or society? If we refuse to understand and confront them, we will have to live with them for the rest of our lives. How often have you seen a bird with an alarm system on its back?

Contemporary businesses and society continually feed our insecurities so that we consume more without knowing why. Do car alarm systems really stop theft? With false alarms being as frequent as they are, we seldom pay any attention whatsoever to their clamour, leaving thieves to get on with their work. As for the protection of private property, the house alarm is all too often triggered by something far removed from the average "break and enter" artist. The culprits are more likely to be birds, squirrels, the wind, rain or more often an erroneous access code. Consider all the new gadgets on vehicles. Do people realize what is wasted in time and money for this *pseudo-protection*? Consider the plethora of life insurance companies who sell people peace of mind on a monthly basis over the course of a lifetime. Are people so inundated by insurance of every kind that they become victims of their own dependencies, and at what price? Fear can truly direct our life and deprive us of important financial resources. The recognition and integration of our different fears can lead us to substantial savings by buying products that address our personal reality and not that of others.

Phobias feed our financial dependencies.

We have gone over what I consider the major problems that prevent us from attaining financial autonomy and in doing so, have shed some light on what is driving society to the financial chaos it is in. What can we now do to assume our full financial autonomy? Here are some practical tools that will bring us financial independence.

Pratical Tools for Financial Independence

A Return to the Source

To return to the source, which is our reason for being, we must recognize our problem of overconsuming on every level and make sure we do not spend beyond our means. To do this, reconsider the major problems dealt with above and draw up a list of what is essential to your life and what is not. Review the list and eliminate the superfluous. It is important to be truthful and honest in conducting this exercise if you truly want to improve your financial situation. We are the only ones who truly know our limits and we all have the power within us to change or overcome them.

Evaluate our real needs to build up our nest egg.

The Family

The family is our most important source of mutual help and financing. This is why we must share and exchange with those around us. Many people experience the same financial difficulties but never think of confiding in others. Sharing our financial problems and discovering that others have similar difficulties can give us moral support to help us overcome our own problems.

Our immediate family can be an important and inexpensive source of financial help. Who but those close to us know our situation better? The financial institutions are there to make money on our business while our friends and loved ones can be there to help and encourage us.

With the help of these contacts, we can succeed in regaining confidence without going into debt. In life, we can only count on ourselves and those close to us to ensure success.

Borrow for success or succeed through mutual support.

Life

To discover and understand that the best things in life are free, we must draw from what is around us: life, the environment, nature, friendship and love. The material aspects of life are accessories to our existence and not an end in themselves. Appreciating the beauty of nature, a child's smile, true friendship and sharing, will allow us to relive the marvels of childhood.

The greatest financial support in our life is life itself. If we capitalize on this fact, we will realize that the essentials are free and how we appreciate them depends on how we use our five senses. Life itself is the essence of our aspirations; it is not merely limited to financial gain but is enriched by experiences of the heart and the events that we encounter on our journey.

It is in the simplest things that we find life's greatest mysteries.

Living Within Our Means

Many people live beyond their means and suffer the financial, physical and psychological consequences. How can we prepare a budget that is in line with our reality? Will it be able to address our dreams and aspirations? How much money do we really need to live? Can we reach our objectives with the means at our disposal?

By beginning with an assessment of our real expenses compared to our net income, we will quickly discover any discrepancies between the two and come up with solutions to improve the situation. The lesson learned by this simple exercise will bring us closer to attaining financial balance.

When we live according to our means, an energy emerges from us... that of the autonomous human. We are less anxious and distressed with life because we have attained financial balance.

Live within our means to attain financial freedom.

Listening to Our Body

What link must be established between listening to our body and becoming financially autonomous? Our body is tied to the financial aspects of our life. In fact, it is the first thing that signals financial woe. Money is physical. Daily financial concerns give way to many problems such as overwork, stress, burnout and depression. All these dysfunctions can be attributed to the physical over-taxation that comes with going beyond our limits. Put simply, we mortgage our health by neglecting it. Our body and its weaknesses are like eyes wide open or an ear to the ground; they can guide us toward financial well-being.

Our body is the financial leverage
to attain our financial autonomy.

Job Security

If you lose your job, what do you do? Roll with the punch, because this setback will allow you to reconsider your dreams and aspirations. When you lose your job or so-called financial security, you will, at first find yourself in a state of shock.

However, it may have been what was preventing you from realizing your dream for many years. Once the crisis has passed, you will realize that you are still alive and there is still life within you. You will find yourself reacquainted with your principal source of autonomy, which is being alive. This disaster can turn out to be the most beautiful moment of your life. You should use it to celebrate your rebirth and your conscious dreams, because from this moment on, you will be able to do what you have always wanted. You will have the time to realize your dreams and desires, contribute to a collective well-being and help those dear to you. When we are caught up in work, we often have no time for those we love yet they are the first to help us through our daily traumas. This change will allow you to express the life within you and to finally be yourself.

Faced with the financial security you have just lost, stay calm, take a deep breath and reacquaint yourself with one of life's truths on earth such as nature. Take time to reflect on the meaning you want to give to your life. Become aware of real financial autonomy and be true to your values and not those that society extols.

The greatest job security comes in accomplishing our conscious dreams.

The Manifestation of Life Within

We must manifest what we aspire to be in life. The closer we are to our essence, the more we understand what animates us. The more we manifest what we truly are; the more we attract like-minded people. How often have we hear it said: "Tell me who your friends are and I will tell you who you are.", "Tell me what you read and I will tell you who you are." and "You are what you eat." Yet these adages take on a whole new meaning in a world where marketing and advertising have twisted them to suit their ends. We are now being led to live, think and act in relation to well-orchestrated paradigms designed to generate huge profits for the sectors concerned. To maximize profits, the food industry relies on additives, processing and genetically-altered products. The entertainment industry titillates us with violence and greed and the chemical industry inundates us with pollutants in the manufacturing of synthetic products that will take centuries to biodegrade. As bad as they are in themselves, all these end-products are designed to direct us away from our real goals. The hidden agenda aims at distracting human beings, to keep them as far away as possible from their true reality so that organizations can benefit from their displacement. Would not a more appropriate scenario see people pursuing personal dreams for an individual and collective well-being? Luckily we are witnessing the birth of a new way of thinking... evolutionary thinking which will bring financial autonomy back to the human by creating useful products and services that are in harmony with life.

In manifesting the life within us for the love of it, we will soon come to recognize these evolutionary products and services as being financially and environmentally beneficial. This understanding will help us to discern what is necessary in our real world rather than what is "wanted" in our illusory world. Only then will we be financially autonomous and have the opportunity to realize our life's aspirations.

We are the financial result of what life animates within us.

WHAT CAN FINANCIAL AUTONOMY BRING TO THE HUMAN?

- REALIZATION OF CONSCIOUS DREAMS.
- SELF-SUFFICIENCY.
- APPRECIATING LIFE FOR WHAT IT IS.
- RESPECTING OUR REAL NEEDS.
- ADAPTING MORE EASILY TO CHANGES.

Financial autonomy lies in our willingness and our ability to listen to our real needs. We can attain it by understanding the fundamentals of existing financial systems, without being professional accountants or other experts in the world of finance. An analytical mind is an asset in understanding the grip the world of illusions has on us, but to truly master our finances, we must control them ourselves.

Financial autonomy is the new power for the human.

What questions must be asked relative to financial autonomy for the human?

1) What are the essential elements in our life? How do we apply them?

2) What are our real financial needs?

3) Why are we so dependent on money?

4) Why do we live in uncertainty regarding our finances?

5) Do organizations help us understand the meaning of money in our lives?

6) Do we manage our finances or allow others to do it for us?

7) Why do we keep a job that does not allow us to be ourselves?

8) Can our conscious dream lead us to financial autonomy?

9) If money is power, can the same be said for autonomy?

10) Are social status, emotions and fear, obstacles to attaining financial autonomy?

11) How can I capitalize on my inner self to be me and not the person society wants me to be?

2) FINANCIAL AUTONOMY FOR THE ORGANIZATION

Why do modern businesses place so much importance on money to realize their projects? What tools can business use to finance acquisitions, expansion, research and development of new products or any other investment? Why are organizations so dependent on financial institutions? At what point do they allow them to control their finances? Do they have access to other sources of finance better suited to their growth? Where does this financial insecurity that so often hinders creativity come from? These questions led me to look for solutions to problems of financial dependence within the organization and to propose a new financial concept that I call the family of enterprises.

Financial Dependence

Financial Institutions

The primary source of financial dependence comes from the power we attribute to financial institutions. In today's world, many companies fall into this trap. They are dependent to the degree that they must answer innumerable questions on their financial situation in order to obtain a loan or keep their credit. In addition, by living beyond their means, they are in constant fear of being cut off from financing, due to poor cash flow, a high ratio of indebtedness, weak sales, in short, poor financial performance.

Financial institutions are supposed to offer financial support to businesses towards realizing their projects. Yet today, the entrepreneurial dream has become a nightmare because financial institutions have altered their way of evaluating a business's financial situation and now impose acceptance criteria which are much more demanding. Not surprisingly, they have become more rapacious and have made enormous profits as a result. Their famous "check list" for loan or credit approval, conceived by them and for them, almost completely ignores human or entrepreneurial involvement which ironically are the guarantee of a project's success.

Unfortunately for businesses, the demands financial institutions impose are numerous. They must:

- assume the required securities, collateral, bank guarantees, mortgages, personal signatures and endorsements,

- pay various transaction fees (opening of credit file, bank and administrative charges, financing, etc.)

- provide documentation such as lists of creditors, debtors, tax liabilities, deductions at source, monthly and yearly financial statements,

- always respect the rules and regulations of the banking bureaucracy which invariably confine you to their parameters.

In short, entrepreneurs are vassals of the financial institutions if they choose to play their game. Under these conditions, how should entrepreneurs foresee their future relationship with financial institutions? With enthusiasm and dynamism or fear and insecurity? There is no question that these institutions can be useful to entrepreneurs but we should never depend on them if it means exceeding our capacity to meet our financial obligations to realize our objectives.

***Recognize our capacity to pay
to retain our autonomy.***

The Real Financial Needs of an Organization

The awareness of a business's financial autonomy begins with the discovery of its real needs to eventually attain its financial autonomy.

Many businesses allow themselves to be caught up in the financial game without properly evaluating what will come of the sales of their goods or services. If the project is so terrific, is their a need for financing? Should the company establish a solid footing and wait for the right moment before launching the business, project or new product? Would it be better to bank on potential human creativity for growth? Take as an example, a company that must assume financing of new equipment. Before buying a new machine, do we ask ourselves whether a used one would serve our needs just as well? What are our real needs regarding the new equipment? Would it be better to wait for initial or major orders before investing in whatever? Is subcontracting a possibility for the manufacturing of a product or service?

This reasoning is based on the principle of controlled spending in view of attaining financial autonomy. Before making an acquisition, the organization must properly consider every avenue available so that every decision can be beneficial. This can be done by:

— Formulating a financial plan in accordance with financial resources that are readily available, such as family, friends or business associates.

— Evaluating the possibility of subcontracting and/or the family of enterprises.

— Ensuring that entrepreneurs are well aware of the creative potential of their employees to solicit their help in finding alternatives to save in production, marketing, sales and other areas.

The foundation of business should be based on the KISS principle for "Keep It Simple and Straightforward" meaning that everything should be reduced to its simplest expression so that individuals, through their creativity, will find different ways to reduce production costs and make their business more profitable. Some companies insist on acquiring the latest technology which is often very expensive and unproven on the market. Beyond assuming major debts, they have no guarantee that their acquisition will have a direct effect on sales, cost or profitability. In truth, the only certainty is that they have another bill to pay and more financial stress.

How then, do we free ourselves from this trap? Can we develop a system that will support our immediate needs and at the same time be free of all the bureaucratic procedures that come with approaching a financial institution?

Creativity can mean an end to financial dependence.

The Family of Enterprises

Why is the family of enterprises a viable alternative in achieving financial autonomy? Given all their demands, the financial institutions have yet to respond adequately to my needs as an entrepreneur. I had to conceive of a new way of financing to allow me to realize my projects. The concept of the family of enterprises was a novel way to self-finance most of my activities and to apply it to all my clients. The concept of family of enterprises can be applied to every type of business, self-employed, professional, manufacturer or company wishing to share their basic skills with other free and autonomous organizations.

The first people I see about financing are entrepreneurs like myself, who understand my situation and see an opportunity for themselves by being directly involved in the process. I would like to share an experience that relates to the financial help the family of enterprises can offer. For more than a decade, I succeeded in marketing inventions locally and internationally without having to go through the traditional financing channels. The golden rules of the family of enterprises allowed me to put in place the network required to self-finance my activities. Here are the principles I followed to develop the structure of the family of enterprises:

- Choose necessary intermediaries for the realization of the project's common goal. Define the role of each one.

- Identify intermediaries' values in relation to the golden rules to be followed. Adopt a code of ethics.

- Establish confidence and delegate responsibilities to the intermediaries. Reinforce mutual respect and team spirit.

- Establish confidence with the clients. Reinforce human relations by personalizing service.

- Establish harmony between family members for client's sake, by respecting the needs of the group. e.g. Consensus among members to respect the pre-established delivery date.

- Create more flexible financial agreements. Respect agreements but have the open-mindedness and integrity to discuss any problems which may occur.

- Maintain encouragement, enthusiasm and mutual help of the intermediaries speaking the same business language.

- Believe strongly that the collective project will come to term.

- Respect the established agreement on profit while remaining free and autonomous.

These rules allowed me to put in place the family of enterprises and to act as a master planner by coordinating the resources necessary to the realization of the concept.

To give a concrete example of how the concept of the family of enterprises works, let us look at an invention I brought to the international market. It was a water canteen for sports or leisure and therefore lent itself perfectly to promotional applications. As a master planner, I drew on the golden rules of the family of enterprises and consolidated the links between the intermediaries in the family. I made sure that all participated and contributed to the collective success of the project.

To illustrate the concept of the family of enterprises, what appears below is a list of the intermediaries and their functions.

The inventor: the idea, the prototype, the product and intellectual properties.
The moulder: manufacturing of the mould.
The distributor: warehousing.
The manufacturers: the components of the product.
The printer: silk screening.
The assembler: the finished product.
The sales reps: local, national and international markets.
The master planner: coordination.
The family of enterprises: financial autonomy.

CONCRETE EXAMPLE OF THE REALIZATION OF AN INVENTION SUPPORTED BY THE FAMILY OF ENTERPRISES

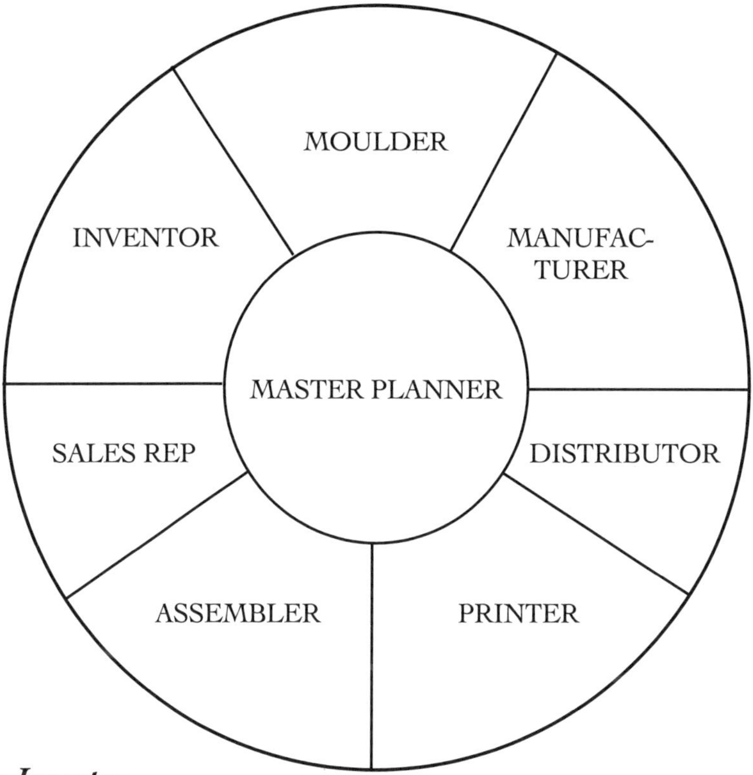

The Inventor

The inventor conceptualizes and draws up the product, then builds a prototype. In our case, once this stage had been reached, a patent officer registered the submission of our industrial design and trade mark. In the meantime, we located all the elements needed for the manufacturing of our product: containers, caps and cords. While the inventor developed his final prototype, I acted as coordinator to create a network of intermediaries to carry the invention to fruition. I took great care in selecting intermediaries who could contribute to the success of the product. The procedure followed the golden rules of the family of enterprises, respecting the principles and essential values to guarantee the project's success.

The Moulder

The second stage required finding a die maker to manufacture our mould.

The Distributor

We then met with a distributor of containers who offered to warehouse our new products. At that time, we did not have all the necessary resources or storage facilities at our disposal. A simple residential garage allowed us to realize our dream. This location was magic because all the small orders were filled under extraordinary conditions. Over time, our distributor became a supporter of both our morale and finances as he allowed us to increase our production capacity by offering us the storage space necessary for our expansion.

Manufacturers

With our mould in hand and the support of our distributor, we met the manufacturers we needed to make the product. Agreements were arrived at according to the time-honoured tradition of a simple handshake and mutual trust without the need for a written contract. Our family of enterprises expanded to include manufacturers of containers, caps and cords. My familiarity with the Japanese concept of "just in time" (which allows for better inventory management) was put into practice. From that moment on, my role was to make sure that all the intermediaries produced top quality products to ensure collective success.

The Printer

The product possessed one particularity: it could take printing on both sides. It was ideal as a high visibility promotional/novelty item for companies. To enlarge our family of enterprises and increase our sales in the area of promotion and sponsorship, we recruited a printer. His participation gave added value to the product and at the same time, allowed us to considerably increase our sales.

The Assembler

The assembly of our products was performed by members of a centre for handicapped workers. Their assiduous and conscientious work was vital to our success. I found these people to be a great source of inspiration and an important lesson in life because of the devotion and enthusiasm they brought to the project.

The Sales Reps

Thanks to the experience I gained overseas, we were able to develop an export strategy for our product. Our goal was to build up an international network, by distributing advertising brochures and commercial samples to various trade shows in North America, Asia, and Europe. Our off-shore representatives joined us because they shared the same values as the family of enterprises. We were able to develop agreements with our intermediaries relative to different commercial activities such as fund-raising and promotion to boost sales.

Being in reality a small business, but adding the weight of each of the intermediaries, my family of enterprises gave me the capacity for production, warehousing, and the financial clout of a multinational. This venture propelled our sales to over two million units in Canada, the United States, Japan and Australia. The experience led us to favour the family of enterprises as an organizational structure, ideal for rapid expansion and unlimited flexibility. We all realized our objectives by sharing a common meaning of business life. This success can be attributed to the collaboration of all free and autonomous members who speak the same business language.

The Master Planner

Very few financial institutions are willing to finance innovations which have not proven themselves on the market. My will and determination as a master planner allowed me to invent a new form of financing by mobilizing the intermediaries around a collective project, by gaining their trust and making sure that each one got their due. I negotiated individually with each intermediary so that they would understand their respective responsibilities relative to the delivery of high quality products via the "just in time" concept. The role of the intermediaries of the family of enterprises, made up of ten independent and autonomous companies, had to be clearly defined since the smallest error could lead to the rejection of the final product by the client and deprive the intermediaries of their revenue. I therefore made sure that the work of the intermediaries was impeccable because I assumed the responsibility of the final sales and the costs inherent. To sum up, the family of enterprises offers the intermediaries the advantage of strength in numbers as they:

- speak the same business language,
- negotiate according to humane and creative principles,
- establish confidence through a common interest in the success of the product,
- help and motivate each other to excel and ensure the success of the concept,
- benefit from extension of term financing,
- benefit from a greater buying power in the acquisition of raw materials,
- benefit from no-cost storage space to stock products on a permanent basis,

- benefit on inventory payable only upon sale,
- benefit from basic skills of each and prosper from the diversity of experiences,
- have the weight of a multinational while remaining a small business, ready to instantly respond to local, national and international orders,
- are able to respond to clients' demands with precision and efficiency by offering exclusive and personal after-sales service,
- as a business, concentrate on basic skills.

As a master planner, my principal role was to make sure that the golden rules of the family of enterprises were respected in order to achieve integrity and credibility to make our collective dream an international reality.

The Family of Enterprises: Financial Autonomy

Ever since I started working in the world of inventions and applying the concept of the family of enterprises, my greatest satisfaction has been the appreciation of each person's talent and the efforts they are capable of to realize their dreams. With regards to our invention, after more than a month of sustained efforts, our family of enterprises succeeded in filling an order of more than 288,000 units in the time allotted, which for us, was a miracle. At that time, we promised ourselves that nothing could stop us from realizing our dream. Together we contributed to the materialization of our collective dream.

"Strength in unity" goes the proverb; which is why together, we can realize our dreams as long as we respect the values and principles which inspire them. In summary, we draw from who we are and we associate with like-minded people. Our clients, employees, entourage, our family of enterprises are in our image.

From my beginnings in the world of business, I have learned that we are all looking for something: well-being, inner peace, power, recognition, financial or emotional security, and so on. Why do some people search all their lives and never find anything while others find without even looking? Whatever your present state of being, the answer will always be found within you. If we do what we really like, those we need will come to us and help us in the realization of our conscious dream.

I would like to conclude with the following anecdote. While I was promoting another invention in California, I was asked what I liked about selling it. I answered in saying I got great pleasure seeing children and adults enjoying the product for its utility and simplicity. It was even bought by a Hollywood movie personality who had her own physical fitness centre. In the end, I realized that it was not the complexity of a product that counted but rather the well-being it provided.

Financial autonomy is the new power of the organization

WHAT CAN FINANCIAL AUTONOMY BRING TO THE ORGANIZATION?

- ADAPTATION TO CHANGE.
- SELF-FINANCING.
- REALIZATION OF COLLECTIVE DREAMS THROUGH MORAL AND FINANCIAL SUPPORT.
- INCREASED BUYING POWER.
- IMPROVED PERFORMANCE BY REGROUPING WHILE STAYING FREE AND AUTONOMOUS.

Today's organization lives a duality between money and power versus values and respect for the life's needs. Faced with this reality, the organization of tomorrow should understand its real financial needs. It should create a family of enterprises regulated by the golden rules and common values and capitalize on common financial resources to ensure their future autonomy.

What questions must be asked relative to the financial autonomy of the organization?

1) What is the organization's real reason for being? Does it aim for money and power or the realization of its dreams?

2) What are the values and principles that support today's organizations?

3) What are the financial needs of the organization? Are they realistic?

4) What is the personality of the directors of your company and how do they select intermediaries of the family of enterprises?

5) How important is the realization of the mission to your business?

6) What are the different sources of financing available to the organization?

7) Can the family of enterprises be a source of financing ?

8) Can the family of enterprises help your company increase its sales and productivity?

9) Do traditional sources of financing take your real needs into account?

10) Do you encourage the members of your organization to develop a network for financial autonomy?

11) Can the family of enterprises bring the organization the collective financial leverage necessary to realize its mission and objectives?

Chapter 11

TOTAL AUTONOMY FOR THE HUMAN

Every life is a voyage and finding our destination is solely our responsibility.

After waking to their dependencies and becoming aware of what connects them to life, humans can now realize their full potential to attain total autonomy. To find their destination, they should free themselves of their dependencies to regain possession of their power to make decisions about their lives: what they want to be, what is good for them, and what values they want to adopt. This chapter will show how to apply the basic principles and values needed in our day-to-day lives to attain total autonomy.

We begin by asking ourselves whether we want to continue being dependent on others and society, or would we rather be autonomous? Can we live totally detached from everything or are we chained to the world of illusion? The road least travelled is our road to total autonomy. Therefore, it is that road we should follow and not someone elses. Why do we have trouble finding our way? Why do so many people postpone the accomplishment of their life's plan? How can we really know if we are truly on our rightful path? What will we need to make this journey?

Humans should find their destination by travelling their road of life.

To understand what this means, I would like to offer five intimately linked elements which play an important role in the discovery of our destination and represent a conductive wire to realize our life's plan. They are metaphorical in nature, stemming from an ancient Asian folk tale which I think is pertinent to our quest for autonomy.

1) The Voyage or the Road of Life

The voyage represents the road of life we have chosen to follow throughout our life. From very early on we must make choices relative to the road to take. The direction we choose must come from within us because it is an integral part of our reason for being. It constitutes who we are.

2) The Carriage or the Body

The carriage represents the physical aspects of the human. What state is it in? Is it functioning or rickety? What is your physical condition? Are you in good shape? The carriage is the physical structure which allows humans to move ahead on their road.

3) The Horse or the Emotions

The horse is the emotional energy we need on our road of life. It is the driving force that pulls the carriage. Its energy, strength and vigour allow us to go forward at our own pace on our chosen path. Is your horse a champion or does it run around in circles? Is it weak or energetic?

4) The Driver or the Spirit

The driver represents the spirit or intelligence which allows humans to choose the road that is best for them. The direction taken depends entirely on the driver. Does the driver master the reins of the horse and keep the carriage in good condition? Does the driver know the destination?

5) The Guide or the Soul

The guide represents the soul of the driver. It is the essence of life itself and each person's reason for being. Does the driver follow intuition? Can the driver master the inner voice, which is the guide within? The guide is the ground that connects us to our life's plan, so that we can reach our destination.

The integration of these five elements will create the symbiotic bond necessary to attain total autonomy.

1) THE VOYAGE OR THE ROAD OF LIFE

Vision

Vision is the first essential element in finding our destination. Have I taken the right road? Will this direction bring me happiness? How does my path appear on the horizon? Is it long, laborious and perilous or is it filled with pleasant surprises of joy and love? Is it a country road or a super highway? In light of all these questions, how would we rate our own road of life? Would we rather be somewhere else? If we find ourselves on a pathway other than our own, it is because we are not in our rightful place. Have you ever had the feeling, when you were out with friends or at work, that you were in the wrong place? How did you behave and feel?

Many people take paths that do not suit them. As a result, they experience much more resistance, snares and slow-downs than if they had been on their own road and travelling at their own pace.

We are caught up in the daily grind where the only answers we have to our problems are ones which are fed to us. Real answers come from exploring what we do not know. Without having a clear vision of our true destination, we find ourselves constantly caught up in the same existential crises. By being ourselves, we will find our direction more quickly and avoid serious obstacles which would otherwise draw us from our original destination. In short, a clear vision of who we are, helps us to foresee our voyage towards attaining total autonomy.

We all hold the key to our road of life and it is our responsibility to discover it throughout the course of our lifetime.

The Evolutionary Chain

Our *evolutionary chain* links us to the knowledge of our ancestors. Understanding our ancestors' past and identifying their strengths and weaknesses will help us focus our vision so as not to repeat their mistakes. In this way, we improve our existence. Understanding the *evolutionary chain* lets us go beyond the problems that have always plagued us instead of continually submitting to them. To manifest our future and attain autonomy, we must integrate the experience of our ancestors' lives.

The key to our life's plan is the integration of the information that comes from our ancestors.

2) THE CARRIAGE OR THE BODY

Eating Habits

One of the important factors to be considered when it comes to our body is our eating habits. Do we take the time to properly nourish ourselves? Do we eat when we are hungry or simply out of habit. Are our meal-times programmed or are they special moments? These questions are aimed at understanding the importance of healthy eating habits to make sure that our carriage will carry us on our chosen road. Many products that we ingest can negatively affect our health, like fast food, alcohol, coffee, refined sugar and all products that undergo industrialized processing. Dietary deficiencies lead to poor health which can obstruct or retard us in attaining our destination.

Having a healthy diet means respecting certain values: take the time to eat properly, choose food for its nutritional value and be aware of your bodily needs. We should always try to capitalize on the benefits nature offers. For instance, we should eat foods that are in season, and avoid produce that has been transformed by industrial processing. We should try to start our day with a few glasses of natural spring water before eating. Our bodily systems will be more efficient and we will benefit by having more vitality and enjoy better health.

In following the road we have chosen, there might be warning signs we should respect. These signs tell us to take the time to understand that healthy eating is a vital element in maintaining good health and allows our carriage to move forward unencumbered. Taking advantage of nature's bounty in our eating habits is a step towards total autonomy.

Nature is our food guide.

Physical Exercise

How much importance do we put on physical exercise in our lives? Are we in shape? Do we respect the rhythm of our life? Can the carriage support our weight or its excess? These questions allow us to reflect on the time we devote to exercising our body to be top performers and more productive. Preoccupations and time constraints often force us to put exercise on the back burner. We practise preventive maintenance on our vehicle to avoid problems yet we forget that our own physical condition is also important. "A sound mind in a sound body." Do you allow yourself the time for physical activities such as walking, running, dancing or sports? The carriage must be in good working order or you are in for a long haul. Our body is the expression of our well-being. Physical conditioning can reinforce our endurance for the realization of our life's plan. By exercising regularly, we will improve our well-being towards attaining greater autonomy.

***The body is the temple of our soul:
it allows us to go forward on our road of life.***

Breathing

Can proper breathing bring more energy to the performance of our tasks? How much importance do we put on it? Can it improve our quality of life? Do we breathe nervously, tensely, irregularly or in a relaxed manner? Do we take the time to develop good breathing techniques? Good breathing allows us to channel our energies to attain greater concentration. Mastering our breathing can give us greater endurance in accomplishing our daily tasks. The relaxation it brings us can be a way to regulate tension, stress, overwork or any other problem we encounter in our day-to-day life.

How do we feel when we work in an environment where the air is stale, recycled or unhealthy? If this is a reality that cannot be avoided, taking the time to leave this milieu and reconnect with nature is essential to our well-being. There are many techniques to help us relax, like yoga, Tai-chi, and meditation. Proper breathing can reduce stress, burnout and overexertion. In short, breathing energizes and regulates our body and pushes it to peak performance.

Breathing is the source of excelling.

Lifestyles

What are our lifestyles based on? Are they suited to a better physical well-being? Can we change them? The body is our primary source of information and is quick to react to our emotions such as sadness, joy, happiness, pain, and so on. How do we interpret its messages? Proper lifestyles can prolong our life expectancy if we listen to our real needs: to eat when we are hungry and sleep when we are tired. This may seem obvious, but a glance at our life will tell us that we eat and sleep according to a programmed routine. It is important to pay attention to the signs our body gives to us. They are always a revelation and we often do not take them into account until it is too late. We are the ones in the best position to determine our limits or our levels of tolerance, so that our carriage is solid and able to roll at a speed that best suits us. Listening to our body ensures greater efficiency, durability and longevity to the carriage. Applying this lifestyle on a daily basis allows us to appreciate a better balanced carriage that will run for a long time on our chosen path. Adopting healthier lifestyles in relation to our real needs contributes to a balance in life propitious to attaining our autonomy.

We should follow lifestyles which are beneficial to our well-being.

3) THE HORSE OR THE EMOTIONS

The Emotions

What is an emotion? It is an affective reaction which overtakes us when we experience a significant event. Can we manage emotions or do they have power over us? Where do they come from? Do we depend on them? What do we do to master them? All these questions make us consider the symbolic horse in us... to reflect on the nature of our behaviour. Does our horse run in circles? Does it make the same mistakes because it cannot master its emotions? What must we understand about our emotions to improve our present situation? If our horse is travelling in circles we will certainly not make much headway on our journey. If our horse does not master its passion and strength, it will take us on a path that is not ours.

Mastering our emotions is essential for continuing on our life's road. Those who fail to master them through neglect or incomprehension, will travel in circles, repeating the same mistakes. If we want our horse to be dashing, full of vitality and energy, we must recognize and be attentive to it and let it be part of our life's plan to succeed on our road of life. The horse will then become our ally and we can channel its energy in order to improve our pace. Each emotion has an origin and to become autonomous, we must find it. At that moment, we will recognize our emotions, accept, integrate and master them so that they are a part of our autonomy.

Emotion is the honey of feeling and the flower of knowledge.

The Nervous System

The horse's nervous system can either stimulate or disturb the driver because it can just as easily speed us to our goal, as land us in the ditch. The more balanced our nervous system is, the more likely will our horse pull our carriage at a proper cadence. If our nervous system is unbalanced or totally drained, our horse will not be able to bring us to our ultimate goal. It will slow down and delay our journey.

What should we do to avoid a power failure in our life? First we must stop to look, feel and listen to what is happening in us and around us. What disturbs or worries us in our life? What should we do to improve our situation? The easiest and most efficient methods are meditation, breathing and introspection. We must find peace within us to regain the mastery of our horse and nervous system. This system is the circuitry that runs through us and gives us a sensibility towards all things. What can we do to capitalize on this sensibility to arrive at our goal? In short, the nervous system feeds us with vital energy. Mastering it helps us to properly use this energy to arrive at our ultimate objective sooner.

The nervous system provides us with the necessary energy to find our destination.

Fears

Fear can be interpreted as an uneasiness that prevents us from finding our destination due to a lack of self-confidence and a fear of failure. Our horse may be dynamic, strong and wilful but if we are afraid, it will sense this and not be able to bring us to our destination. What are our fears and their origins? The origin of our fears often comes from the suppression of emotions which is one of the greatest malaises today. One well-known way of conquering our fears is to confront them. For example, if you have a visceral fear of going anywhere alone, you may well be depriving yourself of an outing that can be beneficial to your life. You should take your courage into both hands and confront the fact that your fear is probably a product of your imagination. It undermines all creativity, self-confidence and the realization of our dreams as well as being responsible for numerous setbacks to the accomplishment of our life's plan. To conquer our fears, we should find their sources and integrate them to finally overcome them.

Recognizing our fears helps us to overcome the obstacles in the path of our total autonomy. To conquer them, we should appreciate what they teach us. We often think that fears are a negative phenomena but in fact they are essential to our evolution because when we confront them, we are led to understand and integrate the behaviours that come from fear and impede us from advancing on our journey. Most fears are a product of our environment and can either be our accomplices or our enemies in attaining total autonomy. We must not forget that our fears have allowed us to become who we are today. By understanding our fears, we make a conscious decision to conquer them and therefore accelerate our evolution toward our ultimate goal. Conquering our fears helps our horse to run at full rein.

***Unconquered fears inhibit us
from reaching our destination.***

4) THE DRIVER OR THE SPIRIT

The Spirit

What is the spirit? Does it have anything to do with intelligence, the unknown world or the intangible? The spirit is the substance which fuels the rational world. It unifies and directs the body (the carriage) and the emotions (the horse) in the direction we have determined to find our destination.

The spirit of the driver is made up of all we have understood, learned and integrated since our birth. The driver should ask the following questions. Am I on the right road? When I reach a fork, which way should I go? Can my horse make the turns I ask of it? Is it still energetic or is it overworked? What condition is my carriage in?

Our strengths are focused because the role of the driver is to guide us in our chosen direction. The driver has to try to be one with the environment by listening to intuition and transmitting the information to the horse. As drivers, we must also stop and take the time to understand the meaning of our lives otherwise we will be going in circles, continuing to make the same mistakes and ultimately choosing the wrong roads.

There are many roads that lead to our destination but we must choose the one that is right for us. If we want to go to Rome, we can take any number of planes and transfer flights in any country to arrive at our destination. The other alternative is to take a direct flight. We can also go to Rome by car, boat, bicycle or even on foot. The choice is ours to make. What will our cruising speed be? The role of the driver is to answer these questions. In short, to reach our destination, we must focus our spirit on the itinerary and mode of transport with the objective of attaining our autonomy.

The plan is what structures the spirit to help us determine our direction.

Thought and Intelligence

Thought and intelligence play a primary role in improving our well-being. What exercises do we do to improve our way of thinking? How much time do we spend honing our thinking skills to become more focused and efficient? Is our method efficient and objective? Tai-chi, meditation and visualization are all proven and effective exercises.Thought and intelligence can be cultivated like any other faculty. The direct result of this exercise can make us more aware of our environment and more accurate with regards to the direction we take toward our ultimate goal. The thought and intelligence of the driver leads to the decision on the direction and pace of our voyage.

Proper reflection prevents us from making a wrong turn.

Intuitive Intelligence

Intuitive intelligence is a conceptual framework allowing the driver to materialize the sense of the inner world into the real world. The driver follows the direction to attain autonomy and is quick to adapt to road conditions and deal with the obstacles encountered on the journey by taking advantage of this faculty.

Manage our intuitions to better choose our direction.

Evolutionary Thinking

Evolutionary thinking is thought which emerges from the unknown, the world of the imaginary, and calls on different sources of inspiration: the soul, intuition, the imaginary and the four kingdoms. This way of thinking allows the driver to materialize these thoughts in order to determine the direction that must be taken.

Evolutionary thinking unites the imaginary to reality.

5) THE GUIDE OR THE SOUL

The guide represents the essence of our existence: the soul which feeds all that is alive in us. It is difficult for us to understand or to sense what lies within us. The soul infuses in us what we must do to become one with ourselves. It is the source which allows us to realize our life's plan and arrive at our ultimate goal. We have to cultivate the soul within us as it leads us to excel and find our rightful place on our road of life. The guide is directly linked to our reason for being. The soul is the conductive wire which allows the driver to be certain that the road chosen will finally bring us to our destination.

Everyone can experience the integration of the body, spirit and soul to become one with their reason for being. Therefore, the direction is obvious to the driver. We all have an innate sense of finding our destination and it is awakened when life gives us a sign. There are no limits in terms of age, borders, time or dimensions. We are the only ones who can identify the light that emanates from us by the integration of the three planes. The greatest justice on earth is that everyone will die one day. In our life, this equity is manifested by the fact that we can all develop the light within by becoming one with the universe.

The discovery of our soul, linked to our reason for being, allows us to find our freedom, autonomy and the light within us. Life is the source of all things and humans, by understanding their reason for being, will transcend life by what they are and will then become one with all that is around them.

The soul guides our life.

WHAT CAN TOTAL AUTONOMY BRING TO THE HUMAN?

– FINDING THEIR DESTINATION.

– BEING IN THEIR RIGHTFUL PLACE.

– REALIZING THEIR LIFE'S PLAN.

– BECOMING AUTONOMOUS BEINGS ON ALL LEVELS.

– FINDING THE MEANING OF THEIR LIVES.

Our understanding and integration of the five elements essential to attaining our total autonomy mark the importance of discovering our destination. To excel, we must understand the link which exists between our soul and our life's plan. The closer we are to our destination, the closer we are to being masters of our destiny. We will thus transcend our soul, our spirit and our body and will find ourselves on the road that was destined for us.

In conclusion, the five elements represent the pathway to follow to arrive at our destination. Each element reinforces our knowledge to help us on our way. The discovery of our destination marks a step towards our total autonomy.

What questions must be asked relative to the total autonomy of the human?

1) What is the state of my carriage or my physical condition?
2) How do I improve this condition?
3) What is my understanding of my fears and emotions?
4) How do I recognize and resolve these fears and emotions?
5) Do I have access to relaxation techniques to make better decisions?
6) What links have I made between the five elements to find my destination?
7) Do I use evolutionary thinking to understand my life's plan?
8) What choices do I have to help me find my destination?
9) What type of exercises must I do to return to my source?
10) What road do I take to find my reason for being?
11) Who am I, where do I come from and where am I going in my quest to integrate my three planes: the body, spirit and soul?

Chapter 12

TOTAL AUTONOMY FOR THE ORGANIZATION

The organization's life mission lies in attaining its destination while respecting life's values.

After awakening to its dependencies and becoming aware of its links to life, the organization should realize its inner potential (human, financial and material resources) to attain total autonomy. To find its destination, the organization must free itself from its dependencies by allowing its members to decide upon the role they want and thus define their rightful place. By stimulating creativity in the members and helping them to realize their individual dreams within the framework of the collective dream, it will find its destination. This chapter will look at the management tools available to the organization to attain total autonomy. What does the organization need to make this journey?

Each organization should find its destination by travelling its road of life.

As we have previously done with the human, we offer the organization five closely linked elements based on the same metaphor which play a pivotal role in the discovery of the organization's destination and constitute a conductive wire for the success of its mission.

1) The Voyage or the Vision

The voyage represents the organization's vision and the road it must follow to discover its destination. Every organization has a road to travel and each one depends on the initial vision relative to a common objective. What road should the organization choose to find its destination? Does the organization have a clear and precise vision of what it wants to become?

2) The Carriage or the Organizational Structure

The organization's structure can be represented by a carriage. Can it hold out against forecasts, changes and new realities? Will the carriage pay for itself or will it be at the mercy of a financial institution, governments or some other system? What is the state of the organization's health? Is the structure properly planned and well built; solid yet flexible?

3) The Horse or the Emotions and the Resources of the Organization.

The horse represents the company's nervous system, reflecting the emotions caused by uncertainty. Are the human, financial and material resources sufficient and essential or are they uncertain? Are they energized, actualized and well managed? Are there training programs suited to the real needs of the members?

4) The Driver or Direction and Daily Management.

The driver represents the direction and daily management of the organization and is the decision-centre or the intelligence that decides on the direction to be taken to arrive at the destination. The driver communicates all information relative to the realization of the organization's mission, presenting different scenarios and choosing the best to mobilize the members to attain the common objective. Is upper management properly oriented and has it mastered the reins of the horse and carriage? Are communications relative to change adapted, improved, reviewed and then updated?

5) The Guide or the Mission

The guide is the life's breath of a business. It is the source of inspiration generated by the organization, since it issues from its reason for being. Is this reason for being integrated to a collective well-being? Are the members in tune with their organization's real mission. What does their organization inspire in them?

The organization should work with its members to obtain the common objective of realizing their total autonomy. The five elements drive the organization to accomplish its mission and that of its members. Why are organizations often delayed in accomplishing their mission? What solutions can they offer their members to find their destination? What steps must be followed for the organization towards attaining its total autonomy?

1) THE VOYAGE OR THE VISION

The Vision

Vision lies in the business leader's state of mind and the employees who influence decisions on the company's orientation. It should take into account the company's history in order to project itself into the future. Why refer to a business's past? Because it reveals the strengths to be energized and the weaknesses that must be overcome. By analyzing its basic competencies, the organization can formulate a vision of what it wants to be in the future in a realistic and efficient manner. To formulate this vision, it must conceptualize through evolutionary thinking and at the same time, consider the members' ideas for overcoming obstacles by adapting to the new realities. The vision's objective is to stimulate the participation of the members in the organization's development. Its clarity and precision will have the effect of motivating the members to its realization. The vision represents the success of the organization because the members will understand its benefit for their growth and will, in turn, be encouraged to contribute to their company's growth.

Lack of vision or an unrealistic vision results in a company that reacts to problems rather than anticipating them. The evolutionary organization manifests its future by foreseeing and preparing for the future instead of reacting to day-to-day emergencies.

The shared vision is the essence of our destination's discovery.

The Evolutionary Chain of the Organization

The modern organization that spends a lot of time managing daily crises would do well to analyze its *organizational ancestors* (their personality, markets, and position in the market) and recognize its place in the *evolutionary chain*. How has it evolved till today in its sector of activity? What obstacles did it encounter? How were they overcome and by what means? With these questions in mind, the organization can now deal with new paradigms to find its rightful place in the market and determine where it stands regarding the competition. The future of the organization depends on its ability to draw crucial information from its past relative to what may impede its progress, or inversely, by identifying success factors to better gauge the future. This foresight can be achieved through *evolutionary thinking* that stimulates all members to discover their destination.

Evolution comes by integrating the past to better manifest the future.

2) THE CARRIAGE OR ORGANIZATIONAL STRUCTURE

Clients and the Market

What is the past, present and future evolution of the market, clients, and their needs? Is our organization properly structured to respond to immediate and future needs? What improvements can we make on our present structures to reduce costs and address tomorrow's real needs? What are our primary objectives? To be resistant to change or to offer modern service to our clients by responding to their real needs instead of their illusory ones? We know that clients, consumers and the markets are always evolving and that their needs change. The organizational structure should be more flexible and adapted to tomorrow's demands. The revision of concepts, markets and clients, will occur with the introduction of new goods and services aimed at making the attainment of total autonomy easier. Tomorrow's organization should direct itself towards the implementation of product awareness programs to facilitate its clients' autonomy in every economic sector. This new vocation will inform clients on the use of new products, their benefits as well as their origins for a better quality of life. In other words, companies in the food industry would have the responsibility of helping consumers be more autonomous by giving them the necessary information to attain better nutritional balance. As an example, genetically-engineered food should be labelled as such. The tobacco industry has already been obligated by law to take this direction by adding warnings on their product, that smoking is harmful to health. The chemical industry should offer products which are less noxious to the environment and sensitize the consumers to change their lifestyles to better preserve nature and life.

Tomorrow's organization will illuminate life through preservation, whereas today's organization eliminates life through destruction.

Economic Sectors

What objectives are pursued in our organization's sector of activity? Do different sectors of economic activity serve only their own interests, or do they also contribute to the collective well-being? Tomorrow's organization will be involved in many sectors of activity through a greater exposure to life's real needs and as a result, will not be limited to only serving the needs of humans. Sectors of activity will be trained to resolve urgent problems such as water, air and soil pollution, the depletion of resources, competitiveness and organizational disputes. These *evolutionary organizations* will have to deal with new realities on a daily basis. They will have to answer to criteria essential to the survival of humanity and put an end to its deterioration. To accomplish this, they will have to apply the new universal values respecting life's needs and as a result, contribute to the collective well-being. Whatever their sector of economic activity, companies will have to organize themselves to offer their consumers or clients, goods and services which will heighten their awareness of and respect for the planet. In addition to being providers, they will now be stewards of all that is precious to life.

The organizational conscience contributes to a universal well-being.

Goods and Services

What goods and services offered in the past will we find in the future? Those which jeopardize the collective well-being or ones which respect the real needs of life? Tomorrow's organization will have to rethink its products in terms of new values. Before even taking the first steps in the implementation of a business, founders and shareholders will have to consider their products or services in terms of the new values which will govern our planet; those that deal with the preservation of life. All goods and services will have to be conceived with their consequences in mind. They will have to comply with the new universal values and life's real needs in order to contribute to the survival of humans by improving their collective state of well-being.

All goods and services should stem from life's real needs.

Technological Change

Is the organizational structure open to technological change? What will the costs and benefits of adapting to these changes be? Will the organization be undermined by these changes through labour confrontations, downsizing and personal conflicts within the organization? Before installing a new technology, we should draw up a list of advantages and disadvantages and have every member participate in making decisions. As well, the organization should offer its employees training in the new technology and allow them to express their creativity by adapting it to the service of humans. Such an initiative would contribute directly to the collective well-being.

Technology should stimulate the Human to overtake, not be overtaken.

Physical and Psychological Balance

Can the organization encourage good physical and psychological health in its members? Tomorrow's businesses face the greatest challenges in the history of humanity. They include the revolution of the information age and natural upheavals that will affect everyone on the planet. We have to be physically and psychologically ready to adapt. The organization should encourage its members to improve their mental and physical condition through a variety of programs on nutrition, breathing, self-improvement and exercise. Good physical and mental health will allow members to adapt more easily to organizational changes. By the same token, they will be less vulnerable to stress, burnout and other illnesses.

Physical and psychological balance leads to greater individual and organizational performance.

3) THE HORSE OR THE EMOTIONS AND THE RESOURCES OF THE ORGANIZATION

Financial Resources

What are the financial resources of the organization? Are they sufficient and do they warrant the organization's success? Adages like "money rules the world" and "without money you are nothing" indicate the importance money has for the organization. The performance of our horse will be affected by the food we give it.

Money is the major preoccupation of all modern organizations and it often paralyses their growth. The organization's growth can be hindered by lack of money, indebtedness, and its search for grants or any other source of financing. Yet we have to remember that money is a means to build a business and not an end in itself. Human creativity is without doubt a company's most important resource. Tomorrow's organization can easily engender economic returns by simply being aware of the potential around it to generate the right financial resources through the concept of the family of enterprises or through innovation. Thus, joining up with other organizations can help your company ensure its growth without being dependent on financial institutions.

There are many ways to self-finance: fund raising, promotions, free media services, knowing a good samaritan or patron, mutual-help networks, word of mouth, family of enterprises and so on. Who knows an entrepreneur better that another entrepreneur when it comes to financing? Before approaching the many possible avenues of financing, the company of the future should take advantage of its existing assets; namely human creativity and the mutual help available through the family of enterprises. Then, and only then will every conscious dream finally see the light of day. Accumulating financial and creative capital allows us to marry what is useful to what is enjoyable while attaining total autonomy.

The accumulation of financial and creative capital is the result of hard work aimed at accomplishing a conscious dream.

Human Resources

How do modern organizations manage their human capital? How do they evaluate this resource? By proficiency management, psychological tests, personality profiles? Are the members programmed like machines or can they freely express their creativity? What does the organization do to stimulate its human resources? Does it interact, communicate and coordinate with them? Is it possible that the main reason for the failure of today's organizations stems from their inability to manage human capital which is vital to their survival? Incessant technological changes, labour problems, endless downsizing, job insecurity, mergers, acquisitions and all the fears that come from this, fill the members with apprehension. The humans in the organization feel themselves inferior in relation to the importance accorded to finance and technology.

How can the organization manage its priorities in relation to the unforeseeable? Organizations often find themselves facing an unscalable wall. They would do well to step back and analyze the experiences that come with disorder. They will then find a new awareness and come to understand the source of their chaos and resolve it. To solve its insecurities, the organization should involve all its members and gain their confidence by agreeing to openly address their fears. It should then enlist their creativity to find solutions to the problems that have been identified. By integrating the members into the decision-making process, uneasiness will vanish and a spirit of cooperation will prevail. The future of organizations depends essentially on their ability to master their insecurities and this must begin with reinstating the human ahead of finance and technology.

The uncertainties that organizations now face have driven a wedge between upper management and the members who often feel abandoned in the midst of this turmoil. A turning point is therefore crucial to reinforce their feeling of belonging to the common mission and thus establish a new order in the organization. The members should feel themselves involved and valued in the formulation of a common vision. Together, they should define new organizational paradigms which will consolidate their creative potential.

Human capital represents life in the organization.
The discovery of this life will determine its success.

Training the Members

Training allows us to teach our horse to excel in its duty: to pull the carriage towards our destination. Do organizations offer training programs centred on developing human potential? What are the real objectives behind their training programs and who are they designed for?

The organization should implement a training program adapted to the real needs of the members to create, invent and innovate with the objective of optimizing their participation in the realization of its vision. Group training will mobilize the members and create a collective awareness of the meaning of their lives as well as the life of the organization. The pursuit of these objectives relies on the growth of the human through *evolutionary thinking*, creativity, the financial health of the organization and its adaptation to new technology. The development of an ongoing training program on organizational creativity is therefore vital to the growth of the organization because it helps itself and its members attain total autonomy by rallying them to a common destination.

Training members reinforces the understanding of their destination so that the organization can reach its destination as well.

Organizational Fears

Today's organizations exhibit a great deal of insecurity about the future and their management is often affected by it. *The evolutionary organization* will train people according to their real needs, by enriching their personal and collective development and giving them the resources necessary to allow them to attain their total autonomy. It will thus stimulate the development of its members by providing a work environment propitious to their development as humans. This new outlook on life will reduce existential crises and make way for the emergence of a new awareness. Organizational insecurities will disappear because greater autonomy among the members will tend to decentralize power, bringing about more participation from the members in the orientation of the enterprise. The members will therefore regain their power to decide on their contributions to the organization. This will in turn, free upper management to concentrate more on the collective destination of the corporate mission.

Organizational insecurities hinder the discovery of the corporation's destination.

4) THE DRIVER OR DIRECTION AND DAILY MANAGEMENT

The Decision-Making Process

Who makes the decisions in the organization? Does the process include every group: directors, employees and unions? Do the short, middle and long-term decisions respect the global vision? Decision-making that stems from *evolutionary thinking* can help the organization find its direction by avoiding the pitfalls that come with assuming success before the fact. Why do many organizations' decision-making processes not include the ideas or opinions of the employees? Unidirectional communication can give rise to many conflicts between management and the employees who often feel misunderstood. A better course would be to seek creative solutions from its members with the aim of sharing ideas and opinions. In short, by availing itself to the knowledge that is already there on the "shop floor", the organization cannot help but benefit. Real and universal participation in the decision-making process will produce results that meet with, if not exceed those that were projected. The ultimate goal is to optimize the decision-making process to achieve their objectives.

Creative power should emanate from every member of the organization. Upper management would have the pivotal role of managing this power in such an evolutionary structure. This will then give birth to original ideas and even save the organization from possible insolvency, poor cash flow or any other problem rising from poorly thought-out decisions based on uncertainties and old paradigms... ones which no longer answer the present needs of the members and prevent the organization from seeing the new reality. The maxim of the carrot and the stick is still very popular as a management technique, however it must be replaced with a more contemporary vision, in keeping with the real needs of the members to attain total autonomy.

The creative power of the members helps the organization to find the right direction to reach its destination.

Communication

How would we characterize communication in our organization? Is it limited, explicative, authoritarian or can we express ourselves freely? Communication has become the commodity of choice in the modern world. What are we to make of this new reality? In today's organizations, the buzz word is "communicate". Everybody hears but nobody really listens. Communication is most often unidirectional and almost always falls on deaf ears. As such it is hardly "communication". People no longer have time to listen, to see, to feel, to taste or to touch. Our five senses no longer have any significance or at best, are reduced to their simplest expression. We become unwittingly computerized, robotic and mechanical entities. We learn to do things by rote instead of seeing meaning or life in anything. However, if our five senses were truly integrated into our life's experiences, we would reach a greater awareness of what surrounds us. The *evolutionary organization* must therefore be a catalyst and transmitter of information allowing members to rediscover their five senses and the world around them. Communication will then be informative and inspiring rather than direct and destructive. *Evolutionary Humans* will see the truth in everything, will understand the incomprehensible, will communicate their truth, transmit their reason for being and feel the beauty of life within them. The *evolutionary organization* will serve its members by seeing their creative potential, understanding their need to express, communicating the universal values and the real needs of life, transmitting information vital to their growth and feeling the beauty of the life that flows from within them.

TABLE OF THE FIVE SENSES IN RELATION TO COMMUNICATION

THE SENSES	TODAY	EVOLUTIONARY
SIGHT	SEEING	SEEING THE TRUTH
HEARING	LISTENING	UNDERSTANDING
TASTE	SPEAKING	COMMUNICATING
TOUCH	TAKING	TRANSMITTING, GIVING
SMELL	BREATHING	FEELING LIFE

If the organization is to employ *evolutionary communication,* it should understand that the real meaning of communication is transmitting the essence of its mission to its members and not euphemistic information that hides the truth. Upper management should quite simply be transparent, and from there, communication will be evolutionary and truthful. For example, an industry that pollutes excessively is certainly aware of its negative impact on the environment. It should therefore admit to its offenses immediately, before specific legislation makes it liable and forces it to come up with solutions to address the problem. The only truthful communication of the organization should be its reason for being, which is to contribute to the collective well-being. Every organization has the power to communicate the truth through its reason for being. In short, the driver is the intermediary between the organization's mission and the direction it should take to find its destination.

Evolutionary communication transcends the truth through action.

The Implementation of the Action Plan

The drivers act out of intelligence, being the directors of the organization's plan and the architects of the structure's functions on a day-to-day basis. This allows the organization to foresee and act on events instead of reacting to them. The plan is the framework which allows the organization to find its destination. What fundamental questions must the driver ask to find the right destination?

— What is my plan to find the right direction?

— Am I acting or reacting?

— Am I prudent enough or do I merely overcome obstacles as they occur?

— In what state are my horse and carriage?

— Am I on the right road?

These questions lead the organization to develop an *evolutionary strategy*; to build a plan aimed at regrouping all the members. The realization of the plan is the keystone to the success of the organization. Most businesses seldom consult their members when conceiving strategies. The strategic plan usually comes from the top and is often not understood because they are not involved in the decision-making process.

The *evolutionary enterprise* will adopt a strategy designed to include the creative input of its members. Creativity, by its very nature, supports the implementation of *evolutionary strategy* and the orientation chosen to allow the organization to find its destination.

The evolutionary plan of the driver is the keystone of the organization's direction.

5) THE GUIDE OR THE MISSION

The Mission of the Organization

What is the company's mission? By realizing its reason for being, the organization will find its destination. Is the mission aimed at guiding the members towards a collective well-being or is it more concerned with return on investments? The businesses that wish to survive in the new millennium should redefine their basic missions through *evolutionary thinking,* by anticipating the consequences and unknown factors which will result from the abuses of the last decades. They must develop an organizational mission where all members should define their personal mission by finding their rightful place to realize their total autonomy. In a sense, the *evolutionary organization* will be the manager of individual creativity which will then be integrated to a collective mission. As a result, all the members will participate in the conceptualization of a global mission, creating a feeling of belonging to tomorrow's organization.

The mission is the guide which determines the road to follow towards the total autonomy of the organization.

The Values of the Organization

What are the organization's values? Are they universal in terms of a collective well-being, or are they monetary? Will they adapt to tomorrow's values or are they rigid? What is basic to these organizational values? Are they imposed and reinforced by upper management? Are they respected, valued and understood by all the members? Do they respect the environment?

Today, we follow the values conveyed by our leaders instead of developing our own value system based on the perfection of this world; nature and life. We blindly follow illusory values associated with the modern world while knowing that fundamental values lie in respect for other beings. Have we perhaps completely forgotten the meaning of our lives in favour of a lifestyle we call freedom of choice. There are well over a quarter of a billion fire arms in circulation in the United States, for protection from whom or what? We have been polluting at will, destroying all that exists, with total indifference to life around us. This state of affairs marks one of the most significant moments in the history of human evolution. It could mean complete self-destruction if we do not backtrack quickly and reassess our situation. Given that humans have created this chaos, can we truly expect them to solve it? Certainly, but we must act quickly by first heightening our awareness through self-analysis so that we may truly understand the meaning of our life and life in general.

The organization of the future will have no other option but to take itself in hand and understand that it must contribute to the awakening and awareness of its members and to society. It will do this by bringing about real solutions and acting on organizational values essential to the collective well-being. The organization should involve itself with policies which are more humane and stem from universal values such as self-respect and respect for life and nature. These values are essential to the survival of the Human and the Organization and we should find a way of spreading them by exercising discernment and tolerance.

Organizational values will become the foundations of its survival.

The Essence of the Organization

The essence emanating from the organization is its reason for being, in harmony with life around it. Life is a whole and we are part of it. We all come from the earth and we will all return to it. Whatever our achievements during our short stay on the planet, we have the responsibility of contributing to individual and collective well-being. Every modern organization should get closer to the essential, which is to transcend the life from which it was born. Life is the most precious thing. Dead or bankrupt, the Human and the Organization can no longer contribute to a collective well-being. They must therefore maintain a balance in everything and understand that we all have a role to play in the development of a better world. Our responsibility is both individual and collective because it is incumbent on all to improve the state of humanity.

The essence of the organization is the conductive wire of organizational values issued from life and nature.

WHAT CAN TOTAL AUTONOMY BRING TO THE ORGANIZATION?

- INVENTING THE FUTURE WITH A CLEARER VISION.
- BEING AHEAD IN OUR MARKET.
- ENCOURAGING ENTHUSIASM AND GROUP SYNERGY.
- CONTRIBUTING TO THE COLLECTIVE WELL-BEING OF ITS MEMBERS.
- ENSURING ITS GROWTH.

What questions should be asked relative to the total autonomy of the organization?

1) Am I allowed to choose my role in my organization?

2) Does the organization's vision take into account the participation of all its members?

3) Will the integration of the five elements allow the organization and its members to find their destination?

4) Does the organization sufficiently capitalize on its human, material and financial resources?

5) Is communication within the organization well-directed? Is there room for the creative expression of the members?

6) How does the organization stimulate the creativity of its members?

7) Would setting up a creativity service for the members be beneficial to the organization?

8) Does the organization have a mission that contributes to the collective well-being?

9) What values does the organization promote? Does it encourage its members to find their rightful place?

10) Does the organization have training programs to improve the performance of its members?

11) What does the organization foresee doing in order to be closer to its mission, members and life's real needs?

Chapter 13

THE HUMAN AND THE ORGANIZATION OF THE FIFTH KINGDOM

By integrating all that exists, the Human and the Organization will evolve to become the Fifth Kingdom.

The purpose of this book has been to make humans accountable for themselves and responsible for their future through the understanding that they are the manifestation of everything that has happened in their lives. By simply being themselves, they will regain the power to decide on their future and become the *Humans of the Fifth Kingdom.*

In the same manner, and by way of extension, the organization will become responsible for its actions by striving for a collective well-being through the stimulation of the creative potential of its members. By encouraging members to choose their rightful place and to excel, it will become the *Organization of the Fifth Kingdom.* By recognizing, understanding and acting on "life" and all its components, the Human and the Organization will be instilled with information essential to their evolution and become the *Human and the Organization of the Fifth Kingdom.*

What is the source of the *Fifth Kingdom*? What is its mission, its reason for being and the characteristics and elements which distinguish the *Human and the Organization of the Fifth Kingdom* from everything else? Who are the *Humans and the Organizations of the Fifth Kingdom*?

1) THE SOURCE OF THE FIFTH KINGDOM

The source of the *Fifth Kingdom* can be seen as the bonding of the mineral, plant, animal and Homo Sapiens kingdoms. Homo Sapiens, being the species that has evolved to become humans in the modern organization, are now on the way to becoming, by their own choice, either "denatured" or the *Humans of the Fifth Kingdom.*

The Human and the Organization are the result of transformations which have occurred over the course of time. The *Fifth Kingdom* will be the evolutionary result of the integration of all the preceding kingdoms. By integrating these four kingdoms, the *Human and the Organization of the Fifth Kingdom* will capitalize on what the earth gives, how plants inspire, how animals teach, as well as what the Human and the Organization of today have learned from these kingdoms, to live in total harmony.

In other words, the *Human and the Organization of the Fifth Kingdom* should discover the reason why each kingdom exists and then give them the respect that is their due. Every kingdom possesses its own natural mechanism to protect itself against predators. It consists of a sensory genetic code. The deciphering of this code will allow us to communicate with each living species and understand its reason for being over the course of time. This access code can be considered as the energy that the kingdoms release through wavelengths or frequencies. By being in touch with these vibrations, we will understand them and perhaps come to understand the problems of our modern age. By deciphering the original source of the kingdoms and by being on their wavelength, we will develop ways to preserve life.

We are all transmitters by the fact that absolutely everything emits waves. For example, we all have a favourite radio station that we tune-in to. With life, it is the same because we can tune-in to it and thrive on the energy that flows from it. To become resonant with the kingdoms, we merely have to tune-in to the right station to be on the same wavelength.

The mission of the Human and the Organization is to tune-in to life.

Briefly, to be in resonance with everything around us means having empathy with all the kingdoms and being able to connect with everything that exists to survive. It means getting in touch with what we once were: a piece of perfection in the greater scheme of things. The kingdoms are a part of us and if we destroy them, we annihilate ourselves. Giving significance to daily events which influence us will help us to understand our original plan or mission, which is the reason why we are here. We must never forget that we are engendered by life and its components.

In summary, being resonant means:

- Interpreting and integrating the messages each kingdom communicates to us: floods and fires, the destruction of the rain forests, endangered species. What the Earth, trees and animals inspire in us.

- Respecting all that surrounds us and determining the strengths and weaknesses of each kingdom.

- Understanding each kingdom's reason for being as well as the respect they have for universal values.

- Recognizing the contribution of each kingdom to our well-being and determining what we can do in return, to help them ensure our mutual survival.

- Appreciating the interrelationship of the kingdoms: water nourishes the earth, plants feed animals and humans.

- Being in tune with the kingdoms by demonstrating empathy towards them. Ask where they come from, who they are and where they are going.

- Understanding the energy we release as transmitters and capturing the energy that emanates from other kingdoms.

In conclusion, becoming resonant is being able to understand the benefits of each kingdom and its direct contribution to the creation of life on earth. Each one of our discoveries and the awareness it brings to us, contributes to the beautification of our garden of life. Everyone among us should be involved in the preservation of the kingdoms and their development. Accepting our insignificance in the universe we are a part of will allow us to understand the meaning of our life and life itself. Instead of exploiting life, we will embellish it and in return, it will reward us with its generosity and abundance. The Human and the Organization should learn to live with their environments and manage the kingdoms' resources with discernment and the respect which is their due.

All the answers to the problems of humanity are found in the kingdoms that engendered us.

2) THE MISSION OF THE HUMAN AND THE ORGANIZATION OF THE FIFTH KINGDOM

The primary mission of the *Human and the Organization of the Fifth Kingdom* is the implementation of a collective plan allowing everyone to thrive and to create a new global order supported by a universal vision of our future. It calls for evolution as a solution, not revolution.

Revolution for more control or evolution for greater awareness.

The advent of the *Fifth Kingdom* will preclude revolution in favour of evolution by making the Human and the Organization autonomous entities and masters of their common destiny.

The Mission of the Human of the Fifth Kingdom

The mission of the *Human of the Fifth Kingdom* will be to:

- Sense, feel, and foresee future events. Awaken humans so that they become clairvoyant in their lives and foresee solutions to counter society's major problems.

- Be a catalyst of information that emanates from everything around them and direct it toward a better collective well-being.

- Preserve humanity's reason for being so that life's needs and the universal values will be in balance.

- Facilitate the understanding of the potential within by integrating the three planes (body, spirit and soul).

- Act as a guide for the preservation of life and for the realization of each person's life plan.

The Mission of the Organization of the Fifth Kingdom

The mission of the *Organization of the Fifth Kingdom* will be to:

- Manage creative human potential based on developmental programs to help the members find their rightful place.

- Spread information necessary for the realization of each members' life plan and show empathy towards them.

- Spread information vital to its survival and growth by forming a universal family of enterprises.

- Participate in the preservation of life by ensuring a collective well-being.

- Act as a guide to lead members towards realizing their life's plan in accordance to their reason for being.

3) THE REASON FOR BEING OF THE HUMAN AND THE ORGANIZATION OF THE FIFTH KINGDOM

The reason for being of the *Human and the Organization of the Fifth Kingdom* will be to solve the problems of humanity through their imaginary world: the only world that is their own. This evolutionary thought process begins with the awakening of their potential and continues through the awareness of the actions to be undertaken towards realizing total autonomy. To achieve this evolution, one being our life's plan and the other the corporate mission, the Human and the Organization must be disciplined and organized. They should determine where they are on their road of life and decide on the direction to take: evolution or revolution?

The advent of organizations which give humans the opportunity to express themselves in all integrity in terms of their creativity and potential will be crucial for our survival. The role of organizations and humans will be to stimulate creativity by spreading information universally so that the people of the global village will capture its essence and become sensitized to the arrival of a new universal awareness of freedom, autonomy and preservation of life.

4) THE CHARACTERISTICS OF THE HUMAN AND THE ORGANIZATION OF THE FIFTH KINGDOM

The *Human and the Organization of the Fifth Kingdom* will be recognized by their virtue, commitment and dedication to the collective well-being.

Characteristics of the Human of the Fifth Kingdom.

- Integrity and creativity represented by virtual knowledge that stems from the invisible world and is recognized by all.

- Balanced and in their rightful place.

- Androgynous, integrating both masculine and feminine polarities.

- Call upon the imaginary world because they are *evolutionary thinkers.*

- Evolutionary and empathic, both generalists and specialists thus universalists: *evolutionary beings, doctors, accountants, scientists* and so on.

- Resonant, possessing the ability to empathize with the kingdoms and decipher the original source of each to discover their respective essence. Demystify each, to communicate in their language and to integrate them into our lives, e.g. the farmer hears the words of the soil, the horticulturist listens to the language of the plants, the apiarist understands the message of the bees.

- Able to decide what they want according to who they are or want to be.

- Close to their essences: their souls, reason for being. Truthful; living to be, instead of to want.

- Alive as sources of energy, catalysts of information and transmitters of positive energy to those around them.

- Awakeners of a new universal awareness in harmony with life's real needs and values.

Characteristics of the Organization of the Fifth Kingdom:

- Reason for being is focused on survival of the planet and being in harmony with the kingdoms.

- Provider of goods and services based on life's real needs, respecting natural cycles and heightening the consumers' awareness.

- Transmitter of information to realize its life's mission and that of its members.

- Integrator of an organizational development plan taking into account the members' life plans.

- Conceiver of an integrated creativity centre to maximize the members' potential.

- Manager of a collective imaginary world.

- Respecter of universal values and life's real needs.

- Androgynous: symbiosis of different polarities; employees and employers.

- *Evolutionary thinker* and creator of an evolutionary education centre with an integrated management system.

- Awakener of a new universal awareness encompassing life.

These characteristics represent the direction the Human and the Organization should take in the future to become completely autonomous.

5) THE DISTINCTIVE ELEMENTS OF THE HUMAN AND THE ORGANIZATION OF THE FIFTH KINGDOM

The essence of the *Human of the Fifth Kingdom* lies in the balance of subtle intangibles which are the vital mental and emotional elements united in life's continuum. To reach the integration of the body, spirit and soul and be united to our reason for being, we must transform our life by understanding what we want to accomplish in it.

The essence of the *Organization of the Fifth Kingdom* lies in understanding the humans that comprise it, by allowing them the opportunity to make choices to find their rightful place. By integrating the body, spirit and soul, it will stimulate and spread the creative energy of its members to attain autonomy for each as well as the collective.

What are the distinctive elements of the body, spirit and soul?

	HUMAN OF THE FIFTH KINGDOM	ORGANIZATION OF THE FIFTH KINGDOM
BODY:	SELF HEALER, CATALYST, CREATIVE. WAVELENGTH TUNER, DEMONSTRATES EMPATHY TOWARDS KINGDOMS. IS IN RIGHTFUL PLACE. MATERIALIZES INVISIBLE WORLD TO VISIBLE WORLD.	TRANSMITTER OF INFORMATION TO MEMBERS. ORGANIZATIONAL CATALYST. INTEGRATE EVOLUTIONARY MANAGEMENT TO FREE CREATIVITY. EVOLUTIONARY STRUCTURE "TREES, FOREST". ALLOWING MEMBERS TO CHOOSE THEIR RIGHTFUL PLACE.
SPIRIT:	EVOLUTIONARY THINKING. LIFE DIRECTED IN TERMS OF UNIVERSAL VALUES AND LIFE'S REAL NEEDS. INTEGRATION OF KINGDOMS.	INTEGRATION OF COLLECTIVE INTELLIGENCE. EVOLUTIONARY THINKING, INTUITION. DIRECTION AND INTEGRATION OF THE INDIVIDUAL AND COLLECTIVE MISSION.
SOUL:	NEW MISSION, PRESERVE THE PLANET. REASON FOR BEING, COMMUNICATION IN THE IMAGINARY WORLD TO REALIZE OUR BEING.	COLLECTIVE MISSION, PRESERVE LIFE AND AWAKEN AWARENESS. INTEGRATE THE CONDUCTIVE WIRE. UNIVERSAL BROADCASTING IN TERMS OF INDIVIDUAL AND COLLECTIVE MISSION.

This chart shows a greater openness towards a collective well-being and a greater awareness so necessary to our survival. The integration of the three planes is as fundamental to the Human as it is to the Organization to ensure their evolution.

6) THE HUMAN AND THE ORGANIZATION OF THE FIFTH KINGDOM

Who is the Human of the Fifth Kingdom?

The *Humans of the Fifth Kingdom* will tend to be faceless, colourless, nameless, without cards, and with thoughts neither objective or subjective yet more neutral and evolutionary, speaking words that are just and true. Pure energy will flow from them eliminating any doubts about their integrity. They will be unified and creative humans, from whom the virtual knowledge that stems from their imaginary world will be recognized by humanity.

They will render the invisible world accessible to reality. They will bring people to a greater awareness of the invisible world and what they manifest will become reality. By working with the invisible world, they will be aware of the source of obstacles that they encounter in their lives such as sickness, indebtedness, divorce, because these problems are born in this invisible world. The understanding of this invisible world will lead the *Humans of the Fifth Kingdom* to solve their existential crises and reach total autonomy. For example, when we take a photograph, the negative represents the invisible which, through the process of development, becomes visible. By understanding this transformation, humans can integrate their problems and free the creative powers within them.

The *Humans of the Fifth Kingdom* will be responsible for their actions. They will recognize and manifest all that surrounds them. There will be no blame for what happens to them in their lives because they will understand that living is being responsible.

We are the fruit of our thoughts.

Each event or experience marks a step in our life. Have you ever asked yourself why you like one person more than another? Why you work for this company in particular? Why you are an artist, painter, doctor or politician? What has led you to be what you are today? Why do you prefer certain foods, colours, animals, the city or nature? The day that humans truly consider the events in their lives and integrate the lessons learned from them, is the day they become the *Humans of the Fifth Kingdom.* People who are honest with themselves think in a fair and just way and will always be in their rightful place in relation to their life's plan. They will become one with all by appreciating all that exists. They will understand that there is no coincidence in life because life is perfect and everything that happens to them is directly related to their lives.

The humans of the fifth kingdom will live detached from everything that ties them to the physical to become one with all.

What is the Organization of the Fifth Kingdom?

The Organization of the Fifth Kingdom will be nameless, replaced by its vital representative energy (its reason for being, colours, its purpose), so that its members evolve at their own pace in terms of their essence. The organization will be known by a symbol or logo that identifies it. It will have virtual proficiencies, enhanced by the inspiration of a collective imaginary world, that will materialize into reality. In this way it will allow its members to express their creativity and deliver their full potential in all integrity. Its role will consist of managing the creative potential of each human while pursuing a common mission.

The *Organization of the Fifth Kingdom* will have no parameters; personal responsability will replace time and space. We will create our own schedules, working when we want and according to our conscious choice. Time hinders people in the development of their creative potential. The *Organization of the Fifth Kingdom* is a product of the *Human of the Fifth Kingdom* and by integrating these two polarities, it will become a realized and autonomous organization. It will be responsible for its actions because its goods and services will respect the environment. Its mission will be to heighten the awareness of humans instead of controlling them. The *Organization of the Fifth Kingdom* will establish links between the confrontational challenges it faces and what is necessary to bring about evolutionary solutions. For example, it will ask itself if its new product is environmentally friendly and well accepted by the market. It will question if it is really acting on its original plan or rather being directed by members who are unconcerned with the needs of those around them.

The *Organization of the Fifth Kingdom* should take a new look at past events and link the vital information these events have provided to its evolution. As examples, it should look at the way the food industry has rendered the soil infertile by abusively exploiting it with pesticides and chemicals year after year to produce a higher yield. It should consider the tremendous changes in our ecosystem due to soil erosion and the disappearance of certain species as a result of the wanton destruction of forests.

The *Organization of the Fifth Kingdom* should connect with all that exists to understand existence and to preserve what is most precious on earth: life. It will understand what the kingdoms are composed of by communicating with them through its members in accordance with their vital needs. Instead of destroying our environment, tomorrow's organizations will enrich it by being the builders of a better world.

The organization of the fifth kingdom is the fruit of collective thinking.

To define the *Organization of the Fifth Kingdom*, and understand its evolutionary structure, we will return to the metaphor of the forest and the tree. The *Human of the Fifth Kingdom* is the realized tree, meaning fully autonomous. It is the master of its fruits. It is the catalyst between the universe (through its branches) and the earth (through its roots), by materializing the imaginary world through ideas and creativity. It becomes the one which transforms the energy of the universe and gives it back to the earth in the form of goods and services. It is autonomous and free. Each realized tree is the human becoming an organization and will be a part of the forest which is the organizational collective or the family of enterprises. Each realized tree will distinguish itself by its fruits (experience, basic competence, know-how, creativity, talent,) and together, the trees will make up a forest.

Complete autonomy of the being and its identity will mean that each realized tree will distinguish itself by its uniqueness and will enjoy group synergy: the forest. The realized organization (human, organization, family of enterprises) will awaken the consciousness of all the realized trees which will become the forest of collective potential. It will lead everyone to transcend all that exists in terms of real needs and universal values taught by life and will create a global force integrated to a common mission: the survival of humanity. In short, all workers will become masters of their destinies in being autonomous and responsible within the organization. The organization's major role will be to manage the creative potential of each tree. It will ensure the transmission of vital information to raise the consciousness of its autonomous members.

We recognize realized humans by their consciousness as we recognize a realized organization by the collective consciousness of its members.

The *Human and the Organization of the Fifth Kingdom* will recognize everything that will happen in their lives and be able to interpret it to serve their life's plan or mission. All the events in our lives will then have greater meaning. Instead of fighting, forgetting or despising these events, we will learn how to recognize, appreciate and integrate them into our lives. We will realize that there is no such thing as chance in life and that everything is perfect because we all come from a world of perfection.

In fact, the *Human and the Organization of the Fifth Kingdom* will be the precursors of the future while living in the present. They will integrate all the keys offered in this book by ensuring that their life plans are truly respected and that in every moment of their lives they will be in their rightful place while respecting the values that stem from this world of perfection.

Every human is a world.
The day we discover this world
is the day we will live together as a community.

Every organization is a world.
The day it discovers the world within it
is the day it will live as a society.

Each human and organization is a world.
The day they discover their own world
is the day they will live together
as the Fifth Kingdom.

Conclusion

What started as a blank page has ended in a real communications tool and at the same time a passport for the world. We have crossed a bridge that has led us to discover the keys essential to attaining our autonomy to become the *Human and the Organization of the Fifth Kingdom.* Like the bridge in Monet's celebrated 1899 masterpiece, *The Water Lily Pond,* there is no beginning or end. In life, there is no beginning or end because the Human and the Organization are part of a continuum. Humans should transform their lives to be alive and the organization should cultivate life within its structure. This process begins with an awakening and the realization of their conscious dreams. They should think about the chaos that is halting their growth on a daily basis as well as their dependencies on different systems.

The awakening for the *evolutionary organization,* which is the family of enterprises, will consist of respecting the autonomy and freedom of each human and organization that chooses this path. We will discover the forest of our full potential when the organization frees the creative expression of the trees which are part of it. To attain this dimension, the Human and the Organization should ask themselves where they come from, who they are and where they are going. The answers to these questions will allow them to recognize, understand and act on their dependencies.

The ongoing process of transformation demands an awareness on the part of the Human and the Organization of all that exists around them. Life is in perfect balance because it emerges from universal values and life's needs. By understanding the importance of balance in their lives and realizing their conscious dreams, the Human and the Organization will regain their essence. To do this, they will have to determine the true meaning of their lives or the direction to take to ensure their growth. The realization of their conscious dreams, stemming from nothingness and taking shape through *evolutionary thinking*, will lead them to take the road least travelled; the road of their own lives.

Evolutionary thinking gave me the certainty that the imaginary, that world which is truly ours, can transform our life by manifesting in today's reality what we will be tomorrow. It is therefore why everything that comes from this invisible world allows us to become who we really are. When the Human and the Organization take all that surrounds them as a model, such as nature and the four seasons, they will discover their true selves.

The realization of the transformation process for humans means choosing a life plan relative to what they are in their soul. For the organization, it means deciding on a mission relative to their reason for being which is a respect for life and the environment. In understanding their reason for being, they will master their financial dependencies and proceed toward total autonomy. Every life is a voyage and we are responsible for finding our destination. In knowing this, humans will regain their power to decide what they want and what is good for them. They will come to realize that they have all the essential elements to assume their total autonomy. The organization should give its members the opportunity to define their individual roles by allowing them to choose their rightful places.

The *Humans of the Fifth Kingdom* have absolute power over their lives. They will be the precursors of life by manifesting their essence. The *Organization of the Fifth Kingdom* will allow its members to express their creativity and deliver their full potential in all integrity. Its major role will therefore be the evolutionary management of the potential creativity of its members.

The third millennium is here and both the Human and the Organization have still not brought any significant evolution to humanity. To reverse this tendency, they should transform their lives by becoming conscious and autonomous entities. Their transformation will give a breath of life to the survival of all the kingdoms. The dawning of the *Fifth Kingdom* will stimulate humans to liberate the potential within them to blossom as fully realized beings. The *Fifth kingdom* will incite the organization to stimulate the creative potential of each of its members allowing it to blossom as a fully realized organization. The realized Human and Organization will have a common vision and a universal message of the fundamental values of life and respect for it. They will guide humanity towards a new world order where Humans will be in their rightful place and where the Organization will respect their choice.

THE POWER OF THE FUTURE
PURCHASE ORDER

PRICE LIST PER UNIT	
Regular price:	29,95 $
Shipping:	5,00 $
TOTAL:	34,95 $

ADDRESS: **Hicom International Inc.**
P.O. Box 833, Station A
Montreal, Québec
H3C 2V5
Tél.: (514) 767-0601
Fax: (514) 767-1107

✂ ....

Please send me THE POWER OF THE FUTURE

______ COPIES, FOR A TOTAL OF $ ______

Name ______________________________

Occupation ______________________________

Name of company ______________________________

Address ______________________________ **Apt** __________

City __________ **Province** __________ **Postal code** __________

Telephone __________ **Fax** __________ **E-mail** __________

I am paying by

❑ **CHEQUE** ❑ **POSTAL ORDER TO THE ORDER OF HICOM INTERNATIONAL INC.**

✂ ....

Please send me THE POWER OF THE FUTURE

______ COPIES, FOR A TOTAL OF $ ______

Name ______________________________

Occupation ______________________________

Name of company ______________________________

Address ______________________________ **Apt** __________

City __________ **Province** __________ **Postal code** __________

Telephone __________ **Fax** __________ **E-mail** __________

I am paying by

❑ **CHEQUE** ❑ **POSTAL ORDER TO THE ORDER OF HICOM INTERNATIONAL INC.**

....

GUY CLOUTIER, entrepreneur, international consultant, speaker, author, educator and professional accountant provides you with personal development tools that will:

- motivate you to make your dreams a reality,
- develop your creativity, (talents, skills and abilities) for personal fulfilment,
- bring meaning to your life by reaching your full potential,
- encourage you to capitalize on your uniqueness to develop self-confidence,
- enable you to become autonomous and self-reliant.

He also offers creative and innovative tools for corporations that will:

- increase organizational performance on human, financial and material levels,
- enhance the creativity of employees and management,
- create a broad-based *family of enterprises* for increased growth and financial independence,
- develop responsibility and autonomy within the ranks, for higher personal motivation and improved corporate achievement,
- generate products and services whose uniqueness will place them on the leading edge of the market.

Guy Cloutier also prepares conferences and training seminars tailored to deal with specific issues affecting your organization.

Professional speaker and consultant for people and organizations who want to live the future today!

PUBLISHED BY
ZONE EVOLUTIONARY CENTRE INC.
P.O. Box 833 Station A
Montréal, Québec, Canada H3C 2V5
Tel: (514) 767-0601 - Fax: (514) 767-1107